LAND AND THE GIVEN ECONOMY

Northwestern University
Studies in Phenomenology
and
Existential Philosophy

LAND AND THE GIVEN ECONOMY

The Hermeneutics and Phenomenology of Dwelling

Todd S. Mei

Northwestern University Press
Evanston, Illinois

Northwestern University Press
www.nupress.northwestern.edu

Printed in the United States of America

10 9 8 7 6 5 4 3 2 1

Library of Congress Cataloging-in-Publication Data

Names: Mei, Todd S., author.
Title: Land and the given economy : the hermeneutics and phenomenology of dwelling / Todd S. Mei.
Other titles: Northwestern University studies in phenomenology & existential philosophy.
Description: Evanston, Illinois : Northwestern University Press, 2017. | Series: Northwestern University studies in phenomenology and existential philosophy
Identifiers: LCCN 2016044883 | ISBN 9780810134072 (cloth : alk. paper) | ISBN 9780810134065 (pbk. : alk. paper) | ISBN 9780810134089 (e-book)
Subjects: LCSH: Land use—Economic aspects. | Land tenure—Economic aspects. | Economics—Philosophy. | Rent (Economic theory) | Phenomenology.
Classification: LCC HD1251 .M45 2017 | DDC 333.3—dc23
LC record available at https://lccn.loc.gov/2016044883

The paper used in this publication meets the minimum requirements of the American National Standard for Information Sciences—Permanence of Paper for Printed Library Materials, ANSI Z39.48–1992.

This book is dedicated to
Joseph Milne and Brian Edwards

Contents

Acknowledgments

This book is a result of years spent pondering what close friends of mine referred to as "the land question," which was posed to me as a problem more important than typical metaphysical, epistemological, or existential questions. The land question was, however, never put formally as a specific question but more in terms of a contradiction in which something essential to all humankind is allowed in most instances to be withheld from general use by conventions of ownership. But rather than pursuing a trajectory of rights and private property, the land question led to matters of economic relations and the philosophical and theological meanings presupposed in those relations. With land always in the background of my research, I soon found what I hope is a coherent and compelling philosophical account of why land matters in ways that we have not really considered.

But how is research able to continue if not by the many kinds of support and encouragement?

I should first like to express my gratitude to the two philosophers who made it possible for me to continue in this profession after receiving my Ph.D. Laurence Goldstein (1947–2014) and Julia Tanney were essential in supporting my teaching career in philosophy at the University of Kent, U.K. I thank you for having confidence in my abilities as a philosopher and teacher.

The majority of this book was written in conversation with my colleagues at the University of Dundee, U.K. (2012–14). The most productive talks were certainly the informal ones—when peering through the office door to say "hello," which led eventually to philosophical discussion. Nicholas Davey, Jennifer Gorrod, Lorens Holm, Beth Lord, Mary Modeen, Andrew Roberts, Brian Smith, Dominic Smith, Jim Thompson, James Williams, and Ashley Woodward are ideal interlocutors—critical yet charitable. My sincere thanks for the years of collegiality and discussion you provided.

Prior to Dundee, I taught philosophy at the University of Kent (2008–12), where my colleagues provided me with a healthy dose of analytic philosophy—rigorous but not dogmatic. My thanks to Tom Angier, David Corfield, Laurence Goldstein, Simon Kirchin, David Marjoribanks, Sean Sayers, Julia Tanney, Robin Taylor, Alan Thomas, Kenneth Westphal, and Matthew Whittingham for the many discussions, most memorable of which are perhaps the ones on MacIntyre. Outside of the Kent Philosophy Department, my thanks to Jeremy Carrette, Benoît Dillet, Laurence Hemming, and Iain Mackenzie.

George H. Taylor and Pamela Sue Anderson were, as always, persistent sources of support, advice, and dialogue. Though little of Paul Ricoeur's philosophy figures in this book, their work in that field has been a productive source for guiding my own research. Moreover, both have been outstanding mentors.

Not being myself an economist, the help of Nicolaus Tideman and Francis Peddle was invaluable. The 2011 Symposium on Global and Economic Justice at Virginia Tech introduced me to wider circles of academic debates on the nature of land.

I have enjoyed the discussions with Robert Scharff on Heidegger over the years. I am not sure Bob will approve of what I have attempted to do with Heidegger's thought, but such is the contingency of being and thinking! Boyd Blundell, with his ability for public outreach in view of questions of justice and ethics, has been an admirable source of philosophical support—often turning my complex theories into more palatable viewpoints when in general discussion with others.

I would like to thank Jeff Malpas and Till Düppe for their insightful and helpful reviews. I hope I have responded to your comments sufficiently. I would also like to thank the blind reviewers involved at various stages during the completion of this book. I benefited from their economic and analytical philosophical criticism.

My thanks to the Philosophy Department at Manchester Metropolitan University, U.K. (2010), the Economics Department at the University of Buckingham, U.K. (2011), and the Centre for Critical and Cultural Theory (Cardiff University, U.K., 2015) for inviting me to present talks relating to phenomenology and economics.

My parents have been faithfully supportive of my research—for what reasons I don't know why! I have benefited from a lifetime of their generosity and love.

For helping immensely to keep me sane within the *circus classicus* that is academia, my deepest gratitude to my wife, Patricia Baker. Much of the keeping me sane involved her introducing me to "the skillful embodied coping" known as windsurfing.

And so, my thanks also to the Wild Times Windsurfing and Sailing School (Whitstable, U.K.), Jason Wild, Ian Wild, Stuart France, Wendy Fitzpatrick, Rupert Kilburn, Rhi Wilmott, and Nick Pardoe for their encouragement and excellent windsurfing tuition while on the shark-infested waters of the Thames Estuary. It all kept me even-keeled throughout the writing of this book.

Essential funding for this book was made possible by the Robert Schalkenbach Foundation (New York). It has been a pleasure working with Mark Sullivan over the years.

LAND AND THE GIVEN ECONOMY

Introduction

> Give me enough of that [land] and I'd fear no one—not even the Devil himself!
>
> —Pahom from "How Much Land Does a Man Need?"[1]

Leo Tolstoy's story of the peasant Pahom culminates in a journey to a foreign village where he is given the opportunity to acquire as much land as he can circumambulate in one day. Taken by the prospect of owning as much as possible, he dies from exhaustion just when reaching the point at which he began. The story may read like a fable about avarice, but it has the quality of a philosophical thought experiment when considered more discretely in relation to the nature of land and its role in human existence. This is because Tolstoy's narrative is not simply a cautionary tale about Pahom's obsession about a means to wealth. Rather, Tolstoy provides a reflection on the fundamental human relation to land as the source of livelihood and production as well as the kinds of practices and conventions that allow for a distortion of this relation. Consider, for instance, how Pahom is a dedicated learner when it comes to land. As Tolstoy recounts, Pahom graduates from a mode of communal usage, to exclusive possession, to freeholding, and finally to speculation. Consider as well, how by this movement, what used to be the source of life is its opposite: land, the source of production and wealth, is the very thing that becomes the source of death. Tolstoy presents us with a peripeteia (reversal) that is philosophically invigorating. And this reversal has every bit to do with the way in which Pahom's movement of understanding only *seems* to be a progression. That is to say, the reversal involves the practices and conventions which treat land in a specific way, no longer as a source of life. And while Tolstoy seems not to provide any answers that may form the basis for social transformation, at least not in the context of the story,[2] he does leave us with the provocation to think further: what is the nature of our fundamental relation to land?

* * *

This book is about understanding land, philosophically and economically. It investigates the being of land—that is, its ontological nature—and how this inclines us to rethink an old idea that gained prominence during the classical period of political economy (c. 1750–1870) but was then summarily forgotten due to the rise of a more positivistic organization of economic theory. The influence of positivism tended toward a marginalization or dismissal of what were deemed to be ethical or normative matters external to economic explanation and prediction. But I do not intend just any way of rethinking this idea, as if a simple reintroduction of its meaning and logic would suffice. Because one of my main contentions is that our current conceptual prejudices prevent us from giving appropriate reflection to this idea's theoretical and practical viability, I propose a specific type of philosophical analysis whose aim is to deconstruct these prejudices in order to elucidate a new understanding.

The idea? Simply that land is a distinct factor of economic production in relation to two other factors—labor and capital—and by this distinctness, it claims a special place within economic theory. David Ricardo (1772–1823) famously identified land's unique capacity in terms of ground rent, or what J. S. Mill later referred to as "Ricardo's doctrine."[3] This doctrine consisted generally in noting how an unearned increment of value arose through the use of land. The intricacies of Ricardo's theory and its subsequent revision by other economists are something to which I will return in the first chapter. For now, it is important to note that "unearned" in this context means a value not attributable to labor or capital and one that can be said to belong distinctively to land. The larger implication of this unearned increment—notwithstanding virulent challenges by economists and philosophers—was that it could not be claimed by labor or landlord. Rather as something arising from use of the land, it was an ideal form of public revenue retrievable through a tax on ground rent.

The necessity to rethink this idea today has arisen due to the challenges presented in both economic and philosophical forums. On the former: the popularity of economic reform associated with land and a taxation on its rent has waxed and waned. Taxation and land reform, often associated with the political economist Henry George (1839–1897), has been described by one able commentator as "anathema to the world of respectable opinion."[4] George's Victorian style of prose, his unorthodox (nonacademic) background as an economist, and the overt prevalence he gives to a lofty style of moral argument have been obstacles to a general, contemporary reception of his ideas. Nevertheless, contrary to those who think the idea of a tax on ground rent began with the

Physiocrats and died with Henry George, one finds a still healthy interest in it. Even F. A. Hayek, reflecting late in his life and notwithstanding some significant reservations, remarked of George's theory that it seemed to him "the theoretically most defensible of all socialist proposals."[5] Hayek confuses George's platform with socialism, but his qualified approval of George indicates that, above and beyond the moral considerations so central to George's political economy, there is a *theoretical* viability to the kind of reform he proposed.

Let us assume that Hayek is correct in his assessment. What would entail an understanding of the theoretical viability of land reform and taxation? The nonspecialist would quickly discover that delving into theory would require, to a large extent, an understanding of calculus as well as a technical use of economic terms. So while economists such as Paul Krugman can say, "Let me be the first to admit that economists have not made it easy for smart people . . . to understand the basics," there is still the requirement that "if you want to be truly well-informed about economics . . . you must go back to school [e.g., read an undergraduate textbook]."[6] This demand sounds reasonable enough. But what is omitted in Krugman's account is the common-sense relation between economics and philosophy that most of us presuppose. In other words, in understanding fundamental economic concepts, we tend to assume that distinct from the technical side of models and formulae—that is, at "rock bottom"—there would be some reflection given over to the kinds of suppositions and implications such concepts might have. And this manner of critical thinking is directly related to, and indeed presupposed by, those types of questions which ask about the ethical, social, and political consequences of economic policies. To question the meaning of welfare, as Amartya Sen has famously done, is not simply to look at alternative models of distribution and preference rankings, but rather to seek to redefine how it is that, in Sen's case, welfare should not be measured by commodities and the kind of utility maximization presumed in acquiring those commodities.[7]

So one gets a sense that involved in Hayek's use of "theoretical" are at least two possible meanings—theory in terms of economic explanation and philosophical evaluation. Speaking as an economist (at least in the context of the passage quoted above), Hayek is clearly referring to the former meaning; but what contribution can the latter make?

On the philosophical forum: because economic theory must assume certain meanings about its concepts, it is not interested in how these assumptions have implications beyond its theoretical scope of explanation and prediction. A philosophical inquiry into any particular aspect of economics would then, and at the very least, involve an identification and investigation of the presuppositions used when constructing its models. As R. G. Collingwood argues, there are concepts that are logically prior to economic analysis, that allow it to be viable. He observes that "economists do not so much derive inductively from facts" as much as they entertain "in their attitude toward the facts" fundamental presuppositions.[8] Understanding these presuppositions and their implications, he goes on to say, is the "task of philosophy." More ambitiously conceived and recalling my mention earlier of prejudice, the philosophical task seeks to expose specific conceptual prejudices that may be extensively and historically determinative; so extensively that they have prevented us from being able to think differently in any significant way. This thought is of course not new. Martin Heidegger comments, for example, "The originary ontological concepts must be attained prior to any scientific definition of fundamental concepts."[9] Heidegger's use of "scientific" denotes not just the natural sciences but any discipline of investigation that uses a method of inquiry where the assumptions and presuppositions of this method are not necessary for the practitioner to question.

Economics, on this account, is a science. More recent philosophies that take on a critical study of its presuppositions include Michel Foucault's analysis of order and representation in political economy and Philip Mirowski's demonstration of the role of physics in neoclassical economic theory. Both studies engage with the historical development of theoretical prejudices which, in turn, lead to significant oversights.[10] One can say that the philosophical forum of investigation that takes aim at presuppositions is one that attempts to clarify how concepts have historically developed and become dominant in order to diagnose how such concepts are involved surreptitiously in our thoughts and practices. I include under this aim any critical form of historical understanding, a form upon which Nietzsche first seized,[11] whether it consists in archaeology, deconstruction, genealogy, hermeneutics, or metaphysics (as Collingwood conceived it). Foucault remarks in relation to his use of archaeology, "such an analysis . . . is an inquiry whose aim is to rediscover on what basis knowledge and theory became possible."[12] In my view, the critical forms of historical understanding share this aim.

With respect to the conception of land, the path of philosophical investigation, as we will see, has yet to be charted adequately. And so while some economists have been arguing for the implementation of land reform and the taxation of ground rent, if my assessment is correct, what is required is neither simply an increased publicity of their analyses and conclusions, nor even the attempt to change the economic convictions of policymakers. Rather, the question of the understanding of the meaning of land must first be raised; the debate about reform presupposes it.

This book will thus deal primarily with the philosophical forum as opposed to arguing about the economic adequacy of land reform and taxation, though I will refer to both classical and recent economic theory when supporting my claims and attempting to address some basic economic questions and misunderstandings. It is not uncommon that these two forms of theoretical inquiry overlap, as for example in the analysis of method or in applying ethics and anthropological conceptions of human nature to economics, and vice versa. However, the use of philosophical investigation into the nature of things (e.g., ontology, phenomenology, metaphysics) is rarely applied to economic theory. Karl Marx was the first and most prominent philosopher to do so, employing his notion of historical materialism to establish a form of economics in which the subject (the laborer) and the object (the thing produced by labor) could coincide without contradiction. As we will see, even with his emphasis on material production, Marx neglects the concept of land. But criticism aside, the significant point that gains prominence here is how a different philosophical understanding of "being and beings" can affect economic practice. This book's wager is that once we gain a better grasp of why land is ontologically unique, we can more ably see how economic revision may be possible only through some radical changes.

Because this book is intended to address a wider academic audience—that is, readers interested in the philosophical implications of economics and the economic implications of phenomenology—I would like to provide some guiding remarks. The first part provides an overview of economic debates. As a philosopher, and not an economist, I have written these chapters so that they should be accessible to those who are unfamiliar with economic terminology. At the same time, I hope that I have offered to the historically minded economist a rather novel way of engaging with and renewing the status of land and ground rent according to clarifications I make in view of Thorstein Veblen, Marx, and early modern natural law. As I do not expect a wider philosophical audience to be familiar with the thought of Heidegger, I use the first chapter initiating my phenomenological analysis (chapter 4) to acclimatize the reader who may have come to this book from another background. Chapter 4 thus begins by situating Heidegger's thought in relation to a more conventional philosophical concern about our relation to reality and how we can relate to things that appear to be given externally. For those readers who have an interest in land via such disciplines as anthropology, archaeology, art, geography, literature, political theory, and sociology, I discuss the recent thought of Edward Casey and Jeff Malpas on the philosophy of place. Their elucidation of the importance of place has reached an international interdisciplinary audience, and I am hoping my engagement with their work provides both a bridge to a wider readership and a critical distinction as to what I am attempting to achieve. Whatever the background and motivation of the reader may be and because the analysis of this book wagers that a current conceptual prejudice prevails, the final part that turns to economic prescription should not be read without at least some recognition of what the preceding parts of the book attempt to achieve—namely, a diagnosis of how and why the concept of land has been misunderstood and an analysis of the basic existential constituency of our being as fundamentally landed.

Argument and Approaches

Let me restate more succinctly the reason for following the philosophical forum in view of the question of land: the philosophical conception of land is logically prior to the economic conception of land. It so happens that the conventional philosophical conception presupposes the classification of land as a form of property, simply in the sense that it can be owned exclusively and in perpetuity. Land's condition of scarcity is only an externality or contingency that, economically speaking, is resolved by the market and, philosophically speaking, is justified according to theories of acquisition and social cooperation.

What follows from classifying land like other forms of property are, of course, specific practices—in this case, that rightful ownership of land means its owner is entitled to its use, the profit arising from its use, and the transmissibility of its title.[13] The second entitlement (profit) would include the unearned increment arising from land use, or what we tend to see in practical terms as periodic payments of rents or fees of lease.

This book, in contrast, will investigate how land ought to be understood ontologically according to the category of givenness, where our relation to land requires a form of appropriate recognition of its givenness as well as a demand to respond appropriately. Land's givenness lies in its capacity to bestow advantage according to its natural capacity or its socially designated status. In the language of philosophy, either case involves showing how land is substantial for *Bildung* (human culture); it is in some sense, *hupokeimenon*, or "that which lies at the basis"[14] of all human dwelling, making, and production. On the other hand, linking its givenness to an appropriate response lies in identifying that aspect arising from land usage which is in one sense "owed back" to land. I argue that the specific contribution that an understanding of land's ontology allows us to see is how the unearned increment arising as ground rent is the general case of an ontological excess resulting from the human use of land's givenness. Beyond the returns to human labor in the form of wages, as it were, ground rent is the remainder of the plenitude offered by land. Land, in this respect, bestows the concrete possibility for human existence in the way of providing us with the ground upon which we dwell and draw in order to exist and create. Precisely because this relation is concrete, the excess of the bestowal is expressed in terms of specific conditions of finitude which I argue are economic ones—that is, ground rent.

Accepting for the moment the viability of my thesis, some significant problems arise with respect to current conventions. Within a society that endorses private ownership of land in perpetuity, the usual practice (if not conceived more strongly as a right) is to allow the owner to retain this excess. Ontologically, my argument is that the excess cannot be claimed to be one's own; it cannot be subject to privation. Yet, at the same time, in its economic form, it cannot simply be returned back to being or to the land. The concluding chapters of this book therefore turn to a discussion about ground rent as the dilemma of the excess, which requires recognizing how the inalienability of the excess can be returned to land through conventional means. Because the excess cannot be transformed back into land, returning it involves a question of our use of it such that it might perpetuate an appropriate relation to land. So resolution of the dilemma involves an ongoing question of how to return the excess through its appropriate use. Taxation would, in this respect, offer a means of allowing the excess to be a matter of public deliberation and investment.

I employ three approaches: hermeneutics, phenomenology, and prescriptive claims about economic practice. In short, it is the task of hermeneutics to indicate how conceptual prejudices have developed, in this case, in the history of philosophy and economics; it is the task of phenomenology to elucidate the conditions for an alternative possibility of meaning of the concept in question; and it is the task of philosophical evaluation to indicate possible prescriptions for social practice. In one sense, this last task is presupposed in how I execute the other two. However, at the same time, I do not think the hermeneutical and phenomenological analyses I offer make the prescriptions I cite a necessary conclusion. To see this more clearly, let me discuss the three approaches in a little more detail.

First, I use a hermeneutical retrieval of the conception of land in classical and neoclassical economic theory. By "hermeneutical" I mean a form of critical historical investigation of texts that returns to the way in which a concept—in this case, land—has been marginalized, misunderstood, or forgotten. Hermeneutics generally involves a rereading of historical sources in view of a question or problem that has been identified as central yet neglected by current thought—and more importantly, remains "unthought" for us in general. Its aim is to provide a critical reinterpretation of the history of a concept in order to gain a better understanding of our current historical situation. As Paul Ricoeur puts it, "Hermeneutics . . . begins when, not content to belong to transmitted tradition, we interrupt the relation in order to signify it," where signification is a mediate form, allowing us to explain and critically interpret the tradition in question.[15] Hermeneutics wagers, in other words, that a substantive change in understanding at the cultural and sociopolitical level can arrive through a critical engagement with, or "destructive retrieve"[16] of, historical sources. To reinterpret ourselves and our possibilities begins with a return to our historically constituted intellectual foundations.

With land, there is a strong philosophical prejudice that prevents a notion of economic land reform from being seen as anything but some kind of violation of an inalienable right to land ownership; it is a prejudice that has its most prominent source in John Locke's account of ownership and natural right and extends up to the present day, most noticeably in various forms of libertarian thinking. Without addressing how this conceptual prejudice has emerged and without understanding the justifications for maintaining this prejudice, the conditions for understanding land ontologically remain severely diminished. There are two forms of conceptual prejudice I discuss as preventing us from gaining access to an ontological understanding of land: (1) the reduction of the meaning of land into labor (most prevalent in Marx), and (2) the reduction of the meaning of land into capital (characteristic of post-1870s economic theory) which directly or indirectly draws on modern natural law conceptions of property ownership.

The hermeneutical retrieval of land nonetheless involves a commitment to, as Ricoeur puts it, "a choice in favour of meaning."[17] What this means is how hermeneutics, in identifying the obstacles to understanding a concept in its historical development, is only possible if it has in view some other meaning of the concept which enables one to be critical of the existing situation of understanding, without necessarily transcending this situation. Hermeneutics therefore has as its complement a phenomenological investigation of the conditions which make another meaning of something possible.[18]

I employ a phenomenological approach to show how land *is*, in its manner of being, and how from this manner of being we can identify the conditions that are determinative of our economic practices. Quite simply put, phenomenology allows us to rethink how our existence is more concretely involved, and moreover, how this involvement reveals the manner in which land occupies a significant formative role. Phenomenology is a discipline with many facets, in both Continental and analytic philosophy, and the version of it I employ is best described as a hermeneutic phenomenology following the thought of Heidegger. If phenomenology in general can be said to be concerned with grasping the conditions for the possibility of meaning, how does meaning arise in the human engagement with reality? Is this meaning merely subjective? Do our thoughts and statements have some kind of traction on what is real? Do our thoughts participate in reality in some subtle sense, perhaps transforming it? A hermeneutic phenomenology maintains that there is no direct knowledge of oneself, one's existence, or reality except through forms of mediation. It gains access to understanding through a detour of what it takes to be inextricably bound up with our modes of perception and understanding. I draw mostly from Heidegger's phenomenology, not in the rigorous sense of a method, but as a descriptive analysis of our human dwelling in relation to that which gives, or makes possible, our kind of being. While I refer to Heidegger's early work I also rely upon his later thought that attempts to disclose a new way of relating to entities, which he places under the aegis of the poetic.[19] (Below I account for my application and understanding of his philosophy.) Phenomenology, as I employ it, thus provides a way of gaining access to that which is taken to be ontologically primary and therefore constitutive of our being-in-the-world in order to understand this being-in-the-world anew. This has been done with respect to temporality (early Heidegger), embodiment (Merleau-Ponty), capability (Ricoeur), and more recently, place and landscape (Casey and Malpas). In this study, I do so in relation to land. And while I do not think there is necessarily a rivalry or exclusivity with regard to other phenomenological studies,[20] it is precisely an understanding of land as we experience it that is lacking. As Heidegger might allege, other concepts have stood "in front" of the concept of land, thereby impeding recognition of its role and access to its meaning.

Finally, as indicated above, I turn to a prescriptive reflection on the taxation of ground rent. This is not simply a straightforward "yes" to a form of taxation, but rather I will endeavor to redescribe how this tax correlates with the phenomenology of land. The move to correlation is what I therefore have called "an economic turn";[21] as a turn it is not necessary, but a maneuver made in order to arrive "somewhere"—that is, at an alternative understanding of economics. This prescription should be regarded in a genuine spirit of hypothesis—meaning, *if* what I have proposed hermeneutically and phenomenologically is viable, *then* it seems we ought to consider seriously its implications in the realm of economic practice. My prescription, in this sense, will remain economically broad, that is, without engaging specific concerns an economist might raise. Present-day debate on economic policies involving land generally refer to a "land value tax." Suffice it to say, there are many versions of this form of tax. While the argument of this book can be seen generally supporting the notion of such a tax, it does not necessarily endorse any particular version of it. It is important to note that my analysis is concerned with the philosophical nature and possibility of a tax on land insofar as one can say that ground rent has the type of ontological excess I describe.

Of course, the danger of this prescriptive move is not only that it can be wrong but that it assumes a type of transcendental privilege claiming validity across history and cultures. While the force of any philosophical investigation has at its center the notion, no matter how latent, that what it is claiming has some universal validity, the philosopher can nonetheless admit an awareness of the historically contingent nature of his or her analysis and remedy. This is in effect to say that a certain type of necessity resides in history, a necessity which can be described as the unavoidable fragility of contingent relations that qualify how we understand ourselves, our past, and our claims to validity. Ricoeur refers to this as a vulnerability of philosophy that makes it "aware of its own lack of foundation."[22] Admission of this vulnerability in this investigation would mean recognizing that the practices proposed are specific to the historical situation in which we find ourselves.

What is interesting to note about practices of land ownership in other cultures is the normative framework in which access to it is sanctioned. Insofar as these norms are seen to have authority, they maintain a form of being-in-the-world in which a sustainability of metabolism and community is possible given their practices of landowning.[23] It is very much the case, therefore, that the question of the meaning of land might never have arisen. Yet, this is not the case for the situation I am attempting to describe for a historically constituted moment in which land ownership is the norm and from which is generated much socioeconomic strain.

This study assumes, in other words, certain conditions under which land has become a more pressing problem for a global community, where "global" denotes separate communities dominated by the same land use practice, than it might have for another culture or society at another time. These assumptions involve conditions of lack of access to land and the absence of ethical precepts that would prevent forms of land monopoly or oligopoly. The advent of these conditions together is arguably co-emergent with capitalism and land enclosure. Whatever the reasons and causes, our current situation is certainly one in which, wherever we go, we do not expect to have access to land without a cost (unless it is commonly held). Rarely do we sincerely question why some tract of land can be withheld from use simply by virtue of the norms of ownership we think to be self-evident, or at the very least, justified.

In What Sense Given?

In view of the three approaches outlined above, I should comment on the book's title. "The Given Economy" plays on a triple meaning of the word "given." In one sense, the economy is given and taken for granted because land has not been appropriately understood and used. In a second sense, according to the unique role land plays in production, the economy is given in a substantial sense that requires we recognize this status. This second sense anticipates the third meaning, which suggests that if we were to respond appropriately to the givenness of land, then a fitting economy would in this sense be "given" or delivered over to us. As the reader may have noticed, these three meanings are respectively the three approaches of hermeneutics, phenomenology, and philosophical prescription.

My use of "givenness" will no doubt raise connections to the studies on gift exchange. There is and has been a great deal of debate concerning the kind of relation involved in gift exchange, mostly in reference to anthropological sources and the intersection joining phenomenology and theology. In this book, I do not attempt to relate land to an economy of gift, though I have attempted to do so in earlier work.[24] And indeed, Heidegger's later work turns expressly to the language of gift and thanking. However, my intention to remain narrowly with the language of givenness has to do with a hesitancy to move too quickly within a discourse that raises, for me, a set of critical questions that would be inevitably distracting.[25] In short, the term "gift" seems to carry an enormous burden when accounting for the way we should relate to certain entities. It may refer to a general orientation of thanking, but in so doing, it loses specificity and can therefore result in a kind of pietism. On the other hand, the idea that land is the gift of nature is problematic insofar as it has been adopted by those for and against land reform. Finally, I have other concerns as to whether or not gift can be genuinely understood apart from religious traditions, their symbolisms and practices.

Having said this, land, of course, is given by no one; it is produced by no one. Recognizing its status of being given is one of understanding the way it remains the presupposition of all human activity and the way this givenness takes shape according to a specific form of value—that is, an unearned increment. Because the givenness of land is already always occurring, we cannot help but be involved with it.

My Use of Heidegger's Philosophy

This section is a digression for those interested in the main argument of this book and can therefore be passed over by those unconcerned with matters pertaining specifically to Heidegger scholarship. The aim of this section is to provide a short apologia for the way in which I employ Heidegger.

This book is neither an exegetical study devoted to Heidegger nor an attempt to derive something like a Heideggerian-styled political economy. I draw upon Heidegger's philosophy in order to elucidate my argument and hopefully persuade the reader of its cogency. Insofar as I have not assumed the reader will have a specialist knowledge of his work and the history of debate surrounding Heidegger scholarship, I attempt to avoid an overreliance on his unique use of terms. Where I do employ them, I make my best attempt to explain their significance in a more generally accessible way.

Having said this, there are two issues I would like to clarify. First, even though I have made it clear that I am not attempting to offer an interpretation of Heidegger's work, my argument cannot help but interpret Heidegger in certain ways. For example, as in my previous discussions of Heidegger, I assume a general unity to his work. This is not to say that there are not significant differences and departures between the early and late Heidegger, but rather that the selection of a specific theme or question determines to what extent one can often find a more or less coherent view, thread, or concern in his works. For example, much of what I want to do with respect to the question of land builds upon the excellent work done by Jeff Malpas and his analysis of the role of place (*topos, Ort*) and François Raffoul and his discussion of the subject and mineness, both of whom argue for some form of unity in relation to their respective topics.[26]

Second, my concern with economics may raise alarm bells in view of what appears to be the attempt to read Heidegger's thought as a practical philosophy. The emphasis on practicality in Heidegger's philosophy, particularly in relation to scholarship on *Being and Time*, has been labeled as an "analytic" understanding of Heidegger or referred to as adopting the "primacy of practice" thesis. Hubert Dreyfus, William Richardson, and Richard Rorty were the first and most prominent commentators to emphasize the epistemological and pragmatic content of Heidegger's early philosophy. To many, the scandal of making such a connection means reversing Heidegger's original and groundbreaking analysis of being-in-the-world. From this point of view (i.e., that of a non-analytic Heideggerian), to be an "analytic Heideggerian" means in some way to take up those kinds of conceptions of human subjectivity and action which his philosophy allegedly overcomes or leaves behind. To overdetermine the epistemological and pragmatic questions and problems of modern philosophy is to inherit the metaphysics and epistemology Heidegger refutes.[27]

From the perspective of an "analytic-Heideggerian," what he or she is endeavoring to do is "put his [Heidegger's] jargon into clear terms" in a way that "stresses simple, everyday practices and how they convey an inexhaustible understanding of being."[28] It is, of course, the idea that Heidegger's "jargon" can be translated that is problematic since, in assuming there is a more accurate translation, one is assuming that what Heidegger really means is something other than what he wrote. Or worse, one is assuming that Heidegger's philosophy is unnecessarily obscure and should be translated into more amenable language. These attitudes, as Robert Scharff has argued, end up reading questions and answers into Heidegger's philosophy that were never there. Scharff writes specifically in view of practices that Heidegger makes nothing "like a preferential turn toward the practical" in *Being and Time* since both the theoretical and the practical are "ways of 'caring.'"[29]

Scharff contends that in addition to the misreading of *Being and Time* performed by Dreyfus and Rorty, the analytic-Heideggerian orientation tends to recognize the importance of historicity in understanding but fails to apply this to its own view. The charge is not that the analytic reading is ahistorical; it *is* historically aware insofar as it is critical of the existing situation of philosophy and how it has developed. Yet, it is historically unaware in thinking that it can gain a perspective above and free from its historically constituted situation, as if it could return after a critical engagement "to whatever was initially obscured."[30] Dreyfus has since revised his position on everydayness, seeing guilt and anxiety in division 2 of *Being and Time* as having a more significant role in resoluteness. Whether this adequately responds to Scharff's criticisms is a question outside the remit of this book.[31]

In view of the above, it might be a criticism of my approach that it, too, not only overemphasizes everyday practice but also forces Heidegger's philosophy to fit a discourse of analysis it repudiates. Phenomenology cannot be fused with economic theory.

Because I am using Heidegger's phenomenology to clarify and

explain the givenness of land, my turn toward economic implications involves a *correlation* by which the two, phenomenology and economics, remain distinct and separate. As co-related, the movement from Heidegger to economics is thus based on a wager motivated by our particular historical situation. In this respect, Heidegger's phenomenology will always remain the same (as a written and fixed discourse) in how it is presented by his texts; yet what changes is the historical situation in which we attempt to understand his phenomenology. This understanding is always an appropriation of a source according to questions and problems in a historical setting. My turn to economics can be considered therefore as a special type of appropriation which recognizes its contingency. It is to say this setting gives to thought an exigency to rethink economics, not simply criticize its theoretical assumptions and shortcomings. This contingency says (to me), let us wager that we can think economics anew with the type of philosophy that thinks being and beings anew. My wager, therefore, is that an economic practice *correlating* to Heidegger's phenomenology is possible; and still more, that it is possible without jettisoning a fundamental concept of classical economic theory.[32]

Synopsis of Chapters

This book is structured in three parts corresponding to the approaches described above—hermeneutical retrieval of the concept of land, phenomenology of land, and prescription, or the economic turn.

Part 1: "Hermeneutical Retrieval." In chapter 1, "Retrieving the Classical Theory of Rent," I explain Ricardo's theory of rent and the manner in which Henry George amends it. I also account for a common poststructural criticism that the discipline of economics is a fiction predicated upon a misguided representation of the human as subject. In attempting to form a science of value creation, the first economists discounted how value is possible only because of a more general human intentionality and relation to reality.[33] I not only defend an aspect of classical economics from this charge but show how Ricardo's conception of land is one that we would do well to recall. Also crucial to this section is the demonstration of how ground rent links up to land value, a point which will be essential in my concluding arguments on dwelling and taxation.

Chapter 2, "Ricardo or Marx?" examines how the distinction of land as a factor of production is compromised by Marx when he places labor at the center of his political economy. His system of economics becomes a way of marginalizing the more classical distinctions in the production of value in favor of the laborer who is the sole producer of value. Because of this, the theoretical situation is one of choosing either Ricardo, because he was correct in identifying how a specific form of value (i.e., ground rent) arose from land, or Marx, because he was correct in identifying how this value is really due to labor. I present grounds for choosing the former.

Chapter 3, "Otherwise Than Capital?" looks at the philosophical preconditions for the post-1870 classification of land as capital. I identify the theories of private property within the modern natural law tradition as the conceptual predecessors of current confusion about the understanding of land. I consider the views of Hugo Grotius (1583–1645), Samuel Pufendorf (1632–1694), and John Locke (1632–1704) on nature and land as property. I describe each philosopher in terms of a "nomological reduction," that is, how each one reduces land to an instrument for realizing what each sees as the aim of natural law. This aim is notoriously cast in terms of self-preservation and socialization. I then consider economic proponents and opponents of the reduction of land to capital, only to anticipate my turn to phenomenological analysis.

Part 2: "A Phenomenology of Land." Chapter 4, "Givenness and Ground," takes up Heidegger's criticism of metaphysics for its inability to think being and how he attempts to redefine the task of philosophy as thinking ground and being more concretely. I argue that essential to Heidegger's notion of overcoming metaphysics is not a rejection of metaphysics per se,[34] but the transformation of thinking such that it is fundamentally concrete in its concern. On this view, the concept of ground we entertain philosophically has ramifications for how we think we should dwell, and vice versa. Because metaphysics thinks ground without regard to existential context, Heidegger attempts to think ground as concretely and immanently as possible. This trajectory leads to the philosophy of place, as discussed in the works of Casey and Malpas, and as I argue distinctly, a new understanding of the priority of land.

Chapter 5, "The Being of Land," draws on Heidegger's notions of earth and cause (*aition*) to argue that, in contrast to conventional conceptions of land, land is best understood as subject, or *hupokeimenon.* I attempt to show that as such, land acts as that which underlies our relation to reality and thus to practical existence conceived in terms of production (*poiesis*). Integral to this discussion is the way land is the subject of both revealing, by allowing us to dwell according to projects, and concealing, by ever-requiring us to take heed of land in relation to specific constraints of finitude.

Chapter 6, "Excess and Gravity," develops further the manner in which land determines our existence. Being-landed is an *existentiale* that I argue is most prominent in relation to the recognition of our ontological possibility-to-be and how the actualization of this possibility owes itself to land. While I employ Heidegger's understanding of mineness (*Jemeinigkeit*) and appropriation to describe the relation between actualization and debt, I introduce the terms "excess" and "gravity" to provide a more vivid account of our being-landed. Distinguishing my approach from Jean-Luc Marion, I discuss how ontological possibility is the excess over which a current situation affords; it cannot be projected except as an excess to a specific standpoint within being. The manner in which this possibility is conceived involves not just something like a personal project, but the place in which this project can be actualized. This place is itself made possible by land, existentially as a ground providing for a manner of dwelling. Gravity accounts for the somewhat ethical bond—if ethical is understood in terms of an ethos for dwelling—in which we owe some form of recognition and appropriate response to land.

Part 3: "The Economic Turn." This concluding part attempts to draw the substantial connections between phenomenology and economic practices. It maps out these relations according to the way in which land's excess is reconfigured in economic activity and how land's gravity appears in terms of a dilemma, which asks of us how we should relate to the excess land produces.

Chapter 7, "Correlating Land," discusses how land's phenomenological subjectivity can be seen at, or correlated with, economics to the degree that it is its foundation. I therefore show how land is presupposed by economic activity at three levels—origin for production, motivation to produce, and economic capacity to produce.

Chapter 8, "Dilemma of the Excess: Rent and Taxation," examines the implications of the phenomenological and economic manifestations of excess. Because the condition of finitude and our human involvement in it cannot transform the economic increment back to its original state, I argue that one way it can be returned to land is through the human relation to it. Ground rent can thus be conceived as a source of public revenue, that is, a tax. In addition to clarifying the meaning of this tax, I address three common questions about its viability.

Tolstoy concludes his story on what seems a rather pessimistic note. "How much land does a man need?"

> Pahom's workman picked up the spade, dug a grave for his master—six feet from head to heel, which was exactly the length—and buried him.[35]

In one sense, Tolstoy seems to suggest that in the end we only require enough land for being buried, and we might then be reminded of certain caricatures of existentialism in which the meaning we ascribe to our existence is really arbitrary and empty. But this interpretation seems inconsistent with the fact that Pahom does not just die; rather, he is buried—a rite within a larger system of eschatological meaning. So, in another sense, one which I think more interesting and certainly in keeping with my thesis on land (and indeed Tolstoy's own), the fate of Pahom is in some manner the fate of those who misunderstand the nature of land. Death need not be taken literally; it can suggest symbolically an end to a specific kind of *human* dwelling—perhaps death is a homelessness on or alienation from the land itself. And yet as Plato knew, philosophy is the *pharmakon* to such an incapacity (*adunamia*).[36]

Part 1

Hermeneutical Retrieval

1

Retrieving the Classical Theory of Rent

My aim in this chapter is to explain the classical theory of rent with respect to its formal inception in the work of David Ricardo and its more extensive application in the work of Henry George. Having said that, accomplishing this aim is not so straightforward. My intention to explain this theory is presupposed by the idea that it can be meaningful and relevant to our current historical situation. This presupposition meets with two types of criticism which rely on different conceptions of historical understanding. For one, history is the subject of a critical exercise of unearthing hidden shifts in thinking. For the other, history is a processual medium in which theoretical knowledge at the forefront most often involves an improvement, if not a refutation, of antecedent theories. According to the second type of criticism, the classical development of rent was generalized in neoclassical reformulation to the extent that land was seen to be no different from other types of capital that similarly gave rise to unearned increments. I will dispute this claim in chapter 2 when examining neoclassical economic thought.

I will treat the first kind of criticism herein. It appeals to a different kind of obsolescence which is not so simply said because it involves surreptitious transformations in historical forms of discourse. Given the classical period, does a theory like rent really explain what it purports to? This question can be described generally as post-structural since it follows on from Foucault's archaeology. Specifically, it takes issue with the way in which discursive formations employ rules and modes of representation that go unnoticed, where "discursive" denotes the non-epistemological conditions and assumptions required for the formation and articulation of practices.[1] Such formations therefore delimit thought and determine the arrangement of social relations. When applied to economic theory, archaeological investigation finds a wealth of material in the kinds of models economists construct and how technical terminology differs or changes depending on what any particular model assumes and excludes (e.g., assumptions about rationality and normativity). Thus the general heading of "an archaeology of economics" would include primarily an identification of the ways in which concepts within models become discursively meaningful. There are no "real," "pure," or "essential" meanings to economic terminology that scientifically ground its method, but rather there are only a series of shifts by which the category of the economic itself becomes viable and autonomous and thus formative of the human agent who is forced to fit this category. Subsequently, economics is no science at all, but a disciplinary fabrication viable only because it has abstracted its objects of observation from their natural, historical, and social contexts. This shift, which Till Düppe claims is the central illusion underwriting an economic formalism that remains intact even today, precludes meanings and descriptions of life not only external to its conceptions but much closer to the elements driving and directing life as a whole, human and nonhuman.[2]

While Foucault's focus in *The Order of Things* was broad in attempting to convey disruptions in the history of political economy, one might expect that looking more discretely at specific terms within political economy might lead to identifying other kinds of disruptions. In his critical study *Land, Labor and Economic Discourse* Keith Tribe undertakes such an examination, looking at how the feudal conceptions of rent and land were transformed in the classical period to benefit the scientific standing of economic analysis, yet only at the cost of distorting the social world. This tension involves the refinement of a formal system for analyzing value and wealth that enables prediction but at the same time marginalizes the life of the human being—most notably, as an abstract producer instrumental to the will of surplus production.

In this chapter I confront Tribe's allegation that a theory of rent is coherent only within the classical ordering of relations that prioritize production and surplus. I accept that disruptions in our forms of knowing require exposure, but I do not believe it necessarily follows from such diagnoses that the objects under investigation are irredeemably confined to its respective form of discourse. Conceptual disruptions can never be so total. So I offer instead a retrieval of the classical theory of rent by tracing what remains undisrupted in it—or, how rent retains a meaning relating to nature as gift. To recall my introductory remarks, I will not argue in subsequent chapters that we must therefore return to a notion of gift. Instead, the elucidation of the role of nature in classical thought will allow me to develop the theory of rent and land according to a different tack.

The first section of this chapter deals with the complexity of the meanings of rent as they appear historically in the transition from feudalism to the classical period. The aim of this section is not to present a history of the theory of rent,[3] but rather to show the clarity Tribe's examination brings to an understanding of this concept. In the second section, I engage Tribe critically in view of methodological problems. The third section performs a type of "positive archaeology" in discussing how the classical theory of rent presupposes a fundamental link with nature and how its bounty entails the production of wealth. Respectively, sections 4, 5, and 6 explain rent according to difference (Ricardo), its application to all types of land (George), and how social progress is figured in the generation of rent (Thorstein Veblen).

Disambiguating Rent and the New "Economic Terrain"

The two basic meanings of rent are (1) the fee one pays for usage of land to its owner, and (2) the value generated as a surplus above and beyond the expenditure of labor and capital. The former meaning inevitably involves various qualifications of legal ownership, usually in the sense of allowing a lessee a right to use and possession of land, but not the right to sell or transfer its legal ownership during the period of possession. It is a meaning more or less pervasive in economic writing since the seventeenth century, though this is contested by Tribe. The latter meaning involves the attribution of value to a factor of production other than labor or capital. While distinct, the two meanings are interrelated. But grasping this interrelation is more complicated than might appear. Certainly, one can make a basic inference: if rent is the fee paid for usage of land, this fee reflects a value that must be based on something identifiable by, and therefore agreeable to, both landlord and lessee. Some general notion of the surplus in production provided by a particular plot of land in comparison to plots of inferior quality would provide a way of determining a range for the fee. This inference is essentially correct. However, explicating this "economically" in relation to the historical development in which land and rent become economic concepts is, as we shall see, a rather tangled affair.[4]

The theory of rent is typically ascribed to David Ricardo (1772–1823), who gave formal expression to it in relation to agricultural land. Yet to say that land and rent were never a concern for economic thinking prior to Ricardo and his contemporaries would be a gross overstatement. William Petty (1623–1687), Richard Cantillon (c. 1680–1734), and François Quesnay (1694–1774) all gave serious attention to the role of land in economic production.[5] One even finds in Aristotle's *Politics* (1318b6–1319a19) a consideration of land usage and ownership for the effective maintenance of agricultural production. Nonetheless, land and rent were not the focus of the kind of economic scrutiny and modeling that Ricardo employed.[6] Spurred on by the debate over the cause of higher corn prices and the concern for circulation of wealth, Ricardo sought a model of explanation that attributed the increase in rents to higher prices in corn.

However, Tribe alleges that this conventional way of characterizing rent is overly simplistic and therefore deceptive. He begins his analysis further back in history in order to show how, with a shift in the conceptualization of rent and land, there emerges a radically new form of representing the human being. So while the notion of rent can be traced back to the pre-classical period of the seventeenth century, Tribe argues that one should not be tempted to assume there are similarities of meanings with the classical period of the eighteenth century; and more radically, one should not see the two periods as being continuous but separated by a decisive break.[7] The classical period thus establishes a new "economic terrain" on which "economic agents" are no longer "real persons" but representations "constituted by relations of labor and capital" geared toward production of surplus.[8] More significantly, Tribe argues that co-emergent with the discursive form of this new terrain are the classical concepts of rent and land which, by virtue of being internal to a closed system of newly defined economic relations, only *seem* to have empirical and therefore law-like qualities.[9]

Put straightforwardly, Tribe's analysis presents a challenge to my supposition that rent, as a historically determined concept, is in fact amenable to something like a philosophical reappropriation. It would be entirely questionable to assert a relation between rent and the ontological nature of land. There cannot be a non-discursive philosophical justification of a discursive form since rent is a practice arising from a discursive social order (i.e., capitalism) while the ontology of land is a non-discursive philosophical description. There can only be a non-discursive form indicating the ordered system of the discursive form.

Tribe's case is quite convincing. He argues that it is crucial to note how each period understands the relation between the two meanings of rent within their respective social contexts. Simply because there is reference to rent in the literature concerned with husbandry in the seventeenth century, one cannot assume there is the same type of organization of relations that we know today in terms of "fee taken" and "use given." Tribe is not alone in this claim. Stephen Marglin argues that understanding the enclosure movements in England beginning in the fifteenth century requires seeing how the shift from a feudal system of rent and tenancy undergoes a significant transformation with the social restructuring of society.[10] Apart from the modern association of ownership with exclusive rights, the feudal period involved a social system in which access to land was extended to those who did not own it. Rent paid by the feudal tenant is not a fee for right of use, but a *tribute* legitimating the sociopolitical system in which tenants, landlord, and monarch all have their appropriate place in carrying out God's work (which is notably not capitalist production).[11] The feudal system conceives of the laborer and landlord as figures whose meanings and roles are constituted by the polity and not by some notion of autonomous economic forces working to produce and circulate wealth. Indeed, the emergence of the concern for a theory of value in the classical period is itself evidence of the removal of "real persons" from production and how specific and local notions of the polity may be the very constituents of value formation.[12] That a theory of value is crowned by the economic good of freedom is only an admission of this deletion, since it is through economic relations that the ethico-political sphere is henceforth constructed.[13]

Following Moses Finley, Tribe's point of contrast is the ancient Greek conception of "economy." In Plato and Xenophon, one can see there is a presumption of organization based on the household, or what is the meaning of the Greek *oikonomikos.* Book 1 of Aristotle's *Politics* is, of course, famous for the identification of household management as the basis for conceiving larger economic relations in the polis apart from trade and wealth-getting.[14] As Dotan Lesham has pointed out, the ancient Greek conception conceives this management "as encompassing any activity in which man, when faced with nature's abundance or excess, acquires a prudent disposition that is translated into practical and theoretical knowledge."[15]

The organization of *oikonomia* is patriarchal and local; even more, it is not concerned with rent in view of economic production and distribution of wealth but with an affirmation of a social bond. And this form of organization is consistent with practices in Europe prior to the classical period. For example, Tribe comments that in the primary historical sources on husbandry during the seventeenth century, "the good ordering of the household is vital to the well-being of the husbandman as representative of the household order."[16] Beyond the local household is the connection to the larger feudal system:

> Far from the agricultural producer being placed in an economic terrain, we have seen that the relation of the landlord to the tenant is conditional upon its conception as a juridical relation, and is not expressed as an economic relation.[17]

How is the shift to the "economic relation" visible?

Tribe focuses on the transition from the small farm to the large farm (c. 1770),[18] where the emergence of the large farm involved diminishing the practices of the seventeenth to early eighteenth centuries, in which the roles of laborer/farmer and caretaker of the land were, if not the same, then intimately bound. To recall from above, the landlord held a social role, not an economic one; rent is a tribute and not a fee. With the advent of large farms, the emphasis on agriculture moves toward profit and stock, that is, economic incentives that replace the affirmation of feudal, social bonds. In turn, with large farms there was the subsequent creation of monopoly by which their owners soon realized they could withhold their produce until a rise in price. This not only reinforced the gearing of farming "technologies" toward profit, but it also had a detrimental effect on the small farms which could not afford to withhold produce. The shift here is notable: while it is arguable that landholding in general may be a monopoly, we see with the large farm a form of subordination that is not political or juridical, but economic. This is not to say in contrast that feudal society was unproblematic, but that its form of subservience had above all a social and political role reinforced by communal norms of responsibility and care.

There was also a change in the nature of production in which the end product of labor was no longer seen within the bond/relation of the farmer to the gift of nature, that is, where one performed a task given by God to reap the bounty of his gift. Instead, the aim of farming was to produce a profit by virtue of a better organized system.[19] Herein, the farm is "an independent capitalist enterprise"[20] where profit is the outcome, and farmers are not liable for rent as an expression of a local subservient legality (tribute), but as a payment in view of maintaining the production of stock. For the feudal use of land, according to Tribe, "'production' is a quality of the individual, and is not a category of economic organisation."[21]

What, then, does the expressly economic rendering of rent do to the conception of persons involved in production and rent? Quite simply, it represents the person in terms of the economic mode of production, no longer having the capacity of self-creation.[22] Tribe sees this form of representation resulting from what post-structuralism generally refers to as conceiving "Man as the Subject." Experience of the person is ordered by a conception of "Man" as a subject integral to a respective form of scientific analysis. Foucault thus notes:

> Man for the human sciences [i.e., biology, economics, and philology] is . . . that living being who, from within the life to which he entirely belongs and by which he is traversed in his whole being, constitutes representations by means of which he lives, and on the basis of which he possesses that strange capacity of being able to represent himself precisely that life.[23]

Foucault here suggests that in order for there to be anything like economics, such a science assumes a conception of the person who lives by means of representing aspects of life back to him- or herself *economically*. This form of representation then acts as the means by which life itself is understood. But this form is at odds with, at least in the passage above, "the life to which he [Man] entirely belongs and by which he is traversed in his whole being." Turning to economics more specifically, Foucault states that in identifying that aspect of life involved in production, Man is subsequently defined by "forms of production."[24] A problem arises when these forms are taken to govern the whole of human existence. Within this economic representation, Man has an agency where he is at once the subject *subjected* to economic production and the subject who is able to form representations of his needs *economically*. This dual role allows for an internal coherency, or what is essentially a science being identical to itself, that can exclude other features of the life to which we entirely belong. Foucault asks, "Can it be said that the subject is the only possible form of experience? Can't there be experiences in the course of which the subject is no longer posited, in its constitutive relations, as what makes it identical to itself?"[25]

In adopting this general attitude, Tribe argues that classical theory operates on a conception of Man geared toward economic self-preservation. According to this concern, aspects of nature and life are isolated and employed to meet the need of this preservation.

> Only where Man is conceived as the constitutive element of the economy—where it is the action of this Man on external objects for the purpose of his preservation—can the terms "land" and "labour" be treated as such essential constituents of economic thought.[26]

As to a remedy, Tribe provides no indication except a mode of perpetual critique of the different forms of "discursive eternalism." It may also be the case that to think one can redefine the human subject is itself a way of falling into more discursive blindness. Perhaps Tribe would therefore agree with Foucault when he says, "Maybe our problem is now to discover that the self is nothing else than the historical correlation of the technology built in our history."[27]

A Critical Response to Tribe

Contrary to Tribe, I believe that rent and land have meanings that are neither reducible to nor meaningful only within a capitalist system of production. In other words, his thesis on dislocation is too strong;[28] and this is apparent at both the general methodological level of the archaeology he employs and the specific level of examples he uses to support his analysis. Let me rephrase these criticisms as questions. Methodologically: does the archaeological form of investigation assume some of the aspects of the discursive forms it seeks to critique and thus become problematic, if not contradictory? At the level of specific examples: does Tribe rely too much on a radical dislocation between historical periods such that it overdetermines his reading of primary texts and concepts?

The perpetual conundrum of any method of investigation is its claim to validity, for in analyzing its subject matter, it must appeal to criteria that do not make it viciously circular. The conditions for which a method can claim validity will differ according to the discipline, and in the cases of archaeology and genealogy, there is a presumption that concealed orders and meanings can be detected without the analyst being entirely compromised by the orders and meanings being investigated and the orders and meanings of his or her own life-world. There are various ways in which one can account for this immunity, and it is Tribe's claim that one can indeed occupy a vantage point external to the subject or discourse one is examining as well as access a non-discursive form in order to analyze a discursive one. He comments, "A discursive order cannot be expressive of a non-discursive order" and "while this book deals with archaic discursive forms, it cannot be said that it is historical."[29] What criteria exist that give this status to his method of analysis?

Tribe does not really specify, though one gets a hint that it is a form of close reading of primary texts in which contradictions and breaks internal to these texts produce a sense of the ordering involved—that is, as Peter Benson and Stuart Kirsch put it, a sense of how "power as a relationship [is] to be understood and renegotiated."[30] Tribe seems in agreement with this approach when commenting:

> I have tried to provide a methodological critique of the traditional approaches to the history of economic discourse, not through a detailed confrontation with the representatives of such history, but by a re-assessment of the material out of which they create their histories.[31]

The impression given is that the archaeologist occupies a role of reading the texts and not a substantive role in constructing a story guided by conventional expectations of chronology and teleology which produce continuity. The archaeologist instead identifies the dislocations; as in the words of Foucault,

> to show . . . in what way, then, our culture has made manifest the existence of order, and how, to the modalities of that order, the exchanges owed their laws, the living beings their constants, the words their sequence and their representative value.[32]

Any claims to order or a set of criteria upon which the archaeologist can rely necessarily puts his or her own study into question. Gary Gutting notes this feature in relation to how philosophical commitments driving the archaeological form of investigation appear latently. On Foucault, he remarks that there is an opposition to "an intolerable aspect of modern social life" without, however, providing any substantial alternative except an "intense pre-philosophical conviction that . . . [certain] practices were morally intolerable."[33]

The idea that disclosure of differences and breaks can be uncontaminated by a discursive form, or more strongly a trans-historical standard, seems suspicious. Alasdair MacIntyre puts this challenge when stating that the archaeological/genealogical approach presupposes some "standards" by which the disclosure of the dislocations can be "intelligible":

> The standards in the light of which such reevaluations are made and such reasoning conducted are independent of the particular stages and moments of the temporary strategies through which the genealogist moves his or her overall projects forward.[34]

On this MacIntyre concludes, "the intelligibility of genealogy requires beliefs and allegiances of a kind precluded by the genealogical stance."[35] For instance, one can say that the break Tribe describes in terms of different modes of laboring—where the pre-classical denotes a concrete self produced within the polity and the classical, an abstracted self subsumed under the category of capital—is explainable because it is intelligible. It appeals to some common stock understanding according to which those who never saw the break before can now recognize Tribe's analysis as coherent. What is this common stock if not ordered by concepts and meanings to which we can generally agree—whether normative, scientific, rational, or logical?

But there is another way of approaching the problems of Tribe's archaeology, and this concerns the manner in which certain meanings or usages of terms sometimes require a rather resolute interpretation of texts that can become tenuous. This may be an expected criticism given that the attempt to identify dislocations sets itself against conventional wisdom and pre-understanding. Regardless, the archaeologist is either in a position of asserting the validity of his or her reading of the texts, or admitting that the validity of any reading comes down to how much one is willing to trust the competence and understanding of the authors one reads. To see this dilemma at play, let us turn to the second question: does Tribe rely too much on a radical dislocation such that it overdetermines his reading of primary texts and concepts?

Because he has to maintain differences between the two periods and various thinkers so strongly, one wonders if the alleged non-discursive formation guiding his analysis is unable to perform any other kind of reading than it does. Because of this, there are two notable lacunae. The first I will only mention briefly: while mercantilism is another form of economic thought relevant to the time period (c. 1500–1776), Tribe does not provide much comment on how it fits within his thesis. The criticism of mercantilism expressed by classical thinkers and its sharp break from feudal practices seems to suggest that it may be another kind of discursive ordering in which rent-seeking is a major constituent.[36]

The second lacuna involves the lack of trust in what classical thinkers aver, as if the discursive content of the classical thinkers is so prejudiced conceptually that they often articulate unwittingly something different to the plain meaning of their statements.

So, while the classical trinitarian formula of the factors of production—land, labor, and capital—is put under pressure by Tribe's thesis, the implication is that these concepts are so discursively formed that really their delineation within a political economy can be nothing but determined by an underlying order that, in the end, seeks to reduce everything to capital for increased production. Classical economy, on Tribe's account, therefore does not really hold the trinitarian distinction despite its various thinkers saying so.[37] Rather, land is really capital. Tribe writes, "For the Classical Economists, land was a form of capital, and capital was defined independently of conceptions of the unique powers of land and labour."[38] But how can Tribe say this when economists like Ricardo, as we will see below, maintain a distinction between land and capital?

Tribe does not explain this in the immediate context of the assertion. But one can surmise that his claim is based upon the argument that classical theories were interested in capital as stock for production. Thus, one can reconstruct the following rationale in Tribe's study: (1) land was viewed as producing a surplus (rent), (2) the capitalist was one who could speculate on this surplus by estimating a fee (rent), and (3) the laborer too was under the yoke of this speculation by having to pay in advance the rent (in both senses of the term) in expectation of future production. Because of the orientation of rent toward surplus production, land becomes a factor of production like capital in providing a future stock of value.[39]

Moreover, if land is a form of capital, neither land nor rent can have any concrete tie to notions of social responsibility and gift, as they did in the feudal period. It is apparent from what has been mentioned earlier that the feudal role of the tenant and landlord was set within a theological account of nature. Production is not a distinct category unto itself but is integral to the use of the bounty proffered by nature—that is, nature as the book of God.[40] Classical discourse may use the same language of gift, but its overtly theological meaning is compromised. And because of their confusion of land with capital, those classical economists who appeal to the description of gift cannot really mean it. Here, the surplus afforded by the gift of nature is no longer a gift in any sense but understood economically as a source of value given gratis to generate more capital. That is to say, it is no longer gift,[41] but value created and determined by the human subject as producer. It is "the rendering of man in the image of God the maker."[42] For the classical period, the category of gift remains an impossibility as long as the economic terrain is a distinct and autonomous sphere divorced from the ties between human labor and nature. And this is only to say, at another level, there is no economy of gift.

Nature and the Underpinnings of Classical Theory

Assuming my criticisms of Tribe are convincing, they still do not make a positive case for retaining the theory of rent. Much of Tribe's argument seems plausible when attempting to give a broad historical view, but such views can themselves be deceptive when sacrificing subtleties that may make the breaks between historical periods appear less clearly demarcated. The subtlety on which I will focus in this section is how classical theory still presumes as essential to its analysis a central role for nature and what this implies, in the following sections, for the possibility of thinking rent and land anew.

In her admirable study of the role of nature in classical economy, Margaret Schabas shows that despite the predominance of mechanistic understandings of nature since Descartes (1596–1650) and advances in the natural sciences and natural philosophy, classical political economists assume to varying degrees a view of nature as foundational to the production of wealth. This is not to say that contrary to Tribe the classical thinkers were unambiguously wed to earlier ancient and medieval conceptions of nature. Rather, it is more the case that the classical period was an ambiguous fusion in which holistic conceptions of nature were integrated with the natural scientific theories that took the human subject to be in some sense above the natural world. Such a synthesis could not ultimately be maintained, but it at least remains more visible and meaningful than one might tend to think.[43]

Schabas's thesis incorporates a broad meaning of nature, tying it mostly to how classical thinkers adopted or used the natural sciences and natural philosophy. Schabas and Mirowski note separately that despite a move toward the economy becoming an autonomous sphere of activity separate from nature, it is not really until the late nineteenth century that nature is fully divested of its priority as a model for understanding economic activities. Schabas refers to this turn as a "denaturalization" of economics, identifying J. S. Mill as the "pivotal figure" who inaugurates a new science explaining the economy mostly in terms of "human agency" as opposed to natural powers.[44] Mirowski takes note of a text in 1883 by Balfour Stewart where nature, once "the bestower of bounteous gifts" becomes a "niggardly paymaster."[45] Nature is no longer a source and provider of wealth but more a backdrop (or "mart" to use Stewart's word) against which humans exchange wealth (or in Stewart's example, energy). The economists inclined toward a more historically nuanced development of their field, such as Jacob Viner and Gunnar Myrdal, also mark the role of nature in classical theory as being decisive, though in a less thematic way.[46]

At some points, Schabas will examine more substantive meanings of nature—that is, how a thinker might interpret what nature is and how it sets a precedent for economic relations. My own intention here is not to align classical political economy with a broad meaning of nature, especially one that is developed through appeals to natural law,[47] but to identify its assumption of nature as a form of gift. This means that however prevalently classical theorists relied on a conception of natural law as operative in the economy, there is also a bias favoring nature understood as gift. It is worth reiterating that this thesis does not commit me to saying that classical political economy is therefore fundamentally based on a theory of gift.[48] Rather, it is to say there is in the classical thinking an account of nature as a unique entity that is best described as gift, and it may be that at the same time, this account was being increasingly crowded out according to the ways in which economic factors and human agency were abstracted from real, concrete social life. In other words, in contrast to Tribe's argument, nature understood as gift remains uncorrupted by the development of more economically specific determinations. Indeed, the persistence by which nature appears as gift enables some classical theorists to identify aspects of economic production that are not attributable to human agency.[49]

For classical theory, the privileged role of nature is expressed in its description. While passive, nature is the source of wealth; it is in some fundamental sense responsible for the production of wealth. Thus in looking back at the classical period, Henry George can say of its conception of nature that it "embraces . . . all natural material, forces, and opportunities" and indeed to such an extent that it can be strictly classified in contradistinction to capital which is not "freely supplied by nature."[50] In point of the problem of delineating clean or clear conceptual shifts, one finds Thomas Malthus describing nature according to images of both mechanism and gift: "The earth has been sometimes compared to a vast machine . . . but yet of very different and original qualities and powers." He later remarks that nature's machines which produce things like corn and raw materials "are gifts."[51]

Much of the prevalence of nature finds its most visible source in the economic thinking of the Physiocrats which gave precedence to "the rule of nature."[52] For the Physiocrats, nature is not just the source of wealth, and thus agriculture the prime activity of production; more importantly, one finds that human production is indebted to nature. In other words, the priority of nature entails an asymmetry in which human production can be seen as owing something back to nature. Hence Pierre Samuel du Pont states,

> Agriculture is the only human labour with which the Sky cooperates without ceasing and which is a perpetual creation. We strictly owe the net product to the soil, to Providence, and to the beneficence of the Creator, to his rain that beats down and changes it to gold.[53]

The net product is, of course, the ground rent generated by the use of the land, and the fact that it is owed to the soil suggests that correlatively rent is caused by the soil and is in some sense owed back. This latter meaning is what underwrites the idea that rent is unearned and therefore an increment that is not privately alienable.

Adam Smith was by all means familiar with Physiocracy, though he departed from it in at least one significant way: Smith rejected the idea that all production of wealth was tied unilaterally to land. Wealth was also produced by human labor, a position that today seems self-evident. Schabas notes that in this regard Smith proposed quite a radical shift, even when compared to Locke who confined his theory of labor to property and not economic value creation.[54] The result, as Henry George notes:

> That there is a natural order he [Smith] saw; and that to this natural order our perceptions of justice conform, he also saw. But that involved

> in this natural order is a provision for the material needs of advancing society he seems never to have seen.[55]

In this respect, Smith retains the priority of nature in his economic thinking; yet with a new (and even natural) prevalence given to the human laborer, nature is subservient to the human subject who holds dominion over the natural order.[56]

But if Smith makes a small advance toward a construction of economic theory based solely on human agency, Ricardo initiates a step back. His formal expression of rent provides not only a more convincing account of how an unearned increment arises from the soil, but also carries with it an ethical position implying that the distribution of rent to landlords is unjust.[57] In any case and regardless of the intricacies of the theories of the classical period, nature is conceived as a passive factor of production. Its passivity is by no means pejorative but denotes its status of priority. It is passive because it has been in a sense given to be used in human production. It is therefore no surprise that classical thinkers can link nature to an aspect of production which was distinct in its own right and has as its correlate a unique type of economic value—a surplus value. That this was indeed the case is only more noticeable in the period of economics just after the classical where, as we will see in chapter 3, land is no longer distinct but reducible to capital. Nature's passivity is of no real concern.

Ricardo and the Differential Nature of Rent

"The clear understanding of this principle [of rent]," writes Ricardo in a footnote, "is, I am persuaded, of the utmost importance to the science of political economy."[58] The debate over corn prices led Ricardo to analyze rent more closely. Rent, simply put, was not a cost of production. Ricardo's comment in his footnote appears to indicate that a clear understanding lies in seeing how rent arises as a surplus. As with all economic models, there are specific limitations. *Ceteris paribus*—that is, all things being equal—Ricardo supposed that given different plots of land, rent could be determined by holding constant the expenditure of labor and capital to produce one type of crop within the same duration.[59] Whether or not this assumption is a problem depends on whether or not the model is able to explain and predict what occurs in the "real" and the mostly non-agrarian world of economic transactions, something I will address in the last section of this chapter.

In its simplest form, one can take Ricardo's model to observe different yields in production due to the quality of soil. Let us consider two plots of land (A and B). Land A has a superior quality of soil and yields 1,000 units of corn (u), while Land B has a slightly inferior quality and yields 800u (*ceteris paribus*). Rent is here the surplus yielded for Land A, or 200u. In other words, if the same amount of labor and capital are expended, the difference in yield is due not to any advantage of applying more labor and/or expending more capital but rather to the advantage provided by the quality of soil of Land A. Thus rent is a surplus to the return of labor and the cost of using capital.

On Ricardo's view, rent is always determined in relation to the land in use that meets the subsistence level of the laborer and has the lowest yield. If a plot of land did not enable subsistence, it would not be worth using. So, we can expand our example to include more plots with varying quality:

	Yield (u)	Rent (u)
Land A	1,000	350
Land B	800	150
Land C	700	50
Land D	650	0

The land with no rent is referred to as marginal land, or the least productive land that is called into cultivation when there is not available land of better quality. Hypothetically speaking, if all land were of the same quality and if there was an unlimited supply, there would be no rent. But, of course, we know this not to be the case.

In addition to the difference in quality of soil, there are two other contingent features that we can note about land: it is scarce and the growth of population will increase its demand. Taken as a whole, these conditions can be more formally expressed: (1) land is limited in quantity; (2) land is not equal in quality; and (3) as population increases, marginal land is called into use. Rent is thus an economic principle that applies only when these three conditions prevail:

> It is only, then, because land is not unlimited in quantity and uniform in quality, and because, in the progress of population, land of inferior quality, or less advantageously situated, is called into cultivation, that rent is ever paid.[60]

Distilling Ricardo's doctrine into more succinct form, George provides the formulation that "the rent of land is determined by the excess of its produce over that which the same application [of labor and capital] can secure from the least productive land in use."[61]

While Ricardo's intention was to show that the value of land did not affect the price of corn and hence was not an exchangeable value,[62] his theory of rent has outlasted this intention. Indeed, it has survived well into the present day. Ricardo's legacy with respect to a theory of rent can be appreciated more when he is contrasted with his predecessors who did not extend nature's original powers to land used in manufacturing. The omission concerns the general supposition by which some of the most significant classical economists understood what constitutes production. In short, only agricultural land is originally productive. George notes that since the Physiocrats, the view persisted that agriculture "grows things" while manufacturing and trading merely change the forms of things. In short, agriculture is "productive"; manufacturing is "reproductive."[63] According to Jean-Baptiste Say, the orthodox position of the political economists prior to Smith was that

> labour produces no value without consuming an equivalent; that, consequently, it leaves no surplus, no net produce; and that nothing but the earth produces gratuitous value—therefore nothing else can yield net produce.[64]

Smith inherits this belief to some degree when writing,

> Food is in this manner not only the original source of rent, but every other part of the produce of land which afterwards affords rent derives that part of its value from the improvement of the powers of labour in producing food.[65]

And as he states later,

> No equal capital puts into motion a greater quantity of productive labour than that of the farmer. Not only his labouring servants, but his labouring cattle, are productive labourers. In agriculture, too, nature labours along with man; and though her labour costs no expense, its produce has its value, as well as that of the most expensive workmen.[66]

Agriculture is thus the original source of value (though not the only one for Smith, as we saw above), a value that is essential for all spheres of economic activity. It enables labor to be employed in other areas of production and reproduction.[67] Indeed, the gratuitousness of nature is unparalleled such that even if human labor produces wealth in some respects, as Smith says, "no equal quantity of productive labor employed in manufactures can ever occasion such so great a reproduction."[68] A surplus of food will always be consumed and used by productive labor. As Cantillon puts it, if there is a "double portion" of food, most laborers will consume the portion for their own maintenance.[69] According to Mirowski, this view is consistent with the classical idea that value, as energy, is original to nature and conserved (and not created) in manufacturing. Consumption, on this view, becomes a real problem: how is wealth circulated when the end activity is the destruction of this wealth? For Smith conservation of value in manufacturing, vis-à-vis consumption, is the saving of stock, which becomes capital for reinvestment.[70]

Furthermore, given this view toward surplus in agricultural production, there is an equally significant belief at work in how the classical economists understood productivity in relation to profit and supply. Simply put, products of manufacturing were observed not to have benefited from their surplus.[71] And because of this, the profit one could obtain from most commodities was dependent on their demand, which in turn was dependent on the growth of the population. This demand, and therefore a commodity's price, was seen to lack significant variation. To be sure, artificial factors could alter the profit for a merchant, as in cases of monopoly; but these were artificial and not a part of the natural functioning of the wealth of a nation. Smith makes this clear enough when discussing the profits of stock in relation to the price of commodities.[72] The inability of manufactured commodities to be profitable with a surplus in supply suggested that manufacturing, and thus the land used for it (since it was not as suitable for agriculture) was not productive. In Malthus's account of rent one therefore finds that the excess arising from agricultural production is unique because it is the excess of food that provisions for an increase in overall economic supply, demand, and exchange. In fact, if any other "machinery," or capital used in manufacturing were to do the same as land in this sense, Malthus remarks that "this excess would no longer belong exclusively to the machinery of land."[73] It is the agricultural land which yields rent and is determinative of the possibilities of subsequent (non-original) uses.

Ricardo, as noted above, appears to be the exception. After citing a passage from Smith on the distinction between productive (agriculture) and nonproductive labor (manufacturing), he concludes, "Does nature nothing for man in manufactures?. . . . There is not a manufacture which can be mentioned in which nature does not give her assistance to man, and give it, too, generously and gratuitously."[74] Yet oddly, because Ricardo formulates his theory of rent with respect to agriculture, a mistaken assumption that it applies only to agricultural land can be easily made.

George and the Extension of the Application of Rent

Henry George's analysis is not solely based upon the excess that provides for the essential metabolism of a society but upon how productive advantage can pertain to the use and possession of any type of land. In other words, with other uses of land, advantage can be clearly discerned; and this advantage inevitably manifests economically in how much one is willing to pay to gain use of the land in question. But to see how George's analysis is coherent, let us approach two other main uses of land—manufacturing (as well as retail) and residence.

With land used for manufacturing, rent is generated due to features that make a particular plot more lucrative than another. As indicated above, this point was made well before George, though he is careful to give it more attention.[75] So while with agriculture, fertile soil is the feature that allows the same application of labor and capital to produce more in a year than a plot with inferior soil, with manufacturing, features such as proximity to the center of commerce provide an advantage over inferior land which may be in a remote trading location. This is obvious in how land that tends to draw more prospective commerce—such as a main thoroughfare in a city center—is deemed more valuable than territory on the outskirts of a metropolitan area. There is an obvious shift here. Whereas the agricultural form of rent is tied to land's natural capacity for production, with manufacturing we find rent dependent on social factors and forms of evaluation.

While Ricardo's model assumed an advantage for agricultural production, we can do similarly for manufacturing or retail. Instead of fertility of soil, one might then look at the advantage of a commercial location in relation to its productivity. Land in the center of a commercial sector gains an advantage in terms of proximity to other services and products or the concentration of potential customers. However, by introducing land used for manufacturing, Ricardo's original model of rent is arguably too simplistic since one now has to account for the way in which land may be lucrative for either agriculture or manufacturing, and how these different categories of production stand in relation to each other when land is determined by quantity and quality.

Yet despite the addition of different types of land suitable for a variety of uses, George maintains that given the three conditions expressed by Ricardo (i.e., scarcity, variation in quality, use of marginal land), in any form of land use, rent will arise. So the determining criterion is not difference in types of production but the rent that any type of production a plot of land will command: "For there is no occupation in which labor and capital can engage which does not require use of the land."[76] In this respect, a plot of land may have the qualities of fertile soil for farming as well as the desirable location for the manufacture of widgets. Perhaps both uses gain advantage due to an adjacent river—one for its provision of water, the other for access to transportation. Its use, as far as human incentive is concerned, is determined by whatever type of production will yield a better return in relation to land at the margin of production. So, George observes, if a plot of land had an equal return for either farming or manufacturing, and the land was currently being used for manufacturing, a factor causing a drop in the return to labor and capital for manufacturing (say, the closure of a nearby market) would provide an incentive to turn the land to agriculture. In one sense, George not only retains the viability of Ricardo's model but generalizes it further:

> And, thus, to say that rent will be the excess in productiveness over the yield at the margin, or lowest point, of cultivation, is the same thing as to say that it will be the excess of produce over what the same amount of labor and capital obtains in the least remunerative occupation.[77]

But how would this work for land used for residence? There is no form of production that takes place on such land.

It is not as if there is no production that can ever occur on land used for residence; rather, it is more accurate to say that land used for dwelling involves a decision to forgo the use of that land for production in favor of some other type of value. As long as the cost of forgoing production or sale of the land is believed to be worthwhile, then the land will be retained for dwelling. In other words, the land used for dwelling either would have a return below that of the marginal land used for production, or if it has a return above the margin, it is worth, in some sense, retaining as land for dwelling. Aesthetic qualities are often reasons enough for doing so. Rent here takes the most visible form as the fee one is willing to pay to gain access or use. Mill therefore marks out this kind of value especially from the "ordinary principles of rent":

> Land is used for other purposes than agriculture, especially for residence; and when so, yields a rent, determined by principles similar to those already laid down [ordinary principles]. . . . The rent which the same land would afford in agriculture, but may be greater than this to an indefinite amount; the surplus being either in consideration of beauty or of convenience, the convenience often consisting in superior facilities for pecuniary gain. Sites of remarkable beauty are generally

> limited in supply, and therefore, if in great demand, are at a scarcity value.[78]

Today, of course, this way of valuing land for residence is most prevalent in terms of high equity retention. The value of the land and house are treated simultaneously as dwelling and commodity that has a resale value.

For George, the role of our subjective assessments of the use of land means that integral to the phenomenon of rent is a process of evaluating advantage.[79] Value is a function of advantage, whatever that advantage may be. As Mill points out above, this can also rely on subjective criteria—for example, aesthetic beauty. How relevant these criteria are depends on the extent to which they are recognized by those who might want use of the same land. Obviously, if no one else thought a plot of land to be beautiful, then its value would be low. Or, it may so happen that while the land might be obtained for little payment, in the future something may supervene to make it of great value. George therefore assumes a dynamic theory of value predicated upon subjective and objective criteria that may change as social and historical circumstances do; but whatever the case, for George the idea that something is desired by someone is the basis of economic value while its price is subject to conventions of barter and negotiation.[80] Land value can be seen therefore as owing to an advantage land originally provides yet only because derivatively there is a community for whom this advantage is meaningful. And this is to say that there is a direct relation between land value and its perceived ground rent.

From an everyday point of view, we do not tend to measure the advantage of land on a comparative basis over a certain duration. But we do tend to form an idea of whether or not the fee paid for the use of land is worthwhile. This form of evaluation persists in less complex matters where something like one's annual wages and expenses determine how much one is willing to pay for rent of land and its real property (i.e., buildings). Or it can be more complex in terms of forecasting loss and profit for a business within the first years of operation and how profit might augment after this initial period. It may therefore be worth the business owner taking the risk of paying a higher fee for the use of a plot of land in the city center, as opposed to the outskirt, with the expectation that this fee will become more affordable as the business gains more patronage. Such gambles are based on expectation of future earnings according to one's labor on the land or, in the case of speculation where land itself is the commodity, the expectation of future earnings in rent (fee paid). As Mason Gaffney remarks in view of this type of forecasting, "To buy title to land, therefore, people pay prices that look very high relative to current cash flow."[81]

There is a temptation to conclude that George therefore adheres to an overly or purely subjectivist account of value. It is perhaps more accurate to say he adheres to a practical theory of value that does not seek a theory of "real" value or a table of pricing. For George, the science involved in economics is aimed at social justice and not simply prediction and equilibrium.[82] In any case, the process of evaluation is not one of asserting some psychologistic content that has no relation to its object. Rather, any process of evaluation takes into account the already given entity land. So land value arises as an interrelation between land and the person requiring and/or desiring its use. We do not, in other words, *create* land value but discover it as a function of recognizing the advantage a given plot of land affords.

This means, furthermore, that while George includes the social sphere of evaluation in accounting for the ability of land to provide advantage, he sees this social layer as being wed to the natural status of land. In other words, the increase in wealth that obtains from the progress of society in its various forms is not wealth produced irrespective of land, but owing to it. Land gives advantage to human activity which is both natural and social. Or can one simply argue the converse? Is the natural advantage really only possible because of the social sphere of human knowledge?

Veblen, Technological Knowledge, and Social Capital

A persistent criticism of the theory of rent addresses its inherent limitation for overdetermining the significance the use of land plays in a modern economy. Even the extension of the theory to lands used in manufacturing and dwelling fail to recognize how such usages depend upon an entirely "non-natural" construction of knowledge. Prerequisite for land used by human labor in agriculture is the knowledge of, for example, how to farm the land in view of a specific crop. Thorstein Veblen (1857–1929) refers to this as the "technological knowledge" "of the physical behaviour of the materials" which, as a collective body, is "beyond what any one individual has learned or can learn by his own experience alone."[83] This knowledge enables land to be used and recognized as valuable, and without this knowledge there would be no discrete application of labor or indeed intent to own or possess a plot of land given its location and natural advantages. The general heading of "economic goods," comments Veblen, "means that they have been brought within the sweep of the community's knowledge of ways and means."[84]

At first glance, the omission of knowledge from a theory of rent seems a glaring oversight in accounting for how marginal uses of land give rise to an unearned increment. It seems, in fact, that rent is really the product of this distinctly human capacity to reflect on different uses of land in order to secure the "ways and means" for existence. That is to say, land is an entity involving only abstract representations of this entity in production, the maximization of utility, and so on. Value and price are phenomena arising due to human thought and agency applied to nature, and they are thus human conceptual creations in which nature plays no part except as the material and provider of certain powers. Veblen's point is not to marginalize the material sphere of traditionally understood "capital goods" or ground rent.[85] Rather, he wants to show how capital goods depend entirely upon human knowledge—that is, how the material depends upon the "immaterial equipment" of society.[86] Veblen argues that as technological knowledge advances with the development of the sciences (broadly construed), the stock of what he terms "material equipment" becomes more important, more desired.[87] But how then might land be conceived along these material lines? His turn to the theory of rent is unambiguous.

The differential advantage involved in land use that is noted by the classical theory is not contested by Veblen. Indeed, he appropriates this theory within his wider definition of capital by showing how technological knowledge in most cases augments the use of land and its differential return. His conclusion does not thus hesitate when citing what he holds to be the genuine reason why rent arises:

> It is only within the given technological situation . . . that any parcel of land has such productive powers as it has. It is, in other words, useful only because, and in so far, and in such manner, as men have learned to make use of it. This is what brings it into the category of "land," economically speaking.[88]

Consequently, the immaterial domain of human knowledge has precedence over the material domain. Without knowledge the opportunity to use anything like natural advantages would not be possible. This primacy given to technological knowledge as capital therefore means the category of land is really a subspecies of capital.

Veblen, in any case, presents a convincing analysis. Is use of land really only possible because of a prior human conception of its use? Yes, this is certainly the case. In many ways this is patently obvious. Then why should someone like George, whom Veblen read with some sympathy,[89] resolutely declare, "There must be land before labor can be exerted."[90] Is it a matter of theoretical obstinacy? Or perhaps blindness due to George's convictions based on religion and natural law?[91] Or is it that because of these convictions, George insisted on keeping economic theory wed to a larger theoretical perspective that was not anthropocentric? If this last question anticipates an affirmative answer, then it is not so much George's convictions that are important but the sense of perspective that reveals how Veblen's argument is incompatible with George's. Indeed, each economist proceeds from different assumptions. Veblen, following what Schabas describes as the trend towards denaturalization, reduces the economy to human agency. Veblen, in this sense, stands as an interesting figure in the history of economics. He seems in agreement with the general neoclassical reduction of the economy to human agency, yet his critical view of the modern economy is more akin to the classical insofar as he opposes monopoly of material means and recognizes any unearned increment as the domain of the community. George, on the other hand, maintains that the science of economy can be formulated only when understanding a larger "order or system" which encompasses it. This, for George, is of course nature. "Human enactments" are thus for George preceded by "natural laws."[92] George, in fact, presents a subtle theoretical distinction with his designation of the human factor as an active agent and nature as a passive one.[93] And while this is a typical classical distinction, George adds that this active-passive relation constitutes the very foundations of political economy. Why? Because in being active the human element produces, but cannot do so as a purely autonomous activity. It must take into account the passive factor which is not only used in creation, but which allows for production. Humans, to use a phrase from Paul Ricoeur, thus have a "dependent autonomy."[94] This dependency is, for George a dependency on natural laws, without which there would be no possibility for the ordering of knowledge and action Veblen describes.[95]

Yet if the appeal to natural laws strikes the modern reader as antiquated—whether anything like it is plausible—one can find in George's convictions a subtler point that provides a counterargument to Veblen. But in order to see the most cogent aspects of his analysis, we will first need to pass through the phenomenological investigation in the second part of this book. This is because phenomenology makes sense of the originary place of land without appealing to natural order, laws, and gift. Instead, it redescribes land's ontological nature, and it will be my argument that it does so in such a way that land can be seen to have a preeminence over humans and their knowledge. I will therefore readdress Veblen's criticism in chapter 7.

A Concluding Note: The Visibility of the Doctrine of Rent

I would like to return to two points left in suspense. The first has to do with the relation between the two meanings of rent, as fee and surplus, while the second concerns a judgment about the viability of Ricardo's *ceteris paribus* assumption.

If we take our cue from George, we find that there is indeed a direct correlation between the advantage afforded by a plot of land (surplus) and the price one is willing to pay to gain access to this plot (fee). The fee for use of land is anticipated as a future return to labor and capital; and in turn, the fee is determined according to the advantage the land provides in relation to the land at the margin. There is no exact science for determining the fee since, if one follows George, it is based upon a person-perspective assessment and a decision of what one is willing to forgo in exchange for use of the land.

Instances of this appear foremost in the form of land speculation where, as indicated above, speculators will purchase land in expectation of the future earnings it will generate either through sale or lease. The seasoned speculator knows that generally the longer he or she can withhold the land from use, the more its value will increase. One need only imagine a finite quantity of land being owned by various speculators, and how as the population grows, the demand for this land—and hence its perceived advantage—will increase. Of course, one need not put so much effort into this feat of imagination. It is more or less the status quo of the modern market economy, perhaps most obvious in the buy-to-rent frenzy. Take the examples of 2008 in Sunderland and London in the United Kingdom, where the removal of a tax relief on property meant landlords who kept their land out of use from businesses would suffer a penalty. For a person not adept in speculation strategies, the threat of a penalty would provide incentive to drop rental fees in order to lease the land. From a speculator's point of view, however, the penalty signals a rise in demand for land such that the government is willing to intervene. Unfortunately in these cases, the government confused a tax penalty on land with one on real property (buildings, etc.). Because the tax fell on the real property, the speculators—instead of lowering rents—destroyed the buildings. It was more lucrative to keep rents up, withhold the land from use, and destroy the real property than it was to drop rents and retain the real property.[96]

Given the above, the matter concerning the validity of Ricardo's *ceteris paribus* is plausibly answered. His simplified model identifies the nature of differential returns to land given the advantage it affords. This is practically instantiated in view of the fees one is willing to pay to gain this advantage—whether for production or for pleasure. If anything is smuggled away by virtue of his *ceteris paribus* clause, it is the assumption that land's status as a natural and original provider for human production was in no need of further justification.[97] It remained, to borrow a phrase from Collingwood, an "absolute presupposition"[98] of Ricardo's times. And this is to say that we must move away from a conception of land as gift, which remains mired in generality, and understand more thoroughly the kind of ontological givenness presupposed by it. Yet in order to undertake this route, we have still to dispel the reductions of land to labor and capital.

2

Ricardo or Marx? The Reduction to Labor

For Marxists, claims that Marx incorrectly negates the value of land in production can be controversial given present-day concerns for the environment. Absent of value, land is arguably of little social concern and open to possible exploitation. That debates over the status of land in Marx's thought involve commentators mostly in the fields of environmental and ecological ethics is therefore no surprise, and apologists for Marx are keen to note two things.[1] First, letter correspondence shows he was very much interested in the status of nature and, in today's terminology, its conservation.[2] Second, and more importantly, his conclusion about land and value is made with respect to exchange value, not value as such. In this chapter, I will be concerned with the latter clarification. Its significance cannot be underestimated since in pointing out that Marx's comments about land are consequent upon his critiques of exchange value and the capitalist modes of production, the rebuttal is that Marx sees nature as intrinsically valuable—namely, as use-value. To describe land in this manner is to recognize a form of value naturally wed to the intrinsic physical properties of the entity in question. These properties appear to us as properties because they are related to human needs. Land as use-value therefore means something like nature as it exists and is used by us in addressing our needs. This argument, in fact, turns the tables on Marx's critics. For it is the categorization of land as use-value that the capitalist mode of production fails to see; and in representing land as an exchange value, capitalism encourages and perpetuates the exploitation of nature, just as it does of labor. As Paul Burkett comments, the form of exchange value "qualitatively and quantitatively abstracts from nature's useful and life-giving characteristics" and it therefore "helps explain capitalism's tendency to despoil its natural environment."[3]

But is all classical thought guilty of this charge? My primary aim in this chapter is to save Ricardo's theory of rent from Marx's historical criticism. This task, nonetheless, is not a matter of simply comparing and contrasting the two on various points. Despite the rough similarity many economists see in Ricardian and Marxist theories, or what is perhaps epitomized in Paul Samuelson's remark that Marx was a "minor Post-Ricardian,"[4] there is an "either/or" dilemma. Because each thinker begins from substantially different assumptions about a theory of value, the possibility of a simple comparison or synthetic analysis is precluded. Indeed, Marx did not want simply to improve on Ricardo's theory, but to present a qualitatively different model. As his correspondence with Engels shows, Marx's critical refutation of Ricardo had been developing since 1851.[5] Building up towards *Capital,* he felt that Ricardian theory was confused and, as David Harvey puts it, Marx "could see clearly where Ricardo had gone wrong."[6] Marx's engagement with Ricardo should not be seen as an attempt to correct existing concepts but one of jettisoning an entirely inadequate and historically parochial representation of value creation. Ben Fine and Dick Bryan thus note that despite any similarity of terms, theories of rent in Ricardo and Marx are categorically different.[7]

In an attempt to respect this difference, I propose first to identify and address Marx's philosophical reasons for defining land as use-value and to show subsequently that these reasons do not save Marx from the general criticism that his economics subsumes nature under human dominion and correlatively reduces land as a factor of production to labor. I will then turn to the question of whether or not Marx's theory makes Ricardo's obsolete. My counterclaim is that despite his historical situation, Ricardo's formal model of rent alights upon a real economic relation when certain conditions supervene. Under such conditions, land is a distinct factor of production that creates value, but not exchange value, as Marx understands this term. In formulating a "Ricardian reply," I will argue that land creates a form of *economic* value which is not exchange value.

Readers familiar with recent studies of Marx and rent will note that I am not engaging in an analysis of the consistency of his theories—that is, Differential Rent I, Differential Rent II, and Absolute Ground Rent. Since I am concerned with showing fundamental differences between Marx and Ricardo, such an investigation remains tangential.[8] Perhaps this strategy of argument does not do justice to the complexity of Marx's analysis. It admittedly confines its scope to his philosophical assumptions as opposed to entering into his system altogether. But this consequence is unavoidable since in refusing to accept the historical interpretation of rent that Marx offers, I am also refusing to admit the remedy which his story necessitates.[9]

Use-Value and Land

Irrespective of debates over Marx's relation to classical political economy and whether or not his own economic theory constitutes a decisive break with the methods and assumptions of his predecessors, he shares with them their theoretical predilection for nature.[10] For Marx, the importance of nature has to do always with the fulfilment of material and biological necessity for humans, and elsewhere I have argued that Marx's identification of nature with necessity is a reductive step which prevents nature from having any other role except as extant material for human actualization (objectification). As Louis Dupré summarizes this problem so well, Marxism tends to aver that "all praxis takes place *within* nature, and there is no dialectic of consciousness *with* nature."[11] If this assessment is correct, then despite the similarity between Marx and his classical predecessors, nature will have in some sense a primary but, at the same time, diminished role.[12] Indeed, what Marx gives to nature as the necessary ground for production, he takes away when maintaining that only human labor creates value.

When Marx states that land is one of the original sources of wealth and the original condition and subject of labor and hence production,[13] he attributes value to land as a use-value. In *Grundrisse,* Marx emphasizes contra Proudhon that because land is and never was a product of labor, it cannot have any exchange value.[14] That it does, as Harvey notes, is to entertain an impossible fiction—namely "that 'rents grow out of the soil' and that land has value even though it is not the product of human labour."[15] Given this categorical distinction, one can argue that Marx's statements on nature are not only critiques of Ricardo's capitalist assumptions but a way of valuing nature under a broader notion of wealth—that is, "in far more universal terms, as consisting of those material use values that constituted the foundations for the full development of human creativity."[16]

If one turns to Marx's earlier writing, one comes across a rather obvious theoretical antecedent to use-value. Actualization involves the development of human consciousness through the objectifying capacity of labor. Objectification, in other words, constitutes the core of a philosophical anthropology—that is, defining human beings by their activity of labor:

> It is only when the objective world becomes everywhere for man in society the world of man's essential powers—human reality, and for that reason the reality of his *own* essential powers—that all *objects* become for him the *objectification of himself,* become objects which confirm and

> realize his individuality, become *his* objects: that is, *man himself* becomes the object.[17]

Assuming that this account of objectification is vital to his later work, *Capital* can be read as an economic translation of this anthropology:

> A use-value, or useful article, therefore, has value only because abstract human labor is objectified or materialized in it. How, then, is the magnitude of this value to be measured? By means of the quantity of the "value-forming substance," the labour, contained in the article. This quantity is measured by its duration, and the labour-time is itself measured on the particular scale of hours, days, etc.[18]

When taken together, the two passages thus indicate an economic anthropology in which human labor is the sole activity by which value is created; only human labor objectifies, and only objectification enables humans to meet their existence through use-values. So far this claim seems uncontroversial, perhaps even too obvious.

However, if use-value is tied to this anthropology of objectification, then its meaning is not as generous as the Marxian apologist wants to believe. Because use-values are essentially utilities,[19] they are attributes of things that arise only because human society deems them useful. Without use-value, things are nothing. It can mean little more than the designation of nature as the means for human fulfillment. In the last analysis, for whatever link there may be between use-value and natural, intrinsic properties, the term "use-value" is defined relative to human agency. Whatever value nature has, it still derives only from the human subject. Indeed, when Marx refers to land as the original presupposition allowing for labor activity, it is not a presupposition whose originality is metaphysically or ontologically significant in any sense, such as first cause. Rather, it is only a material presupposition, a material substratum. And even this aspect of material necessity is diminished when he remarks that really land is an extension of human being.[20] Whether one uses most of a forest for the production of paper or conserves this forest through alternative means of production, it is still only *for* human consciousness. In the language of *The German Ideology*, our relation to nature, or "real life," determines a consciousness which is "for me."[21] Nature as a resource is, in the end, a means to an end for human beings.

To allow nature a more substantial role, which would hold human agency accountable to a degree greater than its mere conservation as resource, would compromise the central, formative capacity of human labor. The actualization of human consciousness, in other words, would rely on another entity giving it substance, rather than human consciousness using matter to form itself. This formation, it must be remembered, is determined by nature, but only insofar as nature provides the means for fulfilling necessity; it is not a substance beyond its material, as if it were like a principle (*arche*) in the ancient Greek sense. If one believes nature fulfills anything beyond material necessity, one is creating an abstraction potentially distorting our real relation to material needs—that is, one is allowing "fancies [to stand] in the place of the real production of the means of subsistence and of life itself."[22] Such a situation is the precursor to the alienation of labor insofar as the idea of nature can stand before and distort how we understand what it really is and why we require it. Indeed, this mistake is made by those classical economists who think land, as nature, is distinct as an economic factor of production. Land is a substance in this regard since, as productive, it generates its own kind of value. But let us see how this allegation works in more detail.

In its expressly capitalist form, surplus value is synonymous with alienation because the modes of production are owned by those other than laborers. To gain access to work, laborers in effect must sell their labor for a wage. The actual product made by labor is therefore substituted with a wage, and this has two consequences. First, the laborer loses possession of the product he or she produces since he or she receives a wage instead. Second, because production is the means of objectification by which the laborer realizes him- or herself, the laborer is alienated in his or her existence. Surplus value thus coincides with alienation. The example often cited is how laborers are asked to increase their productive output per hour. No matter how much more the laborer produces, the hourly wage remains the same. The production of surplus commodities, or surplus value, is then conveniently taken by the business owner.

With land, there is a similar form of alienation. Consider first the linkage between the concept of alienated labor and surplus value occurring in *Grundrisse*:

> In surplus capital, all moments are products of alien labour. . . . The product of labour appears as alien property, as a mode of existence confronting living labour as independent, as value in its being itself; the product of labour, objectified labour, has been endowed by living labour with a soul of its own. . . . Living labour therefore now appears from its own standpoint as acting within the production process in such a way that, as it realizes itself in the objective conditions, it simultaneously repulses this realization from itself as an alien reality.[23]

Second, when Marx says "All ground-rent is surplus-value, the product of surplus labor" and at the same time that this surplus value is the fee paid to the landowner, a direct connection is made between the alienation of labor and the "valorization" of land in terms of exchange value.[24] Within the overall scope of Marx's assessment of political economy, ground rent is a practice through which alienation occurs as rent—that is, a surplus value originally belonging to labor yet given by convention to the landlord. To maintain consistency within his analysis, Marx cannot allow land to have a substantial role in production without acknowledging that rent, as a surplus value, does not belong to labor. Moreover, such an admission would compromise his overarching project showing how capital is, as a "self-expanding value," at the root of economic alienation.[25] Nature provides nothing except the means through which labor can (once again) know itself.

Why There Is No Natural Advantage in Land

It might seem that the foregoing account of land and use-value is enough to understand why Marx had adequate philosophical grounds to dispense with Ricardo's theory. However, this by itself does not really enable one to see analytically how Marx dismisses the commonsensical notion that innate qualities of land—like fertility—appear to contribute to the production of value. In order to show this analytical break, I draw upon a critical distinction made by Mirowski: there are two theories of value, and not one, operative in *Capital*.

The first theory, as discussed earlier, is a general labor theory of value: labor is the only producer of value. The second theory arises with Marx's famous addition of socially necessary labor-time:

> Socially necessary labour-time is the labour-time required to produce a use-value under the conditions of production normal for a given society and with the average degree of skill and intensity of labour prevalent in that society.[26]

But is not this passage simply evidence of Marx surpassing the classical theory, as many commentators assume?[27] Mirowski is not content to accept this conclusion. He sees two theories which cannot be so easily unified. This is because one theory attempts to maintain value as a substance, and the second, as a sociohistorically constituted field, or what Mirowski refers to as real-cost. The first theory of value says that "labor-time, extracted in the process of production, is reincarnated . . . in the commodity, to subsist thereafter [as a substance] independent of any market activity."[28] Real-cost involves the historical dimension of social life where labor value manifests, per above, according to any given condition of production. Mirowski sees the simultaneity of these two theories as a contradiction because an understanding of value as substance involves the transformation of value *already* in one thing into another. To then say this value is determined by what is deemed historically and socially necessary is to say that no real value is conserved in the laboring process; value created by labor really has no substance at all and rather that "present conditions alone determine present embodied-labor values of all commodities jointly and simultaneously."[29]

I will not dwell on the extent to which the co-presence of the two theories constitutes a contradiction. Rather, I want to consider how the two theories are crucial for understanding Marx's dismissal of natural advantage. On the one hand, the substance aspect of his labor theory of value allows him to eliminate any meaningful role nature might occupy. As we saw in the previous chapter, the classical thinkers for the most part retain a special status for nature when seeing it as a gift. The bounty of nature is at the very least a conceptual placeholder for understanding how a passive factor of production is integral to value creation. On the other hand, in order to maintain this theoretical stance, Marx cannot merely aver the obsolescence of the classical view of nature. He has to convince us that natural advantage is really an illusion. The second theory of value thus becomes essential to his argument. Natural advantage appears to exist only because of the historical development of capitalism in which, to be clear, socially necessary labor time and the value it creates are distorted. Per Marx's chapter on Differential Rent I, this distortion occurs primarily through the historically specific institution of landownership—that is, ground rent appears only because a landlord can claim the surplus value. Thus, it is only on the basis of this intervention that it appears a separate value has been generated by the land. Let us examine how the two theories of value relate to land in more detail.

Marx's illustrative example involves a plot of land possessing a natural waterfall. Assuming that various lands within a given society are used to produce commodities by way of steam engines, the waterfall presents a distinct advantage because it provides a free source of labor. Or so it appears that way. Marx writes,

> The value of the commodities produced by water-power is lower because a smaller amount of labour is required for their production, i.e. less labour enters in the objectified form, as a portion of the constant capital.[30]

In accordance with the notion of labor as substance, Marx at first recognizes how given something like a natural source of power, less value must in fact enter into the production of commodities. If labor power, as it were, comes from something other than human labor, and if use-value is restricted to human labor alone, then whatever portion is produced by something like a natural source inversely affects the portion of human labor contained in the commodity. So, whatever has gone into the commodity via a natural source is not value because it was not created by labor. Marx generally refers to this exclusion in terms of the amount of "constant capital" used in production. Constant capital is both raw material and the objectified things of labor used in production. This capital is constant because it "does not undergo any quantitative alteration of value in the process of production."[31] The claim that less labor and therefore less value results from the use of water power does not imply, however, that there is less profit made by the manufacturer relying on water power.

In the following passage, Marx identifies two factors comprising the greater productivity from water power: (1) reduction of capital expended, and (2) reduction of labor expended, both of which, as one might recall, occupy a crucial role in Ricardo's *ceteris paribus* clause (i.e., expenditure of labor and capital are constant across lands of varying quality) when defining rent.

> The labour applied here [in the case of the waterfall] is more productive, its individual productivity being greater than that of the labour employed in the majority of factories of the same type. Its greater productivity is expressed in the way it needs a smaller quantity of constant capital to produce the same amount of commodities, a smaller quantity of objectified labour than the others; and a smaller quantity of living labour as well.[32]

So while less labor enters into the production process when using a natural power, labor is more productive comparatively across a sector of production. Why? Because "a small quantity" of capital is expended; and "a small quantity" of labor is used. What then follows in relation to the majority of factories utilizing steam engines is a difference of "cost price," or the cost of producing commodities, and "price of production," or the price at which commodities must sell in order to obtain a profit. In general, for the labor using water power, the cost price is lower and the price of production, determined by the cost price of the majority of factories using steam engines, thus generates a surplus value. But Marx notes that this way of accounting for the generation of surplus value does not really distinguish the use of natural power from more general instances where cost price can be reduced in the same genre of manufacturing.[33] He argues that factories using steam also employ natural advantage; but even more importantly, they increase the productivity of labor by reducing the cost of the subsistence of labor. So the case of the waterfall really only describes something more general, that is, whenever some form of capital (assuming we can equate land and its natural powers with capital) reduces the cost of production. Faithful to his position on capital and labor, Marx comments that surplus value arises for the land using water power because those manufacturers employing steam engines are using capital which itself has a value (produced by the labor that made them) and therefore costs something when it is used for production. In essence, the natural power as a use-value and as something not created by labor has no value and therefore no cost when used. As Marx states, "[nature] represents no objectified labour and hence no price."[34] The steam engine, to the contrary, is a product of labor and therefore has value; to use it in production is to pay the cost for this value.[35]

Marx strengthens his position by subsuming land under capital (though not in the neoclassical sense to be discussed in the next chapter).[36] In other words, natural powers (e.g., the waterfall or fertility) are only distinguishable when they are employed by labor along with capital. Nature by itself is nothing.

> The increased productivity of the labour he [the manufacturer] applies arises neither from the capital and labour themselves nor from the simple application of a natural force distinct from capital and labour but incorporated into the capital.[37]

So nature in and by itself does not result in increased productivity; rather it is nature "incorporated into the capital." Nature, in other words, becomes productive when labor utilizes it through capital. It facilitates the use of capital, and because nature has no exchange value, it costs nothing. If nature is simply the basic condition for labor, and if nature is in this sense an extant material condition, whatever nature provides by way of varying quality can be in theory equalized through capital investments. So less fertile land can be made more fertile like its superior counterparts through use of fertilizer or more permanent fixtures, such as irrigation canals. To emphasize this role of capital, he notes how the latter, more permanent fixtures often become perceived as part of the land itself; and hence, such fixtures are often calculated into rents as an inflation that occurs at the beginning of a new lease.[38] The coincidence of land and capital improvement is referred to as *la terre-capital*. Harvey summarizes, "capital creates in one place conditions of production that are free gifts of nature elsewhere."[39] Contrary to Ricardo and the Physiocrats, nature is no longer a force of production that provides from its bounty; rather, it is a materially extant means by which human labor can objectify itself. As Marx famously states, "natural force is not the source of the surplus profit, but simply a natural basis for it."[40] Let us frame this more concisely: if labor produces value, it transforms material into value; natural force then is not a cause of exchange value but simply its basis of transformation.[41]

Given this explanation of land as really a part of capital, where does the illusion of the distinctness of natural advantage come from? The answer: monopoly, that is, the second theory of value in which modes of production are determined by certain sociohistorical conventions which, in turn, affect the way the creation of value appears to occur. Thus, turning to monopoly as the cause of surplus profit in the use of nature, we also turn away from the notion of value as substance and toward its historically contingent genesis. Cases of natural advantage, says Marx, are really cases of the monopolization of a natural force. Indeed, Marx notes that even in cases where manufacturing relies on steam engines, the real difference is not the cost of production when using capital made by labor (per above), but the eventual monopoly over natural forces. So while "the manufacturer pays for coal [produced by labor]," he or she does not pay "for the ability of water to change its aggregate state and transform itself into steam."[42] But when these forces are monopolized by the landowning class, then he or she must.

One can also detect the effect of monopoly by contrasting it with a mode of production in which it is absent. For example, in a noncapitalist society, the increased rate of profit originally given to the use of water power would go to the laborer. Yet when ownership of the land on which the water power exists enters into the relations of production, the landowner claims a portion of the production from the manufacturer (who may or may not be the laborer) for access to and use of the land. This intervention gives rise to, as Marx puts it, "an irrational expression concealing a real economic relationship."[43] The irrationality of the intervention is simply the fabrication of the idea of ground rent. To recall: there is only ground rent because there is a landlord who can claim entitlement to it by virtue of legal ownership of the land. "The excess profits," as Harvey notes, "would exist even without their conversion into ground rent."[44] Indeed, let us not forget that a certain sleight of hand occurs with capitalist modes of production. Ground rent, by virtue of being a fee charged based on the margin of profit, acts as a price. So it then appears the land paid for in rent has a value, when really it is only the presence of the landlord causing the illusion. The "real economic relationship" anticipates how Marx will attempt to account for surplus value in terms of Absolute Ground Rent; but for my purposes, it suffices at this point to comment on the historically specific emergence of ground rent vis-à-vis landownership.

As many commentators emphasize, landownership for Marx is a feature of only one stage of the capitalist mode of production.[45] It is clear that his analysis of the waterfall example requires the stage of capitalism at which landownership is a major convention, so much so that, as we will explore in the next chapter, landowning is conceived as a natural (as opposed to conventional or historical) mode of human existence. So what constitutes the real-cost aspect of ground rent is the convention of landownership, or the monopoly on natural forces. This critical assessment is, in the buildup of *Capital,* stated clearly in Marx's introductory comments on differential rent:

> The rationalization of agriculture . . . and the reduction of landed property to an absurdity—these are the great services of the capitalist mode of production . . . . Ground-rent is thus the form in which landed property is economically realized, valorized.[46]

Taking into account this historical perspective on landowning and the substantial claims of Marx that nature contributes nothing to the production of commodities, one can see how both theories of value allow him to break analytically from his classical predecessors. Yes, nature as use-value is fundamental to the actualization of humanity. Yes, we cannot do without it. But no, it has no real involvement in the expressly human practice of economic value creation and only seems to due to specific historical conventions. We thus see the key components according to which Marx describes the nature of ground rent as a fiction.

A "Ricardian" Reply

At the core of Marx's criticism is the allegation that Ricardo fails to see how land operates historically in capitalist modes of production and falters in attempting to remain truly committed to a labor theory of value in which, to quote Ricardo, "the relative quantity of labor . . . almost exclusively determin[es] the relative quantity of commodities."[47] As we will see later, the term "almost" will prove decisive in saving Ricardo. Indeed, despite the two thinkers sharing a general concern for a labor theory of value, Ricardo's conception of rent maintains a significant distinction. He attempts to draw the value produced by land back to labor when conceiving the final effect of differential rents in terms of difference in price;[48] yet he also maintains a multifaceted conception of value which derives from labor *and* land. This last point is essential to my argument since it entails understanding how value for Ricardo is not primarily exchange value, or price.

I offer two arguments in this section. First, I consider the matter of Ricardo's view on the labor theory of value and land as a creator of value. I conclude that Ricardo did not hold to a strong version of the labor theory of value and that the formalism of Ricardo's theory of rent allows one to tie a general form of economic value (i.e., one that is not exchange value) to land. Land has value, both use-value and economic value. Second, I examine specific criticisms of Ricardo made by Marx involving land monopoly and the generation of rent on marginal land.

Ricardo's distinction between rent and labor indicates he was broad-minded when it came to theoretical explanation; he was not attempting to reduce value to the quantity of labor expended. George Stigler remarks that confusion over Ricardo's notions of labor and value derives from the failure to note that he was not making an "analytical" proposition intending to define value: "that labour quantities were the sole regulators of value."[49] Rather, his account is an empirical judgment, attempting to describe an economic phenomenon. On this view, any strong identification of Ricardo with a labor theory of value must contend with direct comments he makes; for example, "Rent, then, is a creation of value."[50]

Such a remark has a rippling effect. Specifically, let us examine the notion that while rent expresses a difference between varying lands, it inevitably manifests as difference between individual production prices and the average production price. In other words, whatever difference in value land use at the margin generates, because the final measure of this difference is the exchange of the commodities produced, it is easy to conclude that Ricardo's theory is one really based on difference in production prices. The land at the margin, the worst land, has the highest cost of production, which determines the rate of profit for superior lands with lower costs of production.[51] Marxist commentary on Ricardo thus emphasizes that ground rent does not arise absent market prices. Why? Because price involves exchange value, and it becomes convenient for Marxists to maintain the expression of rent in terms of exchange value since, within capitalism, rent directly relates to the market value of land.[52] This equation cannot be overlooked since it omits a more basic observation of Ricardo's theory, one that does not require price and exchange value.

Fundamentally, Ricardo is examining production in terms of the use of capital employed by labor. His theory need not invoke exchange value, at least not at the most basic level; for what is being produced by land and labor is essentially a product, and not necessarily a commodity in the capitalist sense. Less the costs of production, what remains irrespective of market exchange are the products themselves.[53] When land use is factored in, what then arises is the variation in the production by labor, since lands of different quality or advantage will produce a greater return given the equivalent expenditure of capital and labor on inferior land. In these rudimentary terms, superior lands create a value not yet represented by exchange value but expressed as products. Furthermore, on Ricardo's view an aspect of the profit obtained in the use of superior land is technically owed neither to labor nor landlord. Though he never says so, one can venture to say it is owed, as it were, to the land.

There is a more obvious difference that emerges when insisting that Ricardo's formalism takes varying levels of production rather than prices as fundamental to his analysis. This formalism, as discussed in the previous chapter, is something that can be extended to all types of land, whether for agriculture, manufacturing, or dwelling. Marx, to the contrary, seeks to find the difference resulting in surplus not in differential rent extended to all types of land, but the difference in capital consumption between agriculture and industry. In this respect, Marx assumes that differential rent does not apply to the industrial sector.

What force lies behind my attempt at clarifying rent in terms of economic value? Precisely the weakening of Marx's materialist appeals to a labor theory of value. Ricardo, in other words, cannot be criticized from a Marxist perspective for failing to carry through the implications of the labor theory of value, or what Marx states as "Ricardo's failure to understand his own principle."[54] If Stigler is correct, then Ricardo's approach is one in which a unilateral theoretical commitment to one theory of value is absent. Whatever room remains in Ricardo's political economy for other sources of value becomes a potentially significant issue, not just for better understanding his overall economy but, in this case, seeing how his theory may be more dynamic than popularly thought. To aver that Ricardo was confused and could not begin to work out what Marx had then appears a disingenuous claim.

As to my second argument, let us examine two of Marx's reasons for rejecting Ricardo's theory of rent: (1) the claim that ground rent arises only with the presence of landed monopoly, and (2) the worst (marginal) land pays rent.

Marx writes when commenting on Differential Rent I that it

> presupposes precisely the monopoly of landed property, landed property as a barrier to capital, for otherwise the surplus profit would not be transformed into ground-rent and would not accrue to the landlord instead of the farmer.[55]

I discussed above how this way of describing rent involves the historical development of capitalist modes of production and how, within this development, the landlord as a social convention is deemed in some sense integral to production. As John Kenneth Galbraith comments, Ricardo may have recognized the problems with landlords taking a portion of the production to which they contribute nothing, but he thought "there was no evident alternative and certainly none was better."[56] While for Marx rent expresses a "swindle"[57] that is possible only with landed monopoly, for Ricardo rent can be easily explained in the absence of landed monopoly.

To follow Ricardo requires keeping distinct the two meanings of rent—that is, rent as surplus and as fee. Marx's conclusion about landed monopoly conflates the two: surplus is the fee taken by the landlord. Recalling that for Ricardo the application of labor and capital are held constant, the varying qualities of the soil will result in a difference in yield. Here, rent is not a fee but the designation of a surplus on nonmarginal lands. Any "excess," as Ricardo remarks, "is itself rent."[58] To be sure, Ricardo at the same time fails to see how rent may be detached from the fee taken by the landlord when he insists that rent is a creation of value and not wealth. By this he means its creation benefits its possessors (i.e., landlord or laborer), but not the general wealth of the society in terms of its infrastructure.[59] In any event, it is apparent that the definition of rent as excess is prior to that of fee; there can be no fee without the excess.

In his opening comments about Absolute Ground Rent, Marx dismisses Ricardo's theory for a second reason:

> In our analysis of differential rent, we proceeded from the premise that the worst land pays no ground-rent, or, to put it more generally, land pays ground-rent only when the individual production price of its product is below the production price that governs the market, giving rise to a surplus that is transformed into rent.[60]

Marx argues that the notion that the worst land pays no rent is fallacious. In his analysis of Differential Rent II, he puts forward the possibility that different amounts of capital can be invested in lands of the worst quality. The worst land can produce a rent so long as application of more capital results in a market price above the production price.[61] For instance, swamp land can be drained and improved in order to make it suitable for farming.

This position departs from Ricardo's *ceteris paribus* clause, which holds application of labor and capital constant for the same type of production on lands of varying quality. Why does Marx make this departure? Because it does not make sense to entertain the possibility that land creates any surplus value. Commitment to the labor theory of value in this sense requires that excess value can be generated by labor on any land, especially the worst. The only way of accounting for this in Marx's system is to show how surplus is wed to the difference between production price and market price. So given the limit of the governing, general market price of a commodity, use of additional capital can enable labor to increase its productivity such that something like an average profit may result. This, in turn, allows Marx to dispense with the idea that fertility of land contributes to the production of value. It is quite clear in his examples that the application of additional capital acts in the same capacity as natural advantage, for it increases the fertility of the land.[62]

Ricardo, of course, accounts for additional applications of capital in order to augment production. He refers to the presence of improvements in knowledge and methods (or Veblen's technical knowledge) to increase productivity, on the one hand, and to reduce the amount of labor, on the other.[63] Whatever variation there may be, the Ricardian model always maintains a margin, even in cases where successive applications of capital fall on the same land. So with the worst type of land, the expenditure of capital held constant for all types of land for the same production is considered the first application. Its rent is zero. Given an additional amount which yields a surplus above the constant rate, that surplus is rent. Yet this additional use of capital and its surplus yield in no way contradicts Ricardo's assertion that the worst land has no rent. This is because the *ceteris paribus* clause provides the measure. Ricardo's formal model requires that any additional capital used to improve inferior land result either in (1) taking that additional amount applied in usage across all types of land used for the same production, or (2) marking the additional capital in terms of a successive application of labor in distinction to the labor applied in attempting to cultivate the land in the absence of these improvements. From the start, as Ricardo makes clear, the basis of his differential analysis, while relating to market price, is established on the difference in "the proportion of the produce" on varying lands.[64] So in the instance of drained swamp land, investment of capital to improve the land would be measured against current land used for the same production. This comparison is neither trivial nor avoidable. The incentive to convert the swamp would not occur unless land suitable for farming in its natural, unimproved state were not available. Indeed, one need only imagine how given a choice between using lands of superior and inferior fertility, a farmer would most certainly choose the land that required no capital investment in order to bring it to the same production levels of its superior counterpart.

Yet why is the maintenance of this *ceteris paribus* measure important? In one sense, it provides a point of reference by which one may decide to employ unused land. In another sense, it indicates the value of the plots of land used in production. If the worst land requires additional applications of capital to yield a surplus, then despite this yield, it is still of less value than lands of superior quality. As I discussed in the previous chapter, Ricardo's notion of the margin is in fact what is employed, usually unknowingly, when determining prices in the land market. According to one critic of land monopoly, prediction of the prices in land conforms to "Ricardo's Law."[65] Yet this is not to say that a land market, in which ownership of land is held privately in perpetuity, is the necessary condition for rent and land value as Marx held.[66] Even in an economy where ownership of land is prohibited or absent, value would express itself as the desire to use that land on which a more lucrative use could be made given the same expenditure of labor and capital across other inferior lands. So from a Ricardian perspective, what is ignored by Marx is the decision to use one plot of land over another. If land of inferior fertility requires additional investment of capital in order to make it competitive with lands of superior quality, this investment does not result in equalization, certainly not in such a way that the distinction between natural and artificial can be collapsed. The investment in capital is, to the contrary, a cost paid in order to make labor as productive as it would be on a superior plot of land. The two types of land, one with natural advantage and the other with artificial improvement, are never the same except in the perception of their yield, certainly not when accounting for the expenditure of labor and capital.

My responses to Marx's criticisms suggest that the formalism of Ricardo's theory is not as historically parochial as Marx would have it. If awareness of historical relations is lacking in Ricardo's account, it can nonetheless be claimed, as I have, that his theory of rent describes a basic economic relation between land, labor, and capital. My placement of Ricardo's formalism and Marx's historical analysis in opposition is, of course, somewhat selective. It is not that formalism triumphs in this instance, but rather it is to say that the formal relation articulated by Ricardo has, despite the following anachronistic description, a *phenomenological* grounding that has yet to be explored.

3

Otherwise Than Capital?

When economists like Vilfredo Pareto and Mark Blaug make unequivocal statements such as, "Land capital does not enjoy any economic precedence over other capital" and the classical definition of land results from the confusion of "thinking in physical rather than economic terms,"[1] one might wonder why I should devote any attention to the way economic theory since the 1870s has by and large reduced land to capital. The default attitude seems unambiguously self-evident. In what follows, nonetheless, I treat this self-evidence not as a testament to a general attitude of agreement but its unexamined nature.[2] Beyond the frame of economic theory, why do we generally and readily accept land as a form of capital?

That one can handily make the distinction between the physical and economic, as if the classical thinkers made a category mistake, presupposes a philosophical milieu—or imaginary—in which the sphere of the "economic" is understood to deal with realities separate from what is physical or natural. The economist might argue that because economics deals with human relations of exchange, natural definitions have no relevance to its enterprise. But I think this response is possible only because what has been accepted as cogent is in fact a separation between the economic and the natural. So what then gives cogency to this distinction? It most certainly has something to do with the alienability of land and how it is understood today as an entity primarily constituted by social and economic relations. Land, in other words, appears to us first as an entity arising from these relations. Whatever alternative meaning it might have is secondary to this. Meanings—pertaining to nature, gift, or givenness—are therefore seen as trivial or irrelevant.

In the first half of this chapter I want to explore how this shift occurred in looking at the philosophical imaginary which makes it possible. I will discuss this imaginary in relation to three of the most prominent thinkers of the seventeenth century who formulated the foundations for theories of property—Hugo Grotius (1586–1645), Samuel Pufendorf (1632–1694), and John Locke (1632–1704)—and how their philosophies *enable* the present-day understanding of land as capital. The second half of this chapter will then consider the main economic arguments since 1870 for maintaining this attitude and those skeptical or critical of it. It is important to note that I will be using the term "private property" in a very general sense—namely, that an entity is alienable. I am calling into question how and why this term has become so readily applied to land. In most theories of property—and the three natural law thinkers are no exception—land is a special instance of private property which obeys the general rules of ownership. Such features as land's scarcity and immobility may distinguish it from things (*choses*) commonly understood to be property; but these features do not preclude its definition as property—a feature which persists in current economic theory, as we shall see.

The Philosophical Imaginary

There are many ways to show the influence of philosophical ideas and arguments. Conceptual influences need not occur through evidence gleaned from extant references to such sources; and such influences need not be consciously received or affirmed. Borrowing and adapting the term from Michèle LeDoeuff,[3] I refer to the "philosophical imaginary" as the context in which certain concepts and the delineation of these concepts in philosophical debate give rise to meanings through which we begin to conceive and experience our relation to entities. Following to some extent the example of Charles Taylor,[4] I want to ask, what makes it possible for the belief that land is classifiable as capital?

The imaginary is in this sense a conceptual landscape which conditions the possibility for certain meanings—what can be thought and what cannot. This imaginary does not necessarily have a direct historical cause-and-effect relation that one might find as we did, for example, when Margaret Schabas linked classical economic conceptions of nature to the literature on scientific investigations. While this kind of direct relation might exist, the imaginary is broader, even if more ambiguous. It is constituted by a variety of texts which have a variety of interpretations, which in turn generate and affect the ways we think after these interpretations have sedimented themselves in our traditions and canons. This is only a very basic way of making a central point of hermeneutics after Heidegger. Yet what also follows upon the conceptual determinations made possible by varying interpretations is, of course, a no less Heideggerian point: our mode of being *is* interpretation. And this is to say after Hans-Georg Gadamer and Paul Ricoeur that the primary medium through which our mode of being is interpreted is through texts. Thus, given an understanding of philosophical sources, it will have a direct relation to our existence and our use of things in existence. This kind of use, as Heidegger discusses, is ontological since it declares, or reveals, a type of relation in which our understanding and valuing of existence is disclosed and enacted through our practical activities.[5]

There is a philosophical flip side to this historical relation to interpretation; and this involves how we critically reread those texts viewed as constitutive of our traditions, canons, and present situation. For example, the social philosophy of the seventeenth century is dominated by what C. B. Macpherson famously called a "possessive individualism," which in turn informs the "possessive market society" we have today.[6] While critical reaction to Macpherson is extensive, to argue that his interpretation may not be accurate in depicting the original position or perspective advocated by the likes of Hobbes or Locke is to miss the way traditional texts engender meaning beyond the immediate horizon of their historical audience. Such texts have meanings emergent in and through history—that is, in and through the way we as readers attempt to read them as meaningful with respect to a certain set of questions and problems we bring to these texts. And often, these questions and problems may not be things of which we are consciously aware.

Rather than dismissing Macpherson's claim as anachronistic or false,[7] it might be fairer to say that his claim is a way of making sense of seventeenth-century philosophy according to what he perceives to be the problems of the twentieth century which, above all, have not arisen ex nihilo but through a process of understanding that draws on its historical sources. Macpherson's decision to (re)read major figures in seventeenth-century philosophy is, of course, not arbitrary since the works of Locke are often called upon by those who defend the kind of individualism Macpherson attacks. I therefore think an important philosophical exercise lies in seeing how, apart from the accuracy of interpretation, a critical understanding of a present-day problem can be traced back to historical sources. This task is not a way of laying philosophical blame on a thinker, or advocating a specific historical narrative or genealogy, but of seeing how historical sources have made possible a specific understanding of our relation to things despite whatever original intention these sources may have had.[8] Critical forms of historical understanding thus wager that a better diagnosis of our present situation comes through an analysis of our relationship to past sources.

In view of this chapter's argument, what I wish to convey is how Grotius, Pufendorf, and Locke prepare the conditions for thinking land as alienable in the sense that we readily understand it today as a form of capital. I identify in the three a general remit under which land is understood as a gift of God and as a means for achieving what is deemed to be a human good. The former involves the gifting of the creation (nature) by God. The latter is linked (in)famously to sociability and self-preservation. For Grotius, Pufendorf, and Locke, land is given and alienable only because it serves the purpose of ensuring human socialization. I argue that this is a reduction of the gift of land to a means of fulfilling their conception of natural law: because natural law is determined by the ends of sociability and self-preservation, land is essentially related to our natural ends (willed by God). But as an entity about which we form various conceptions, it is distinct from these ends. It is a means, an instrument, or what is finally an entity that has meaning only in relation to something else. I refer to this way of conceiving land as a *nomological reduction.*

One final note: there is another prominent reason that can be attributed to the transformation of the understanding of land. In the modern natural law tradition, land is understood within a theological context which applies specific limitations or provisos to human appropriation. When this context is surpassed and the practice of land appropriation persists, the originally conceived practical limitations are lost, and potential abuse of this practice can emerge. As is often the case with historical transformations of concepts, the theological context is often abandoned, or what Max Weber famously notes as the process of disenchantment or rationalization. However, I will not be investigating this aspect of the subject matter if only because the fact that we no longer appeal to the "substantive" (in Weber's terminology) theological framework unique to the thinking of Grotius, Pufendorf, and Locke is patently obvious. Today, justification for the ownership of land draws on a notion of the individual detached from this framework—that is, the individual free to realize him- or herself economically. Karl Polanyi's work has explored this type of transformation in great detail.[9] Another reason involves an assumption on my part. The voluntarist tendency, at least in Pufendorf and Locke, anticipates a transition to secularism with its separation of nature from its divine source. I therefore take for granted that these two reasons attest to the problem at hand, as we will see when I discuss voluntarism; but in the deepest respect, it is a problem that requires still a fuller understanding beyond the lament of the loss of a certain theological, metaphysical, and ethical perspective.

Land as the Gift of God

That land (the creation) is understood by the likes of Grotius, Pufendorf, and Locke to be the gift of God is well known. They are all agreed that this donation was to humankind in common, though each theorist will devise different justifications for the progression to private property. Understanding land as a divine donation may seem an obvious feature of the Judeo-Christian tradition since it is founded on a cosmology in which the natural world is caused by a supernatural source. However, this view is not limited to creationism; it can also be consistent with emanationism, or what is a metaphysical perspective deriving from Neoplatonic thought which describes the creation as a direct emanation of the One—either through his will or intellect. Whatever the case, this cosmological understanding does not entail any specially designated human practices when it comes to property. Such a development relies on the direction that theological reflection and doctrine assume. For example, the importance of dominion (ownership) can be interpreted from two significant passages in the Hebrew Bible. According to Psalm 24:1, "The earth is the Lord's, and the fulness thereof; the world, and they that dwell therein." And in the Year of Jubilee, Yahweh says, "The land shall not be sold for ever: for the land is mine, for ye are strangers and sojourners with me. And in all the land of your possession ye shall grant a redemption for the land" (Leviticus 25:23–25).

There is an implicit ethical meaning in the passage from Leviticus that severely limits the practice of owning and selling land. In today's economic terms, one can say that whatever value accrues to land is Yahweh's. Taken with the cosmology of divine dominion, God is not only the owner of the land but also its source of productivity (divine bounty). What this means in terms of more concrete social practices is debatable. One such practice may in fact be returning surplus value (rent) in the form of a tribute to God.[10] Yet what we will see below in terms of the three modern natural law thinkers is a different tendency. What seems to be a rather substantial way of defining land as God's gift is really, in the end, empty.

Nomological Reductions

The nomological reduction consists in how land is recognized as a divine gift, but only in a perfunctory and instrumental sense as a means to the natural ends of self-preservation and sociability. Each thinker develops this reduction in a specific way where the law is fulfilled according to historical necessity (Grotius), adventitious moral concepts (Pufendorf), and as a direct response to God's commandment (Locke). In all three there is a tendency to see land's gift status as requiring little more than a reflection on how to use it for our human purposes.

Grotius: Historical Necessity

For Grotius, what appears as a purely human convention is justified in terms of an original right. This original right is not a right to private property, but it will develop into one through his notion of historical progress. In *Mare liberum* (1609), God is the "founder and ruler of the universe" who provides a natural law that is "the common mother of us all, whose bounty falls on all, and whose sway extends over those who rule nations, and which is held most sacred by those who are most scrupulously just."[11] In his *De jure belli ac pacis* (1625), Grotius states that the gift of creation entails a right over it: "Almighty God at the Creation, and again after the Deluge, gave to Mankind in general a Dominion over Things of this inferior World."[12] These two works are seen to constitute respectively the cores of Grotius's early and late theories of property. Stephen Buckle notes that one of the main differences between these periods is a shift in tactics of justification. The former establishes use-right developed through a conception of occupation, while the latter turns to a more historical account of the development of private ownership through agreement.[13]

Grotius's historical thesis can be seen as originating in the concern to provide a common ground for all humankind upon which a discussion of private property rights can occur. Given the diversity of nations and their interests, and the conflicting claims to property arising from this diversity, the demand of moral science is to explore the possibility of a common ground, a common account which will appeal to all nations on the basis of commonly inherited faculties (e.g., reason and character traits) and a plausible account of social development from a common origin (i.e., the state of nature). In *Mare liberum,* this origin is at once a common ground and a common state of dominion: "For God had . . . given all things . . . to the entire human race."[14] In *De jure bellis ac pacis,* Grotius elaborates this origin in terms of a common use-right to nature, or what is a common inheritance: "There are some Things which are ours by vertue of a Right common to all Men."[15] As Buckle clarifies, it is not a joint ownership of nature but a use-right held by all—that is, we all have a right to its use.[16] However, there is more informing the common origin and use-right. Grotius's discussion occurs under the umbrella of human sociability, which will figure crucially in his turn toward history. In the opening address of *Mare liberum,* he writes,

> God was the founder and ruler of the universe, and especially that being the Father of all mankind, He had not separated human beings . . . but had willed them to be of one race and to be known by one name; that furthermore He had given the same origin . . . in order

> that they all might recognize their natural social bond and kinship. . . . He had drawn up certain laws not graven on tablets . . . but written in the minds and on the hearts of every individual.[17]

Grotius speaks of a "natural social bond" and indeed emphasizes, like Pufendorf and Locke, the common and natural aim of sociability. But on what authority is the role of sociability proclaimed? Innate to God's creation is the inclusion of a sociable nature in humankind; it is, along with reason, a unique trait which distinguishes humans from animals.[18] Speech is a way of enjoining and further utilizing the two. Grotius comments that the mature person has "an exquisite Desire of Society, for the Satisfaction of which he alone of all Animals has received from Nature a peculiar Instrument, viz. the Use of Speech."[19] God therefore wills humankind in a certain way so that they are sociable.

The impetus for Grotius's historical analysis can be seen in how the present state of affairs at his time is taken to be an advance from the original condition *through* sociable nature. Thus, it appears that whatever Grotius is describing as the content of natural law is conveniently in accord with an existing state of affairs of our sociability. The present state of the world is not to be fundamentally questioned, as conflicted as it may be, but clarified in view of how sociability can be affirmed and enhanced. I think this relation to his historical present is decisive: it provides a medium for reflection through which Grotius can elaborate the notion of a common historical origin and use-right in the direction of the present state of affairs.

I therefore want to add a bit more conceptual detail to my argument and allege that Grotius's investigation is, above all, *verificationist-revisionist* in its methodological outlook. It is verificationist out of the interest to defend a current state of political and religious affairs.[20] It is "revisionist" since it represents our common historical origin in a manner that accommodates the moral truth of the existing world. Commenting on Pufendorf's account of the science of morality, Buckle notes that this science "does not ask, What sort of moral world ought there to be?, but What is the origin of the moral world (we have)?"[21] This may be one of Pufendorf's original developments in the history of philosophy, but arguably it is detectable in Grotius's approach. In this respect, what should not be overlooked is Grotius's concern to rebut moral skepticism. It forced him to shy away from substantially redefining what appears to be the actual state of affairs of human social reality.[22]

What does this mean for the possibility of explaining private property? Unfortunately, it suggests that whatever is taken to be private property at his time will not be understood in any radically different way, certainly not as gift in any substantial sense. It will be, simply speaking, subservient to the task of resolving another issue—that of rights: "And such a Use of the Right common to all Men did at that Time supply the Place of Property, for no Man could justly take from another, what he had thus first taken to himself."[23] This passage suggests at a methodological level that as far as private property is concerned, the results of Grotius's moral scientific ventures are predetermined. He will read sacred history and natural law as verifying private property: "When property or ownership was invented, the law of property was established to imitate nature."[24] The reduction of property to this plan means (1) natural entities are predetermined as rightfully subject to individual ownership, and (2) these entities serve the purpose of realizing the nature of humankind willed by God. Given these two defining foci, property can be little else than the material divinely given to fulfill a divine will. Property—especially land—is the means to fulfilling natural law, and it can be nothing substantive in itself; for to allow it this stature might mean altering the conceived aim of human existence. That is to say, the meaning of land might outrun the importance of sociability; indeed, the latter might be the effect of our relation to the former.[25] But such speculative counterargument is here outside the remit of my analysis.

Grotius is clearly not concerned with the status of nature except as a thing that may or may not be privately owned. The historical progression toward increased sociability entails growth in population. This growth requires the institution of private property which enables the distribution of goods.[26] What makes distribution problematic are two factors: (1) our flawed human nature, and (2) the finite and therefore unequally distributed state of nature. Human nature possesses traits that are both "good" and "bad" in the sense that they may tend toward self-interest, envy, maliciousness, cowardice, and so on and therefore generate conflicts; but because of this conflict, they create the conditions according to which our good traits can enable us to attain resolution and sociability.[27] Grotius refers to these as our "internal Principles" which are "justly ascribed by God" in that they aid our reason and can in fact aid those in whom "strict Reasoning is weak."[28] To make divine will more consistent to this end, Grotius explains how divine providence did not equally distribute goods in order that we would have to work to achieve social harmony. It is the natural tendency in history for humankind to expand and diversify such that inequality of goods becomes an impetus to social cooperation.[29] In summary, private property, as an institution historically deriving from a natural right, is the natural institution enabling us to achieve social equilibrium despite our limitations.[30] Indeed, reflecting on the necessity and emergence of the private ownership of land, Grotius observes that "the Division of Lands produced a new Sort of Right."[31]

Pufendorf: Adventitious Entities

In Pufendorf's work there is a noticeable change in the purpose of natural law. Whereas for Grotius natural law enabled us to manage our social lives despite our limitations, for Pufendorf it assumes a corrective role. The anthropological picture is therefore starker. Our natural traits do not enable us to fulfill the dictates of natural law; they need to be curbed by it. While there is no mention of the fear of death, as in Hobbes, Pufendorf is nonetheless quite clear in *De officio hominis et civis* (1673):

> So then Man is an Animal very desirous of his own Preservation; of himself liable to many Wants; unable to Support himself without the Help of the other of his Kind; and yet wonderfully fit in Society to promote a common Good: But then he is malicious, insolent, and easily provok'd . . . . Whence this must be inferr'd, that in order to his Preservation, 'tis absolutely necessary, that he be sociable, that is, he join with those of his Kind, and that he so behave himself towards them, that they may have no justifiable Cause to do him Harm, but rather to promote and secure to him all his Interests.[32]

The desires for self-preservation figure so strongly that they can only be corrected by the recognition that an individual's self-preservation is better served through social cooperation. This correction is, of course, natural. After speaking again of strife and dark passions in the state of nature, Pufendorf qualifies, "Now though it was the Will of Nature itself, that there should be a Sort of Kindred amongst all Mankind."[33] This shift augments the marginalization of land, for it gives it a narrow role in the realization of our duty and obligations. Ownership of land is not a natural necessity, but a social one. This means that Pufendorf will argue that private property is necessary for our social existence but, at the same time, that the practices and concepts we develop to facilitate this existence have no direct relation to natural law.

This separation is visible when Pufendorf comments on the origin of the natural right to property. Unlike Grotius, who recognizes a common use-right that later develops into the right to private property, Pufendorf argues that rights concerning property are not derived directly from natural law. As Buckle observes, "there is no original right to all things."[34] Pufendorf himself remarks, "It ought not less carefully to be observed, that the Grant of Almighty God, by which he gave Mankind the use of Earthly Provisions, was not the immediate Cause of Dominion."[35] He cites as a reason that even nonhuman animals have "Divine Permission" to use and consume nature's resources. Strictly speaking, there is no such thing as an original right to ownership that can be observed in nature. He goes on to elaborate that any such rights derive from a "Human Act" which should nonetheless comply with God's authority; for the earth must be used, humankind must subsist and procreate. Accordingly, we have "an indefinite Right to all these Possessions [of God]."[36] As Buckle clarifies, Pufendorf's categorization of property under an indefinite (or imperfect) right requires some form of agreement, tacit or explicit, between citizens in order for there to be use and possession of a given thing.[37] It is no surprise that one of the difficulties of Pufendorf's philosophy is how his reliance on convention weakens the moral force of natural law.[38] But it has also another implication that undermines any strong notion of self-sovereignty. With such a strong commitment to convention, Richard Tuck comments: "It was of course tantamount to the repudiation of the whole history of rights as *dominia*, as active rights expressing their possessor's sovereignty over his world."[39]

Indeed, Pufendorf affirms a general anthropology in which natural things in themselves are only meaningful according to the provisions of tacit or expressed agreements about their use and possession. Much of this view relies on his distinction between natural and moral entities. The former can be considered as physical substances created by God and having causal powers, while the latter are seen only by humans to be substances and are in that sense additions to the natural world, and therefore ultimately adventitious.[40] Pufendorf states that "Property and Communion are moral Qualities which do not affect the things themselves, as to their instrinsick Nature, but only produce a moral Effect."[41] Because of this gap between the natural and moral worlds, land occupies a dual role. It is natural, provided by God; and it is moral insofar as its alienability derives from a moral quality which is integral to our sociability. The physical, natural substance of land therefore causes a moral effect that does not arise out of direct or absolute necessity. It is, as J. B. Schneewind explains, a hypothetical necessity.[42] Why? Because the moral as adventitious cannot be natural; rather, it is a mode of and analogous to the natural. We find this expressed when Pufendorf accounts for the physical substance of place (*Ubi*, here, there)—which can also be taken as land—and how it manifests naturally as "immovable Substance" and adventitiously as a State, or moral entity.[43] Natural substance allows for the erection of a moral space—that is, the State. He also comments more generally, "the Law of Nature is suppos'd to approve all Agreements made by Men about the possession of things, provided they neither imply a Contradiction, nor tend to the Disturbance of Society."[44] The link between nature and convention appears very weak, indeed. The approval of nature is not self-evident in our contemplation of the meanings of things, but is recognizable in retrospection, whose basic criterion is presumably noncontradiction of self-preservation and sociability.

This separation of property from the natural realm is deeply voluntarist and, like Grotius, instrumental. It is voluntarist because it seeks to maintain a diminished role for human reason. Our social conventions derive from the human intellect and cannot, by virtue of its imperfection, understand God, his will, his intellect, and his creation. Moreover, we cannot discern an ultimate plan or design to the creation (nature). Reason can, however, observe what is "plain and clear"[45]—that is, the necessity of the preservation and promotion of society. Knud Haakonssen summarizes this as "sociability . . . understood as a given" which subsequently "dispense[s] with any role for the Deity, except as creator."[46]

This voluntarism only enhances the instrumentalism of property insofar as reason in its reduced role adheres to a more technical purpose. It is practically oriented in applying conventions of property in attaining sociability. Rather than contemplating meanings that transcend our finite condition, it performs the role of finding and using the means for fulfilling the end of sociability:

> And since he that designs the End, cannot but be supposed to design those Means without which the End cannot be obtain'd, it follows that all such Actions as tend generally and are absolutely necessary to the Preservation of Society are commanded by the Law of Nature.[47]

In this sense, Pufendorf's comments in *De jure naturae et gentium libri octo* (1672) appear much more suggestive: "But it was left to the Reason of Men to determine what Measures should be taken to prevent any Discord for their own Use and Service."[48] Property, though a convention, just so happens to be necessary to the kind of existence God has willed us. Or as Jeremy Waldron summarizes, "Though God did not give the world to man *as* private property, He gave it nevertheless *for* private property."[49] In the last analysis, land, as a natural entity subject to the conventions of private property, has no substantial meaning in and for itself.

Locke: God's Commandment

In Locke's labor theory is the strongest articulation of the nomological reduction. Put simply, the use of landed property to fulfill the natural aim of self-preservation is derived directly from God's commandment. The divine (natural) law in Grotius and Pufendorf was more indirectly involved in appropriation, buffered by historical conditions and moral concepts (respectively). In Locke's philosophy there are three features that prove crucial to his view on land: self-ownership, labor, and his empiricist-colored voluntarism.

I will not say much on self-ownership and labor, which have been discussed in great detail by others, save the way the two place human agency at the center of this outlook and affirm his voluntarism. For Locke, the self is ontologically prior to nature since it exists undivided, as an individual, and therefore forms the locus according to which relations with and meanings of external things are defined. This is most evident when Locke describes the undividedness of the human body as what is originally one's own and is therefore the epicenter of interaction with nature:

> Though the earth, and all inferior creatures, be common to all men, yet every man has a property in his own person: this no body has any right to but himself. The labour of his body, and the work of his hands, we may say, are properly his.[50]

The Lockean framework, despite whatever provisos or references to community he later uses to qualify his analyses, begins with this individualistic core whereby all things natural are made subordinate. In this respect, Locke is radical not just for formulating the role of labor in a way not previously conceived; he also provides a form of justification for appropriation that does not rely on abstract processes of history or morality but on a basic, concrete act. The naturalness of appropriation lies not in the ruminations of the moral scientist, but in the brute fact of what it means to be a person who can act. In contrast, Grotius never really sees labor to be a significant factor in rights of ownership,[51] and Pufendorf's explicit conventionalism about the right to private property prohibits any kind of claim that ownership of things results from one's labor, since this would be a claim based upon a discernible natural relation and right.[52] It is no surprise, then, that Locke reacts critically to the idea that consent, on which both Grotius and Pufendorf rely, can provide the basis for ownership. It is simply unrealistic for a growing society since it requires "assigning to everyone his particular part."[53] Instead, Locke states that when things are held in common, an individual's labor takes what is held in common and appropriates it for him- or herself.

Aside from self-ownership and labor there is, moreover, the shift to an expressly empirical-voluntarist argument for natural law. This disposition will allow Locke to articulate God's grant of human dominion over nature in a way different from the others. Unlike Pufendorf's voluntarism which maintains a separation between the natural and the social realms, Locke's empiricism interprets the voluntarist view of creation in a radically different manner. While both thinkers acknowledge our incapacity to understand God's will, Pufendorf reads this gap as a necessity causing the adventitiousness of our moral and social constructs. Locke, in contrast, reads it as the condition under which nature teaches us through the most straightforward means—the use of reason and the senses. From this we learn, as we will see, that appropriation of land is therefore a commandment.

While Grotius and Pufendorf cite observation of nature as the most immediate way we can discern natural law, Locke makes the empirical approach fundamental to grasping this law and its justification. Grotius's characterization of natural law as "written in the minds and on the hearts of every individual" relies on a version of innate ideas that Locke famously rejects: "For if they were innate, what need they be proposed in order to gaining assent."[54] Locke elaborates in relation to natural law:

> There is a great deal of difference between an innate law, and a law of nature; between something imprinted on our minds in their very original, and something that we, being ignorant of, may attain to the knowledge of, by the use and due application of our natural faculties.[55]

Pufendorf's account can be understood as a transition from Grotius to Locke. On the one hand, he rejects the idea that knowledge of the law was "implanted in the Minds of Men."[56] As we saw earlier, he maintains that such knowledge derives from clear and plain facts that force our assent. Reason, in this sense, has a role in understanding natural law, but not in any grand teleological way. On the other hand, Pufendorf does acknowledge to some degree that natural law "is written in the hearts of Men"; yet he takes this to be not an idea or knowledge but a "Sense . . . instill'd into us."[57] He does not say much about this sense except that it, along with reason, inclines us such that "no other option of our knowledge of this Law" is possible.[58] In the end, the thought that this knowledge is innate is an illusion owing to the fact that we cannot remember when we first attained this knowledge and so believe it to be given with our existence.

With respect to Locke, the role of the natural faculties cannot be underestimated in understanding how land is reduced to a mere means of conforming to the natural law. Consider first how Locke will appeal to these faculties not only in establishing an epistemology but also the conception of social and political equality.[59] Discernment of the aim of self-preservation through our natural faculties is simply a matter involving the observation of facts about our existence, something which informs, as we saw, his criticism of Grotius's and Pufendorf's reliance on consent. But the role of empirical method plays a more decisive, even if subtler, role in relation to land. Similar to Pufendorf, the creation is not be interpreted in terms of a divine plan or meaning; it does not reveal to us anything more than the means and conditions for the flourishing God intended for us. Our knowledge is too feeble to attain anything so great:

> Men may find matter sufficient to busy their heads, and employ their hands with variety, delight, and satisfaction, if they will not boldly quarrel with their own constitution, and throw away the blessings their hands are filled with, because they are not big enough to grasp everything. We shall not have much reason to complain of the narrowness of our minds, if we will but employ them about what may be of use to us; for of that they are very capable.[60]

God has thus "put within the reach of their discovery, the comfortable provision for this life, and the way that leads to a better."[61] And this by itself constitutes for Locke sufficient "knowledge of . . . [our] Maker, and the sight of . . . [our] own duties."[62] Unlike Pufendorf, there is a strong relation between this diminished (or perhaps modest) role for the knowledge of God and how it focuses on our duties in view of preservation. Land plays the essential role as the means for self-preservation. That land is alienable through our labor only ensures this reduction.

Much of this depends, of course, on the manner in which Locke interprets revelation to endorse human dominion over the means to self-preservation. In contrast to the passages from the Hebrew Bible quoted earlier, it is interesting to note how Locke begins his chapter on property with Psalm 115:16: "The heavens are the heavens of Yahweh; but the earth he has given to the children of men."[63] In fact, Locke does not refer to the first part of the verse involving the heavens. His focus is dead set on the donation of the earth to humankind for self-preservation. He famously writes in the *First Treatise*:

> God having made man, and planted in him, as in all other animals, a strong desire of self-preservation, and furnished the world with things fit for food and raiment, and other necessaries of life, subservient to his design, that man should live and abide for some time upon the face of the earth, and not that so curious and wonderful a piece of workmanship, by his own negligence, or want of necessaries, should perish again, presently after a few moments continuance; God, I say, having made man and the world thus, spoke to him, (that is) directed him by his senses and reason, as he did the inferior animals by their sense and instinct, which were serviceable for his subsistence, and given him as the means of his preservation.[64]

Waldron concludes that "what God is supposed to have commanded, what reasons tells us, and what our instincts incline us to do, amount more or less to the same thing."[65] As Locke himself declares in the same work, "the fundamental law of nature" "willeth the peace and preservation of all mankind" with "man being to be preserved as much as possible."[66] As the *First Treatise* develops its argument, Matthew Kramer observes that Locke "became more assertive, and indeed left no doubt that God had fully approved the exercise of mastery over nature by human beings."[67] Indeed, Locke eventually concludes in the *Second Treatise*:

> God and his reason commanded him to subdue the earth, i.e. improve it for the benefit of life. . . . He that in obedience to this command of God . . . thereby annexed to it something that was his property.[68]

The relation between our self-preservation, which requires improvement of land for the "benefit of life," and the natural law is much stronger in Locke than in Grotius and Pufendorf. If self-preservation is a commandment of God, property is neither a historical development of an original use-right (Grotius) nor a moral entity created adventitiously by us in accordance with our nature (Pufendorf); rather, it is the original form of relation intended by God. In Locke's identification of the two, the reduction of land to the law is therefore most immediate and intense.[69]

To be sure, Locke is careful not to say the ownership of land is a universal right in the sense that everyone should be a landowner. Land is necessary for self-preservation in general, but this need not imply that every citizen of a community own and use land.[70] He also offers provisos to prevent the abuse of monopoly and waste of resources.[71] Despite these qualifications, what tends to prevail in the philosophical imaginary today is more the aspect of Locke's philosophy that strongly links the right to self-preservation with the appropriation of landed property.[72] Given his proviso that appropriation should not result in the disadvantaging of others, one wonders to what extent right-libertarian philosophers, who appeal to Locke's arguments in some form, refuse out of sheer conviction to see land monopoly and enclosure as problematic.[73] Whatever the case may be and despite the interminable debates regarding private property, Locke's framing of landownership—or more accurately, the predominant interpretation of it—remains entrenched in the philosophical imaginary. If land is a means to self-preservation, it is but a small step from this characterization at the physical and social levels to its definition as capital at the economic one. That the implications of the reduction of land in the modern natural law tradition did not manifest immediately and completely is evident in the mixed views of land in the thought of the classical economists that we saw earlier.[74] But we can no doubt see emerging the conditions for the possibility of land's meaning as capital.

Imagining Land as Capital

When discussing different types of atheism, Alasdair MacIntyre uses the term "passive" to describe a form of inherited belief in which the original reasons for rejecting theism have been forgotten.[75] Atheism thus becomes a passive outlook, and as such, somewhat difficult for the believer to assess internally. MacIntyre does not say what is sufficient to cause such passive beliefs to be "active" and perhaps critically revised. Whatever the case may be, I think he alights upon an interesting way in which some beliefs work. Heidegger, for different reasons, referred to passive beliefs according to a fore-structure of understanding in which what we believe is not evident to us conceptually but rather present in how we act.[76]

I think this way of describing the modes that beliefs can take is helpful when trying to understand why land is readily conceived as private property and how this belief subsequently underwrites the economic conception of land as capital. In the first half of this chapter, I have attempted to make the case for seeing how Grotius, Pufendorf, and Locke articulate the conceptual conditions according to which it is possible to categorize land as private property. In general, all three anticipate this designation when explaining how land acts as an essential means to realizing our self-preservation and sociability. Notwithstanding challenges to this designation from the socialist, distributivist, and Marxist schools of thought, one can say this relation to the land dominates the fore-structure of our understanding. In other words, we are placed within an existential and social context in which practices, values, and beliefs figure alienable land as one of the major constituents of the functioning of the world. In Marx's thought, we reproduce ourselves in terms of this abstract social relation. To this end, it is no exaggeration to say that economic analysis largely presupposes the private ownership of property. Indeed, it does so in terms of capital.

While it is true that all forms of capital are not privately owned, economic models work on the assumption that the most significant forms of capital are in fact so.[77] So even if these models are not uniform and can be imaginative in creating new ways of understanding economic relations, their formalistic nature prevents them from questioning the substantive meanings of their terms. Such terms are narrowly economic.[78] Moreover, this mode of conceptual reproduction, to remain with Marx's term, instantiates itself historically in our practices. It is therefore no surprise that the private ownership of capital is augmented and reinforced by our economies which require the use of such capital to finance production and the speculative exercises which figure into this financing.[79] The land market—that is, land as a capital commodity—is an integral component of this.

On this view, the passivity of belief for the majority of economists is one in which the designation of land as private property never comes into question. In fact, this is so much the case that some recent theorists tend to want to dismiss any discussion of land altogether.[80] The arguments for doing so may be various, but they often involve, in some form or another, the urge to disregard salient features of land in order to affirm its classification as capital. Historically, this has involved a dismissal of any special properties one might want to attribute to land as a distinct factor of production—for example, scarcity, immobility, its unproduced natural state.

It is nonetheless true that no matter how passive a belief is, it cannot endure without sufficient endorsement and support from other beliefs. In the case of atheism, it may be that passive nonbelief in God is supported by de facto epistemological pluralism in which, as Taylor has noted, God is one option among many.[81] What, then, might be the case for land in economics? How is its designation as private property reinforced? It is reinforced through arguments and analyses which want to see the core of the economy in terms of relations to capital.

The main historical case for this shift involves the neoclassical adaptation of Ricardo's theory of ground rent. Mark Blaug begins the section on Ricardo's theory of rent in his comprehensive *Economic Theory in Retrospect* with the observation that "the core of the Ricardian doctrine of rent is still with us, though in attenuated form."[82] His ensuing analysis makes it plain that "attenuated form" means the removal of any special status given to land and the rent it generates. Instead of a special case made for land, Ricardo alights on a more general principle—that is, marginality.[83] But maintaining this position, as Blaug also makes clear, relies on the validity of a competing economic theory to explain away land's special status: "In long-run stationary equilibrium, the total product is resolvable into wages and interest as payments to labor and capital—there is no third factor of production."[84] In other words, ground rent may arise in the short run as a surplus; but in the long run, it resolves into wages and interest. However, Blaug's account appears somewhat circular. Let us use a model that depicts production narrowly in terms of wages and interest in order to show how there is no such thing as ground rent. This complaint is, of course, a bit simple. A much fairer accusation might be that the model on which Blaug relies assumes value is resolvable into categories that presuppose private property. Wages belong to labor; interest belongs to the owners of capital. That land can be described as belonging to the landowner means it is only a subspecies of capital; it is an entity that generates value like privately owned capital.

Enabling this view was Alfred Marshall, who famously demonstrated in his *Principles of Economics* (1890) that rent has a broader meaning that applies to "agents of production"[85] garnering an unearned increment of value. Ricardo simply failed to see that his doctrine was not specific to land. While the term "ground rent" had been used to denote rent relating to land in the classical period,[86] it was not really until after the 1870s that the term "rent" gained a wider usage. Ground rent was, to quote Marshall, "the leading species of a large genus."[87] And land was nothing but "embodied capital."[88] The latter transformation of terminology, where rent denotes interest, appears to have occurred as early as 1907 in the work of Irving Fisher and is utilized by the likes of Frank Knight.[89]

It may seem foolish to attempt to rebut Marshall's theory of rent with the classical version he was claiming to surpass. Nonetheless, it is important to emphasize Ricardo's presumption. Because land was a unique factor of production, it led him to specify rent as that which was solely generated by land. In other words, he was entertaining a different philosophical conception (presupposition) of land than Marshall. For Ricardo, land is "original" and "indestructible," while rent, he notes, "is often, however, confounded with the interest and profit of capital, and, in popular language, the term is applied to whatever is annually paid by a farmer to his landlord."[90] Though this position requires one to treat land distinctly, it does not preclude the possibility that surplus arises with respect to other agents of production. Modern proponents of Henry George's thought, for example, maintain the distinction between ground rent and other forms of rent without losing the special place the former has in economic distribution.[91]

Is it possible that Marshall himself was a victim of a passive belief in landed property? If, as some prominent critics allege, economics is determined in advance by the noneconomic beliefs economists hold,[92] then one might be able to find noneconomic reasons for collapsing the distinction between land and capital. While neoclassicism wanted to reject any naturalistic and hence fallacious descriptions of land,[93] for Marshall, the English practice of land tenure was not just economic but ideological—a view also assumed by Malthus some one hundred years prior.[94] To be sure, Marshall wavered on the role and significance of land.[95] Yet at the very least, one can say that Marshall's view readily associates land enclosure with economic progress:

> [Land tenure] afforded great advantages to a country, which pioneered the way for the world in the development of free enterprise; and which therefore was impelled early to adopt all such changes as give freedom and vigour, elasticity and strength.[96]

The identification of economic freedom with land tenure is itself questionable; but more to the point is what Karl Polanyi notes as a general contradiction in the notion of the market economy. Appeals to economic freedom seem to miss how such freedoms impose certain types of restraints.[97] These restraints come not just in a form of state control which modern capitalism requires for the provision of security,[98] but a basic contradiction where the visible wealth generated by tenure comes at a cost—in this case, the "unfreedom" resulting from the expulsion of people from the land. What Marshall saw as an advance, George saw as a contradiction: "Where the conditions to which material progress everywhere tends to be most fully realized . . . we find the deepest poverty."[99]

Perhaps more germane to recent trends in economics and finance is the type of reduction which presupposes the neoclassical identification of land with capital. This concerns how price is the main form of representation of production employed by economic models. This is not to say classical economists were not concerned with price. But it is to say that they were concerned with price as derivative of value creation. The various theories of value provide the foundation for understanding price, something evident as we saw in Ricardo's analysis of high corn prices and how the underlying causes were determined by clarifying the roles of the different spheres of value production (e.g., rent). Despite the cogency of Ricardo's argument within the history of economic theory, the overall problem with the classical representation of production had to do with its focus on principles underlying economic processes. A familiar split abided in classical theories: explanation and prediction did not necessarily require an accurate theoretical account of natural or physical (and even metaphysical) entities and processes. As Mirowksi argues, the inability to account for value creation as a physical substance in classical thought led to a concern for price—or value conceived *as* price.[100] The difference for the neoclassical paradigm is that there is no need to find where value persists physically in entities (indeed, one cannot); rather, "the only phenomenon that can be said to persist through time is the psychology of the transactors." That is to say, what persists is utility measured as price, which is "not explained, but merely treated as given by transactors."[101]

If a major portion of the history of economic theory is driven by, at first, the concern to develop a theory of value; and subsequently, by the inability to do so; and finally, by the replacement of a theory of value with that of price, then its correlative effect is to focus on production in terms of cost and price. On this view, the classical concern for factors of the production *of value* is obsolete. Factors of production, under the aegis of price, are input costs affecting price.[102] In other words, the economic models utilizing these terms do not have the internal means to distinguish purely mathematical calculations of profit and costs at the margin from the natural and social bases that are ontological prerequisites for these calculations. Land, labor, and capital as natural and social entities are nonexistent.

Unease and Refutations

Economists wed mainly to the thought of Henry George in some form or another have been the most outspoken critics of the identification of land as capital. Mason Gaffney argues that despite the various transformations since 1870, economics remains trapped within neoclassical idioms. He traces a general and pervasive resentment of George's radical views on land value and reform to a host of economists—from John B. Clark (1847–1938) to Paul Samuelson and beyond.[103] However, there are other branches of economics interested in the primary role that land plays, as for example, in ecological economics, which generally holds that land is first in energy provision and production.[104] It is true that ecological economics can be seen as complementing my arguments against conceptual prejudices; yet there is, in my mind, a subtle and significant difference. It is questionable to what extent ecological economics appreciates land beyond the designation of essential resource. (I address this issue in chapter 7.) Given the historical picture I have drawn, it is sufficient to focus on how the debate over land as a factor of production involves the question of whether or not it can be accounted for sufficiently as capital. This debate rests not on philosophical arguments about the nature of land as an entity but the problem of whether land, economically understood, fits the criteria defining capital. There are two basic differences that I will discuss in this section: capital's derivative nature and rent's incontrovertibleness.[105]

Capital Relies on Land and Labor

This argument requires to some extent an abstract form of analysis because it conceives of a precedent relationship between the three factors of production deduced from the present. This relation, as Knut Wicksell (1851–1926) put it, is one in which "capital itself is almost always a product, a fruit of the co-operation of the two original factors: labour and land"; or as he says later, "We may thus regard capital as a single coherent mass of saved-up labour and saved-up land."[106] First, there cannot be capital goods without the relation between labor and land where things used in production must be fashioned by some combination of labor and land (e.g., a hammer made from stone and wood). Wicksell therefore refers to a "non-capitalistic" mode of production in which the technical use and development of capital is extremely low. Second, because production can be understood abstractly in terms of the primary relation between labor and land, the generation of capital in its more advanced forms, which in turn augments overall production, really means that capital is a transformation which stores up labor and land. This storage is both physical and historical. The steam engine, for example, retains its power to propel a ship based upon the labor which made the engine and used land in doing so. This relation to labor and land is not specific to the engine itself. Historically, the engine is an accumulation of the preceding economic and social progress of society, or all the advances which utilized labor and land. Capital is thus like a capacity; it lies in wait in order to be used in production. On Wicksell's view, capital's reliance on land and labor means it is the least substantial of the three factors.

However, Wicksell can be accused of merely favoring one side over another. In contrast, Frank Knight maintains that the term "factor of production" presupposes that as a factor it had been produced some time in the past. With respect to land, he argues that it is a factor of production only because it was the product of the human efforts of discovery and development that give it any economic application.[107] In a similar spirit, Philip Wicksteed comments:

> Just where we have an area of the earth's surface which, physically speaking, owes little or none of its value to anything that has been done to it or on it—for instance a bare site in the centre of a great city—we find that its value depends more than ever upon capital, that is to say, upon the results of accumulated effort.[108]

We saw earlier a version of this in Veblen's theory of knowledge, and it is not an uncommon rebuttal to the classical notion of land as original and indestructible. So is the matter just an "either/or"—take capital or take land as the defining factor? Only an argument showing how one factor is more originary than the others can resolve the dilemma. This will be the task of the remaining chapters. Let it then suffice to reiterate a point made in chapter 1: Veblen, Knight, et al. espouse a position which goes too far since it neglects that precondition for production, which is the grant of land—or, in Heideggerian terms, the givenness of earth that provides for our being-in-the-world.

Rent Is Not Interest

The confusion of rent with interest stems from the reduction of land to capital since interest is the surplus owed to the latter. But this is not simply a category mistake predicated upon a definition of terms. It is also an economic mistake. Henry George argues that if one maintains there are different factors of production, each factor has its respective return—wages to labor, rent to land, and interest to capital. His treatment of these categories is set against a variety of misperceptions which he seeks to rectify in the first half of *Progress and Poverty* (1879), the best known of which is the notion that wages are a cost of production. With respect to interest, George beckons the reader to consider a modified form of Ricardo's example of rent, that is, "where the production of wealth went on without the aid of labor."[109] One is asked to imagine the varying outputs of farms due to variation in soil quality. With labor deleted from the model, production can only be represented in terms of the return to capital investment and rent. Given the limiting stipulation, the landed context of marginal production is highlighted: "[Capitalists] would get, as return for their capital, the whole amount of wealth it produced only so long as none of its produce was demanded as rent."[110] Where and when rent does arise—that is, when the land employed produces a surplus when compared to the poorest land in use for the same type of production—the rent arising claims a portion of the overall surplus of production. This distills into a general law for George: as rent increases, interest must decrease.[111] The confusion of rent and interest therefore falls prey to a contradiction insofar as it misses, as Gaffney summarizes, how "capital and land are rivals for the same pie"; and he concludes from this, "It is hard to see how any forecasts of the results of economic policy . . . could have any value without keeping focused on this distinction."[112]

The foregoing clarifications of ground rent account for two of the more convincing economic arguments. If rent is a genuine category, then within a theoretical framework, there lies a distinction according to which a form of production surplus can be imagined in a different way. But they are only economic considerations whose cogency requires further philosophical development in view of and against the general disposition that takes land as alienable. I have tried to convince the reader that underlying economic thinking are philosophical determinations of land as property which are drawn from the natural law thinkers of the seventeenth century and comprise the imaginative fore-structure of modernity.

At root, therefore, is a specific philosophical relation to reality that requires, in my view, engagement and alteration by philosophical means. Moreover, because this relation is not just philosophical, but more precisely ontological, it requires a new application of thought to our mode of being-in-the-world. It requires rethinking what makes possible the kind of being that we as humans have.

Part 2

A Phenomenology of Land

4

Givenness and Ground

While the preceding chapters present good reasons to reject the Marxist and neoclassical reductions of land to labor and capital, these reasons do not necessarily provide an alternative way of understanding land that might clarify the nature of its distinct status. Indeed, if there is something like a lesson to be learned from the story I have attempted to tell, it is that land is original in some profound sense. It is clearly involved in the production of value in a way that labor and capital are not. As we saw, the attempt to distinguish land from the other factors of production was made by a few classical thinkers who designated land according to its *natural* originality. But as we also saw, the status of "natural" was dismissed by later thinkers on the basis of claiming that their classical predecessors confused the noneconomic (or natural) meaning of land with the economic. There are no natural entities for economics. So how then should we conceive of land?

I think the most direct and forceful philosophical route is to establish land's originality as an *ontological* one. Land provides for human existence not just materially but ontologically in the sense of constituting our existence and our understanding of what it means to exist.

The second part of this book attempts to rethink the ontological originality of land according to the phenomenology of Martin Heidegger. As I mentioned in the introduction, I think Heidegger's philosophy is especially apt because it attempts to redescribe human existence according to aspects of reality we have taken for granted. It is not simply that we can readily rethink these aspects according to new concepts or definitions. Rather, because our existence has been ordered and determined in certain ways, Heidegger wagers that we have to reorient how it is we describe what it means to exist, which includes above all what it means to refer to and speak about reality. To do so allows a new understanding to change the way we dwell since, for Heidegger as I mentioned earlier, interpretation *is* our mode of existence—to exist presupposes an understanding of what it means to do so. In this second part, therefore, I attempt to employ aspects of Heidegger's thought to initiate this reorientation by changing the way we think of what grounds thought and existence.

Each chapter of this part advances this project by degrees, first examining how our pursuit of understanding entities involves a search for grounds that can never finally rest with abstract reasons to explain this relation. Rather, Heidegger takes the meaning of ground, and therefore the grounds for something's being, to be concretely manifest. The remaining chapters follow this momentum respectively by examining how this notion of concreteness progresses from grounds, to earth, and to land and how land can therefore be understood as ontologically providing for our existence.

The opening argument of this chapter concerns how things appear to us in an existential context. For Heidegger, entities are given in a special way that has specific implications for us. We are not simply passive observers of a neutral or objective reality. As indicated above, what Heidegger gleans from the way we are involved with entities is that they have a ground that is formative of our existence and understanding. As we will see, for Heidegger philosophy tends to conceive grounds abstractly and therefore lacks in giving appropriate attention to existential context. Heidegger will thus move from this abstract dimension to a way of envisioning a jointure between ground understood philosophically and as it is experienced in our *concrete* being-in-the-world. To think how being gives itself is to think it in the most concrete manner. Ultimately, I see this move as having been initiated by Heidegger but not carried out in a more decisive way.[1]

The term "concrete" is key to my argument, and by it I understand how thinking the philosophical meaning of ground is directly involved in our manner of existing. Whatever is identified as a ground in terms of philosophical conception means that this conception is indivisible from what is physically present. The concrete is not just a token of the concept, or vice versa, but inseparably linked to it. Ontologically speaking, between the concept and the concrete, there is no passage. Heidegger thus remarks at one point, "In truth, what is 'philosophical' is concrete, and the descriptions are abstract, that is, removed from the ontological meaning which sustains them."[2] The way we account for the philosophical conception of ground requires seeing how it is invested in our understanding of the way we settle, dwell, and inhabit the earth. Heidegger points out that philosophical reflection is originally concerned with what appears concretely to us in existence—the appearance of being as phenomena. Yet the use of concepts, which are limited, provides descriptions which tend toward representing the concrete abstractly. In part this has to do with the tendency of thought to look behind the appearance of entities to find their cause, in the constant redefinition of concepts arising in debate, or in the attempt to refer to something novel in a new vocabulary.[3] So thinking concretely suggests not just a harmony between thought and action, but a mode of thought that apprehends how existence is indebted to an origin that is both philosophical and concrete, as opposed to metaphysical and abstract.

Indeed, Heidegger's reflection on the nature of grounds for philosophical thinking highlights how modern philosophy tends to think it is the human subject who gives grounds through its analyses, methods, and uses of language (i.e., propositions about entities). Grounds therefore constitute reasons and justifications for a certain way of describing reality which generally provides us with an understanding or sense of why reality is. Heidegger terms this general orientation as the concern for "the truth of being,"[4] but he sees the concern for grounds as it has come to unfold in the history of philosophy as misled, focusing not on being itself but on the composition of beings, or entities. (I use these terms interchangeably.) Apropos to this errancy, *one* way of describing Heidegger's movement of thought is to say it begins at the earliest stage of his career with an interest in dispelling the increasingly abstract definition of ground which arises from a conception of entities as significantly separated from our existentially and materially constituted existence. This abstraction culminates in the role ascribed to humans as the masters and givers of meaning and truth. The concrete in Heidegger's thought becomes most pronounced in the moves he makes from the primary role of temporality in *Being and Time*, to a questioning of ground in relation to metaphysics just after *Being and Time*, and then to a development of his notions of poetic dwelling and earth (*Erde*).

So in employing and elaborating aspects of Heidegger's thought, my argument begins with a basic epistemological problem understood from an ontologico-phenomenological perspective. Given the finite nature of our knowledge, we can never entirely grasp the fundamental way in which reality, or being itself, is given to us. Nonetheless, this conundrum does not so much mean that human knowledge is irredeemably flawed or inadequate, but rather that being itself is fundamentally constituted in such a way that it prevents anything like certainty, absolute knowing, or infallibility. So when seen from this ontological perspective, we are asked to rethink what it means to understand what is given and what it means to make claims about the nature of what is given. In what follows, my argument takes into account the way our knowledge is involved in a paradox insofar as it is derivative of what is given; how we are asked to think differently about what grounds being itself; and how this difference entails a move to a more concrete analysis.

It is important to reiterate the comments made in the introduction. I am not claiming this movement as the most accurate way of reading Heidegger; it is only one way of doing so that I believe to be consistent with what he thought the task of philosophy, or thinking, is: it attempts to say what has not been explicitly thought.[5] And what has not been explicitly thought in this case is how Heidegger's insights have concrete consequences beyond his (and commentators') specific examples often drawing on craft, building, art, and ecology. In the concrete, I will maintain, is the germ of an economy.

The Paradox of the Given

What I am calling the paradox of the given is a *manner* of speaking of what Heidegger calls the ontological difference, yet with particular emphasis on an active, donative aspect constituting reality and existence.[6] The paradox simply put: what is given to us seems to be there passively for our understanding, yet because it ontologically precedes one's existence, one's understanding is derivative and cannot attain the kind of mastery one might wish in a project of knowledge or science. Heidegger seeks to attune our thinking to this paradox by taking note of the active, disclosive nature of being. Attuning does not mean resolving the paradox but learning to think how our dependency on what precedes us qualifies significantly what it means to know and understand. In this section, I clarify the meaning of this dependency according to two points: the tendency of our understanding to focus on entities and the finite nature of our use of concepts when discussing entities.

One of the root meanings of the term "theory" relates to spectacle and how in being a spectator (*theoreo*) one is witness to something that inspires wonder and reflection. While there is no such thing as a completely neutral mode of witnessing, the fact that something has been given over to us to witness entails theoretical questions—namely, what concepts and modes of reflection we use to understand that to which we bear witness. Involved in the act of witnessing is, of course, not simply a straightforward feat of observation; for we can contemplate two questions simultaneously: What is the nature of this thing we are witnessing? and What are the meanings and limitations of the concepts we are using to understand this nature? For example, if Plato is the first thinker to develop a comprehensive philosophy, it is not by accident that the main focus of his thought is the nature of the polity. This is because the concept he uses to understand human dwelling is the Good (*to agathon*), or what is a concept overtly tied to the virtuous constitution of the polis. Heidegger refers to this critically as designating the Idea of the Good as that which "offers a view to what is present."[7] In other words, whatever concept we privilege or rely on involves a philosophical wager that it can illuminate an essential aspect of what is real, what is present, what we witness. Suffice it to say, the finite and historical nature of our understanding makes any substantial reliance problematic. Consequently, one of Heidegger's main worries is that we fail to see how the use of concepts and ideas in explaining what is present is a form of determining what is in fact present. I develop this thought by alleging that the metaphysical concern for concepts becomes overdetermined when, being enthralled by the sufficiency of their definition, it becomes divorced from how we understand what it means to dwell. While this separation is evident by virtue of the term "meta-physics," this does not necessarily mean that as a branch of philosophy it *should* be separated from its relation to "physical" existence. To recall a typical criticism of Platonism after Aristotle, a main worry about the metaphysical Idea of the Good is that it is not practicable.[8]

Heidegger uses the concepts of ontological difference, being, and beings to speak of what is present and our relation to what is present. That which gives itself to be witnessed in the most fundamental sense is being itself. In traditional metaphysical parlance, being itself is "the first" since without it nothing is; and to say that something causes or gives rise to being would mean that this antecedent is being. Our mode of finite understanding, as I have explained in part above, cannot help but see being in terms of the entities that arise within it or in terms of the predicates or features of entities existing in being. This noncoincidence—where we are in being and yet perceive it only specifically in terms of beings—is the core tension constituting the ontological difference. "The first [being itself]," says Heidegger, "is accessible in a different way than beings."[9]

What is given over to us for thought is primarily mediated through a concept which gives us access to it. It is questionable as to what kind of access is given or whether we should be concerned with improving the accuracy of concepts, even if this is possible.[10] While this point can be taken epistemologically as an endorsement of indirect realism, where we rely on concepts to make sense of what is given, this conclusion would be a mistake.[11] Indirect realism, traditionally conceived, assumes a representation of the human subject's relation to reality that phenomenology in general does not. For the former, what is given to the witnessing subject is an external object that impresses an idea of the object upon the perceiver's mind. The nature of the object's externality is one largely governed by the human subject since the idea, even if impressed, resides in the human subject. Hence the dualistic nature of indirect realism is one in which we have access to a representation of an external object but never the object as it really is. The crucial difference for Heidegger does not lie in problems of dualism, however. It lies in how such a view thinks objects exist.

In the early stages of his career, Heidegger refers to this as making use of a picture of an entity in thought. Its limitation is its specific view of a thing which, by virtue of being thought of as a mental picture, frames it in such a way that it is encountered as something other than as we experience it. The picture, in other words, is not an exact portrayal of the entity, but a view of it, and a somewhat distorted one at that. While one thinks the picture has accessed the genuine context and being of a thing, it has produced instead an abstracted and disengaged one because it presumes that the relation between the observer and the entity is one where we internally produce an image of the external entity, and in so doing, necessarily picture it in the context of the mind's eye as opposed to "out there" where it is. Heidegger therefore emphasizes how the picture is not the thing itself, but an entity presenting a view of the thing.

> It all goes against the plain and simple findings about the simple apprehension of an object to interpret them as if I first perceive a picture in my consciousness when I see that house there, as if a picture-thing were first given and thereupon apprehended as picturing that house out there. There would thus be a subjective picture within and that which is pictured outside, transcendent.[12]

Yet, as indicated above, it would be misleading to think that Heidegger believes phenomenology should resolve the relation between external entities and the representational contents of the internal mind.[13] The relation of "subjective picture" to the "transcendent outside" is a wrong way of representing our relation to entities in the world.

For phenomenology in general, the external object is understood to disclose itself actively to the observer. This feature is often referred to as ontological truth as manifestation.[14] In other words, the relation between the human subject and the entity observed is constituted with meaning due to an active interrelation between the two. It does not arise as a result of the human subject proposing something about an entity. It is not simply that the observer is trying to unlock the essence or qualities of an object external to his or her mind. The relation, to the contrary, is interactive: the human subject actively desires to know the entity and the entity actively discloses itself to him or her. Heidegger thus speaks of the desire to know in terms of our concernful involvement with things.[15] Concern entails a specific relation to those entities with which we are concerned. In this respect, there is not the same logical problem for epistemology of how the observer knows he or she has an accurate idea of the external object. Because we are concerned with an entity and because this entity actively discloses itself phenomenologically, the interactive relation can result in a revision of the concept we use to understand it. How so?

Not in the sense that someone might instruct another when an error is made. Rather, because of our concern, the entity in its context elicits a further investigation. This context is one in which the entity simultaneously means something to us and yet reveals the entity as not fully understood. So while the so-called epistemological "argument from illusion"—in which we mistakenly make assertions based on an illusory appearance of an entity—deems the appearance to be problematic for the sufficiency of our perception and also our claims to justification and truth made through perception, phenomenology sees this limitation as revisable because the fuller encounter with the appearance of something is played out and "thickened" by our involvement with it. This involvement is not simply abstract; it is certainly not an abstractly conceived instant in which an entity faces the observer statically. Something like a stick which appears bent by a pool of water reflecting its image calls for further investigation. The stick in its context discloses itself as possibly bent and as something which can be more closely examined if the situation merits. Perception involves decision and judgment made in and through existing.[16] Heidegger comments,

> To reside in what is readily available is intrinsically not to let the concealing of what is concealed hold sway. Certainly, among readily familiar things there are also some that are puzzling, unexplained, undecided, questionable. But these self-certain questions are merely transitional, intermediate points in our movement within the readily familiar and thus not essential.[17]

To clarify the contrast between a phenomenological approach and a traditional epistemological one, the correctness of propositions we make about things is not the criterion for truth since these statements can change according to the manner in which we decide to interpret and engage the entity in its situated context. Agreement between what the observer asserts propositionally about the object, as Heidegger remarks, "posit[s] that which grounds in the first place."[18] The grounding that Heidegger has in mind is one which presupposes the reasonability and correctness of the assertion.

In this view, there is a prior ontological ground and context that makes the assertion both understandable and revisable. Heidegger notes this difference historically when referring to a certain prejudice in the history of philosophy to ground truth in the correctness of propositions. In contrast, truth, or *aletheia* in Greek, means unconcealing, or truth as the manifestation of being itself (which includes beings). This, for Heidegger, is a far cry from truth as correctness since correctness presupposes manifestation. On this point, Denis McManus comments, "The activities of the person are not constituted independently of the relevant objects; and thus, between them, there can be no question of fit or correspondence."[19] Indeed, Heidegger notes that the opposite of truth as unconcealment is not error and falsity, where our propositions about things do not fit them, but hiddenness, where things already fit by virtue of existing together but where our view of this fit is only partial due to first-person perspective as well as the finite nature of being. That is to say, the opposite of *aletheia* is not *pseudos* (falsity) but the way in which being hides itself and requires further investigation.[20] This distinction cannot be underestimated. The property of truth does not lie in the correctness of an assertion made about an entity. Truth already exists in that it allows us to make an assertion about an entity. Truth, in this ontological sense, is not a property of a thing or statement but the precondition for our relation to things.

Yet equally as important is how being conceals itself. Being is therefore not absolutely disclosed but only partially so according to the conditions of finitude. Given these conditions, the obstacle to understanding this disclosure, this truth of being, is therefore not making an incorrect assertion about entities. Propositional truth has merely to do with the correctness of the assertion from the perspective of the observer *within* a specific frame of observing. As McManus notes, such frames entail methods of observing which presuppose "the mastery and adoption of a particular kind of 'measure,'"[21] where measure includes but is not limited to arithmetical data. Measuring is generally a way of gaining access to the way certain entities are in their manner of being. In this respect, the correctness of an assertion is a matter only within the frame of measurement adopted by the observer, whether this be scientific, metaphysical, theological, and so on.

Furthermore, Heidegger's ontological understanding of truth means that it is being itself which gives or allows any frame of measurement. This can be gleaned logically when no frame of measurement can be absolutely validated, since any attempt at validation presupposes the use of its forms of measuring to do so. But the logical point is not Heidegger's main concern since it is derivative of a larger ontological issue—namely, as McManus clarifies, a frame of measurement must be already given in order for a comparison to be made.[22] The giver, in this sense, is not the human subject who measures reality but the orderliness inhering within being itself that makes itself accessible, perceivable, and measurable through entities we encounter.[23] What this means for truth becomes clear especially in Heidegger's later work. We, as the beings concerned with truth, make assertions according to the many ways in which being itself manifests as entities. The real matter for concern is not whether these assertions are correct—since this question is pertinent only within a respective frame of measurement—but how being itself, when giving us access in one way, conceals itself in another. In this respect, the matter for thought is how to remember this dynamic "revealing-concealing" relation in our various modes of gaining access to entities, that is, through our frames of measurement.[24]

Historically, if philosophy is the activity of reflecting on being, and if philosophy is perennially pervaded by the limitations expressed above, then the history of philosophy is in one sense an attestation to the struggle with these limitations. Heidegger of course thinks so, and in the next section I consider his infamous discussion of metaphysics, not in order to advocate his *provisional* reading of the history of philosophy,[25] but as a means of explaining the way he illuminates how prior to philosophical reflection is a source or origin which not only makes possible this reflection but must also be taken into consideration in a special way in our attempt to think.

Questioning the Abstract Conception of Ground

Gaining access to what is given requires understanding its ground since its ground is the cause or reason for the being of an entity. Heidegger's discussion of ground most often involves that which we fail to notice as ground, and indeed, metaphysics has unfortunately misconceived what this ground is. Since Heidegger assumes the default state of philosophical affairs is a kind of ignorance or oblivion on our part, the rhetorical orientation of his thought is one which describes what needs to be heeded or noticed as that which is absent. In other words, in our ignorant mode of understanding, we are not aware of what needs to be heeded. It is absent and thus it can be said to be "nothing." As for a remedy to this oblivion, his later works often emphasize a turn or transformation of understanding which culminates in a new relation to ground through language.[26] Despite this well-known emphasis on language, I want to assume (instead of argue) its importance in order to focus on another aspect of this transformation. If well at the center of Heidegger's critique of metaphysics is its abstract language, then crucial to his attempt to arrive at a philosophical language is a way of speaking that is conceptually meaningful and concretely relevant. Ground, in this sense, is not just a term accounting for philosophical foundations. The transformation Heidegger wishes to initiate is a form of understanding where the philosophical conception of ground is seen to be involved in our dwelling. Foltz observes that this move toward a greater degree of contact with dwelling is consistent with Heidegger's understanding of the Greek term *zoe. Zoe* does not just mean life; it is the intensification of that origin and process that grants life. For humans it thus consists in "a special self-opening whereby living things are open to what is around them, make contact with it, and simultaneously enter back into themselves along with something outside them."[27] The movement toward the concrete is a way of joining our thoughtful concern for being itself to our participation with everything around us.

In his early work (pre-1930), Heidegger speaks of ground as a way of rethinking being itself. However, this rethinking is oblique since it cannot directly grasp in discourse how being appears as given. At least in *Being and Time,* this oblique path seeks its articulation in the analysis of temporality as the primary mediation of our access to being. After *Being and Time,* Heidegger considers three ways in which ground is understood: "projection of the world, absorption with beings, and ontological grounding of beings."[28] The first concerns his well-known thesis in *Being and Time* that in order to understand anything at all, we require a fore-structured world in which things can "appear" to us as meaningful and of concern. The second follows from the manner in which we are already involved in a concern for the entities that appear to us in the world. We are, in this sense, absorbed by beings because they are a part of how we live and carry out projects. Heidegger then comments that because the first and second ways in which ground manifests entail a form of relation where we question the ontological possibilities of entities as they appear to us in projects, we search for the third sense of ground as that which explains their manner of being. The third sense is distinct because it seeks a foundation apart from how we are engaged practically with the entities in question. In other words, it abstracts. This third sense is not in itself pejorative or inauthentic; in fact, Heidegger sees it as necessary.[29] Nonetheless, the ways in which this third sense accounts for ontological grounds can be problematic.

Indeed, these three meanings of ground all presuppose a more originary meaning; and Heidegger intends to indicate this originary meaning negatively by showing how the history of philosophy has overdetermined these three meanings and therefore made the originary one significantly difficult to notice. He takes up the third meaning of ground when it becomes a manner of seeking some principle or cause to explain why entities appear as they do. In thinking grounds in this way, we miss *how* entities appear to us; and consequently, we miss how our seeking of grounds involves a specific relation to entities that may in some sense be unnatural, inauthentic, or inappropriate.[30] To emphasize the importance of how things appear, Heidegger contrasts it to the "why?" of beings, or what is the search for the reason for something's being and the presumption that understanding this reason constitutes the entity's ultimate ground. In other words, the preoccupation with "why?" assumes a myopic view of the entity, like a picture-thing, in which we believe an entity can be understood most adequately and correctly if we take it "by itself," and furthermore, take an aspect or property of this thing as the focus of understanding. Conceptualizing about an entity by itself requires selecting that view which constitutes its enduring and therefore most real being. Through whatever frame of measurement we adopt—dialectic, Idea, substance, essence, qualities, and so on—we then select those features we perceive in the entity as most important. These features allow us to speak of the ground of the entity as, for example, when we posit that the real being of an entity is its Idea.

It is the concern for a why that narrows thought such that the spectacle of being is seen in terms of specific features and traits. Yet according to Heidegger, such determinations are derivative of something more originary.[31] In what sense derivative? Recalling what I noted about entities actively disclosing themselves, derivative is meant precisely in the way that any beings, which are the subject of an investigation, must make themselves available to us for such an investigation. They are not merely given, as if displayed on a pedestal. Entities appear within an irreducible context of temporality, place, and interrelation with other entities, while it is the general metaphysical view that strives to describe entities apart from this context. We cannot disengage an entity from its context because the two, taken together, are what give us access to the entity. Above all, Heidegger states, it must be remembered that such investigation does not give us access to beings; instead, "they [beings] must be manifest *before* . . . and *for* it."[32]

Heidegger therefore speaks of the truth of being as its openness, or how it actively manifests itself.[33] As such, it is prior to any determination of beings, or what in a more general sense is the priority of ontological truth over any form of metaphysical truth. And because the intelligibility of entities is presupposed by this openness, he is concerned with an account of *how* being itself manifests to us.[34] This is a central responsibility of philosophizing since it "awakes in a more originary manner."[35] Responsibility, which can be taken in this context as having both care for our manner of questioning and the ability to respond to that which provokes our questioning, is a mode of relating to being itself that is unique and cannot be trivialized. This is because its mode is one of witnessing how things appear to us and what this witnessing can then reveal in terms of understanding how to exist in relation to these entities. If we do not understand how our relation to things is constituted, then the matter of acting, deciding, and existing is thoughtless (a form of *hubris*). In other words, how are we regarding that which gives itself? And how does this manner of regarding stand in relation to that which gives itself?

Suffice it to say in relation to the subtle sense of how, these questions are perpetually open-ended for Heidegger. This open-endedness is a sort of plenitude or abundance which, as he indicates in his later thought, is a genuine source for questioning.[36] Moreover, because we are ignorant of it and because it has a fundamental role, its absence from our thought results in a sort of law-like consequence. Its absence haunts us in terms of historical failures to understand how to be. Modern technology is, of course, a paramount instance of this for Heidegger. But staying with the issue of metaphysics, the contrast between the how and the why comes out most provocatively in Heidegger's use of the term "nothing." If metaphysics has typically asked "Why something instead of nothing?" Heidegger argues that in doing so being itself, as what is given, is not thought. This is because in seeking reasons to explain the appearance of being according to the features and qualities of entities, it forgets that being has given itself. In fact, Heidegger refers to the history of the meaning of the ancient Greek *hupokeimenon*, which is translated in Latin as *subjectum* and in English as *subject.*

Hupokeimenon is a way of speaking of ground in terms of what is subject, and Heidegger understands *hupokeimenon* as a way of designating that which underlies and makes possible our witnessing and speech about entities and being.[37] Being itself is subject and underlies that which we encounter in the world. Yet within the history of philosophy, Descartes is the figure who becomes most identifiable with reversing the place of *hupokeimenon*, though this transformation had been building with Scholastic thought.[38] The modern age of philosophy is marked by the reduction of *hupokeimenon* to the human being; thus the subject is no longer "out there" in reality, as it were, but in the human being itself, that is, the human being as the human subject: "Man is the referential center of being itself."[39] Moreover, Heidegger sees this shift corresponding to the drive for certain knowledge since the attainment of certainty relies on locating the act of judging in the human subject; otherwise, on what grounds can we claim such knowledge? Heidegger at one point comments:

> The preference given to a *sub-jectum* (that which lies at the basis as ground) which is preeminent in that it is, in an essential respect, unconditioned, stems from man's demand for a *fundamentum absolutum inconussum veritatis*; for an unshakable ground of truth, in the sense of certainty, which rests in itself.[40]

So when ground becomes the human subject, Heidegger sees this as consistent with traditional metaphysics which, while not entirely erroneous, forgets to think that which is prior to the human subject.

This forgetting is evident in how what appears to us most readily is a concern for beings and their underlying features. Returning to the use of "nothing" mentioned at the outset of this section, Heidegger alludes to this persistence of forgetting negatively. In our ignorance, what gives itself (being) appears as nothing; and because it is the source of beings and our thought about them, as long as we are oblivious to it, this nothing persists, eventually revealing through history the inadequacies of our thought—that is, the "nothing itself nihilates."[41] Nothing is so perplexing precisely because it is absent and cuts against our tendency to want to represent being itself in terms of entities and their properties.[42] On this view, Heidegger is not alluding to a mystical nothingness that we need to intuit; rather, nothing persists as a reminder of the limitations of our thought at any given historical moment. And this is to say its perplexing nature is not absolute but hermeneutical; as a limitation and a mystery it is productive insofar as it names how being itself is ever-present but cannot be totally grasped or made the object of a knowledge claiming certain ends. Using the metaphor of night, Heidegger refers to nothing as both darkness, in the sense we cannot see it, and nearness, in the sense that it is what secretly binds everything together.[43] So what we notice in lieu of the nothing is how beings are made visible to us according to the features which certain forms of measurement bring to the fore. These features mean that we take beings to be the objects of our investigation, all the while forgetting about being itself: "Beings in general are the ground in the sense of the foundation upon which any further consideration of beings takes place."[44]

But if our thought persistently faces the problem of not being able to think its ground, or the being that gives itself to be thought and the being that has made possible anything like our thought and existence, what then is it to think the more originary meaning of ground? And hence, what does it mean to think what is given?

The Turn to Ground Understood Concretely

My response to the foregoing questions involves understanding how Heidegger sees ground as the presupposition of thought which persists in every form of thought: ground is the condition for the possibility of our being and thinking.[45] As such, it therefore requires to be understood philosophically and as the basis for human dwelling, that is, concretely.

Indeed, if being thrown into existence constitutes the existential condition of our being, and if this condition means we cannot master existence because we had no choice as to whether or not we should exist,[46] then as Heidegger's philosophy moves toward the more concrete, one would expect this thrownness to be conceived more definitely in relation to dwelling. No longer abstract, Heidegger will in fact speak of thrownness in relation to ground and finally, as we will see in chapter 5, earth.

Because concepts are derivative and conceived by finite minds, or as the famous maxim of *Being and Time* runs, we arrive "too late" in the attempt to carry out this project of thought,[47] the question remains as to whether any concepts can adequately think being. Heidegger proposes to offer such concepts and avoid the trappings discussed above by using a "pre-ontological" understanding that can form "ontological concepts" and that can give some indication of ground.[48] In other words, adequate concepts would derive from the disposition that does not take for granted how being itself is given to us. They make the question of this giving (or its how) as foundational and allow us to think from that instance. (Recall that for Heidegger any adequate concept is bound by its historical and finite context. As his own work attests, such concepts may prove obsolete as an understanding develops.)[49] In some sense, their adequacy lies in being able to attest to the givenness of being at a specific point in our historical existence. In contrast, metaphysics, Heidegger asserts, forgoes this givenness and thinks it has surpassed and mastered givenness through its representational concepts—*sub specie aeterni.*[50]

How is it then possible to remember this givenness? In part, the task resides in understanding ground as presupposed in everything we do and understand. Heidegger writes:

> Because being [itself], as understood in advance, "intrinsically" *grounds* things in an originary manner, every being [entity] as a being [entity] in its own way announces "grounds," whether these are specifically grasped and determined in an appropriate way or not. . . . Ground, however, belongs to the essence of being because being (and not beings) is given . . . as a grounding that finds itself in a projecting world.[51]

Heidegger refers to the way grounds seem to be in entities while really what grounds entities is being itself. Let us recall that metaphysics erred insofar as it sought the meaning of being in acquiring reasons explaining beings, or entities. The focus on beings directed philosophy away from the question of being itself. Yet because ground is presupposed in everything we do, it shares the same precedence as being itself—it precedes us: "Insofar as being 'is' what grounds, and only insofar as it is so, it has no ground/reason."[52] In this respect, any reasons we offer—whether for being itself or for beings—arrives too late. And we can therefore never ground that which precedes us. Heidegger names this perpetual elusiveness *Abgrund*, that is, how the originary ground cannot be grounded, or is unground.[53] In this respect, the identity of being and ground is not a simple one. While being and ground are "the same,"[54] to see what is the same as two distinct things conceptually implies seeing what is most originary for our existence in terms of differentiation. In other words, what is originarily a unity becomes differentiated in our thought about it.[55] Because thought recognizes this difference, we subsequently recognize how this difference is relevant to our life and thus played out existentially.

Indeed, the differentiated identity of being and ground suggests another differentiated identity between ground and human dwelling. Consider how ground provides the "upon which" beings can manifest, or what Heidegger describes in relation to their "standing there" or presencing—as opposed to the way traditional metaphysics represents entities as objects that "stand over against" or as merely present.[56] In allowing entities to manifest in their specific manner of being, ground donates a sense of locality—hence beings "stand *there*." The existence of entities is, as he says, a kind of repose in their outward appearance. As standing-there "being means appearing. Appearing is not something subsequent that sometimes happens to being. Appearing is the very essence of being."[57] Heidegger thus notes a contrast between the modern and ancient Greek regard for entities. The ancient Greeks

> address beings as the "stable" [*das "Ständige"*]. "The stable" means two things. On the one hand, it means whatever, of and by itself, stands on its own, that which stands "there"; and at the same time "the stable" means the enduring, the lasting. We would certainly not be thinking like the Greeks if we were to conceive of the stable as what "stands *over against*" in the sense of the objective.[58]

What Heidegger describes as the stable refers to how entities in the ancient Greek sense are apprehended as self-revealing. They are stable precisely because they do not require something in addition to enable them to show themselves. This stability allows them to "stand there" in the sense that they give rise to location and places or can mark occasions. The way in which an entity appears cannot be understood apart from its specific locality, or situatedness.

This difference is so significant for Heidegger, as the philosophers of place have argued,[59] that it provides him with the basis for conceiving space as that which emerges from the situatedness of entities. Space appears only as a result of there being entities; or, as he says, entities *make* space since, by their situatedness in a place and in relation to other entities, space can be said to emerge or inhabit a specific location. Heidegger refers to this creative or productive feature of entities as gathering and admittance.[60] Entities gather elemental material in a certain way where their standing-there configures a place. By virtue of configuring, this place admits a certain presence.[61] This is most overt in different forms of architecture which give rise to, or presence, respective atmospheres, environments, and occasions. According to Heidegger, we are not simply isolated bodies moving within a void populated with other entities.

> Rather, we always go through spaces in such a way that we already experience them by staying constantly with near and remote locations and things. When I go towards the door of the lecture hall, I am already there, and I could not go at all if I were not such that I am there. I am never here only, as this encapsulated body; rather, I am there, that is, I already pervade the room, and only thus can I go through it.[62]

The already constituted locality of places is primary in this sense, and the competing notion of space as a homogeneous void is a representation of our experience after the fact of our already being placed in existence. Space is not filled but emerges from the already given (as in natural locations) and constructed places (as in the world rendered by work). Even the Cartesian representation of space is not possible but from a place that is something like a view from nowhere. Heidegger's challenge, in this sense, is one that begins from the ground up.

While place appears to prove essential to Heidegger's thought, as I will discuss below, his attempt to think being in terms of an intimate participation with our surroundings indicates that he wants to drive toward thinking being in the most concrete and immanent sense as possible. It is as if to think being as ground shifts the emphasis of our thinking and looking such that we no longer tend toward entities and their properties by themselves, but these as they are inextricably bound to being itself. Indeed, one way this shift can be seen is in Heidegger's desire to express a subtle relation between how we understand the meaning of being and the involvement of this understanding in our situated existence. To redescribe human dwelling as bound in this sense to a ground outside itself severely reduces the sense of certainty or privilege by which we can claim to have a monopoly on truth as a human-specific phenomenon. The truth of being grounds our manner of dwelling.

But this conclusion has its own difficulty. For the unity of ground and dwelling implies that our thought about existence can no longer be concerned merely with abstract possibilities. In other words, the task of remembering ground cannot proceed by reflection alone, as an exercise of the private mind. Ground must be understood as manifesting in human existence as well.

This move to the concrete recalls the irreducible role that humans occupy in Heidegger's ontology, a role which is not jettisoned in his later essays. Heidegger uses the term *Dasein* as a way of highlighting the unique mode of being we have. Seeing a "there" that is given by entities is the basis for our active engagement with the world; in fact, we cannot help but see entities in terms of "there" since we are always involved to some degree in a way of interpreting our existence according to ends, projects, and locations. His use of the term "Dasein" is a play on the more typical German *Dasein*, or "existence."[63] We do not just have existence, like a rock, but a manner of existing that discloses through interaction. In such disclosure, as Heidegger says, is "the openness where beings can be present for the human being, and the human being also for himself."[64] This placement is both a placement within a project for being and a placement in a locality in which a project for being has context and meaning ("there"). Heidegger famously describes the practical dimension to our being-there with respect to our tendency to make things near through the use of entities, which he terms equipment (*Zeug*), and how this practical relation mediates the distance and orientation of our being with things. Through distance (*Ent-fernung*) and orientation (*Ausrichtung*) we form a bond between things in our location. Malpas remarks:

> The distance and orientation that are characteristic of being-there thus capture the way in which being-there is situated with respect to the ordering of things in the world as that particular configuration of that "there," a particular "nearing" of things in a specific activity or task.[65]

Through use of the fishing boat, for example, the sea has a different sort of distance than it does when one fishes from the shore; we see the sea *as* a source of livelihood in a different way according to the fortunes and perils brought by fishing away from land. As well as with the force of winds and sails, a strong breeze can be made "near" through the right rigging or type of boat.

If humans are those who participate in the "thereness" of being through their engagements and activities, this role is a manner of accommodating our dwelling to what is understood to ground existence. Heidegger refers to this in terms of play: through what he calls "the leap" of recognizing that being is ground,

> thinking enters into a breadth and depth of that play upon which our human nature is staked. . . . The question remains whether and how we, hearing the movements of this play, play along and accommodate ourselves to the play.[66]

Play is, of course, no abstract experiment, but a playing out of an understanding that lives according to what grounds it. Playing is, in this existential sense, an enacting of an understanding which would do well to remember its relation to being and ground. As McManus argues, in the early Heidegger remembering takes heed of the question of being (*Seinsfrage*).[67] In the late Heidegger, remembering recalls how to dwell poetically. While the relation between the question of being and poetic dwelling has been discussed elsewhere,[68] here I wish merely to point out that in both cases practical activity is a way of enacting an originary relation. To be, for humans, is to be constantly enacting that which we remember as what constitutes the meaning of being. Heidegger thus speaks of memory as a "making inward" in order to arrive "into the widest compass of the open," that is, where the open is the thereness or habitation we disclose in our understanding and activity.[69] In this sense, the turn to ground is a way of attempting to infuse a philosophical interpretation of the meaning of being into our existence, as a foundation for our projects of dwelling.

There is, however, a problem with the attempt to remain with the term "ground" as an adequate expression of the concrete: it is inevitably tied to the notion of the human as subject and as the one who gives grounds. And though we can see Heidegger making efforts to distinguish ground in a different way, there seems to be a recognition on his part that clarification of the concept is not enough. Both the historical sedimentation of the human as subject and the drive to think being and ground more concretely pose a new project for thought. So to what can Heidegger turn to rethink ground in a new way that distinguishes it from the human subject, or decenters us as the masters of meaning?

A Turn to Place?

The significance of place in Heidegger's work, but moreover in our general relation to existence, has been explored in relation to art, the environment, and identity. The aim of these studies is to dispel prevailing misconceptions of place which might in turn liberate us into new modes of being—a more grounded, local, and poetic existence. Ed Casey remarks at one point that giving serious philosophical thought to place requires thinking in either a premodern or postmodern context.[70] He explains that a proper consideration of place involves suspending the modern pre-understanding of reality as if it existed within a homogenous void.[71] Space, for the modern mind, is like a container in which things appear; and places consequently tend to be defined as mere positions within this container. That this pre-understanding is so dominant is evident in how it is difficult for us to think of reality and our existence as being anything but contained in space. Historical and philosophical reasons for the pervasion of homogeneous space are several. Casey, Malpas, and others note the problems with Cartesianism and Newtonianism and the central role ascribed to bodily extension which results in a form of "objective spatiality."[72] By this Malpas means how we tend to see space as a containment of the measurable extension of things. Such entities are not seen in relation to their specific situatedness but as an object of standard measure—that is, as entities represented as standing out from their context in order that they can be measured in a certain way. In contrast, as we saw above, Heidegger's reference to equipment was employed to demonstrate how contrary to objective spatiality, we find not objects in space but a fore-structured region constituted by practical and theoretical relations. Space thus emerges from this region. This engaged and involved form of spatial relation is "existential spatiality."[73]

In his *Place and Experience*, Malpas sets out to clarify place apart from space, noting how both terms suffer from the assumption that their meanings are clear. Of place, he notes that it "is inextricably bound up with notions of both dimensionality or extension and of locale or environing situation."[74] Ultimately assuming a Heideggerian position, Malpas argues against the prevailing idea that places are more or less physical locations in space. He shows instead that space arises from place, not as a projection from the mental life of the human subject, but as the "wherein" we as human beings have our sense of dwelling.[75] To think of ourselves and to think at all is possible because we exist "in" a place from which we have a reflective vantage.

Also contributing to our pre-understanding of space as homogenous is the prevalence given to a linear conception of time which reduces places to points defining temporal intervals. The linear notion removes the singular identity of locality, representing it merely as an interim in a temporal sequence. Heidegger refers to this as the one-dimensionality of time in which its intervals are not simultaneous but "one after another."[76] So long as this conception of time orders our everyday affairs and determines our psychology, anything having depth and breadth beyond one dimension is, to use Kierkegaard's term, leveled down. Casey notes the multidimensionality of place in terms of its four cardinal directions and the manifold ways in which different landmarks and landscapes manifest different senses of temporal locality.[77] In view of this, Malpas highlights how Heidegger's *Being and Time* is involved in at least two projects—one that rejects the linear notion of time in favor of a lived and historical temporality, and the second which rejects the notion of space consistent with linear time. While *Being and Time* famously, even if incompletely, develops a thesis on temporality, Malpas shows how the development of an alternative to homogenous space is inchoate and in fact cannot be achieved within the limitations of *Being and Time*. He convincingly describes this as a failure to find a perspective and discourse that can give equal regard to both the human being and place without reducing to subjectivism or objectivism.[78]

Because the notions of homogenous space and linear time dominate scientific formalism, the focus on and recovery of place is crucial for addressing conceptual prejudices which can be tied to forms of environmental and even sociopolitical exploitation. In general, the philosophical revivification of place resists the tendency of the scientific worldview which represents entities abstractly and formally. To see entities, especially humans, as situated and defined by their locality is not only to break with this "spirit of abstraction," to use Gabriel Marcel's words, but also to reconceive the kind of subjectivity we have. No longer do we conceive our consciousness as transparent, mastered, or unified. It is limited, bounded, situated and therefore subject to, defined and decentered by place. It is the opening by which we are shaped.

Having said this, one might think that the turn to the analysis of place would prove a substantial foundation for my own phenomenological investigation of land. Yet, this is true only to some extent. The studies of Casey and Malpas make significant progress in rethinking our relation to land, yet they do so without seeing the deeply ontological and economic implications of what this relation means. This is not to say that they ignore it or to dismiss the cogency of their work. Malpas and others, for example, are very much concerned with the relation between place, environment, and power, while Casey briefly discusses "the Great Economy," describing this as an economics of household management (*oikos*) in line with nature, or what he at one point refers to as "selective husbandry" as opposed to stewardship.[79] Nonetheless, by focusing on the specific kinds of disclosures and events arising from this situated kind of dwelling, these studies tend to elide discussion of the material condition for the possibility of place. What grants place? On what does place emerge? To what is it subject? Before seeing how I distinguish my approach to land from their meditations on place, let me refer to a few examples for clarification.

Casey maintains that the priority of place is ontological, meaning that there is no being and no conception of being without place.[80] One can say being itself is always tied to the particular manifestations in existence, as entities. Whatever entities we wish to examine occur not in a neutral void but are situated in a place. Collingwood puts this well when challenging the traditional notion of metaphysics as the science of being as being. He argues that there is simply no way of discussing being as being without reference to specific entities and their temporal and spatial locality.[81] This is to say more specifically, our perception is bound by and to place, something John Sallis observes in terms of the singularity of place which cannot be conceptualized since each place is a unique gathering of people, things, and the elements.[82] And while the common practices local to a place go a long way in determining our understanding of dwelling, it is not enough to say that place is specific to cultural norms, especially when scientism claims that the abstracting power of reason can transcend any kind of placial particularity. An appropriate philosophy of place clarifies instead that place allows and constitutes the gathering together of an event like observation, reflection, and speech.[83] (In this sense, the scientist speaks from a place which, despite the specificity of the experiment, is defined abstractly by the regularity of nature.) Place, it can be said, is not synonymous with relativism but the manifold and rich paths by which we come to understand, that is, the many ways in which being can be said.

In addition to this priority, Casey often notes how place involves land, especially in relation to indigenous and aboriginal peoples who have an intimate relation to nature. Implicit in his discussion of the legal and moral rights we might ascribe to land—as opposed to our rights to land[84]—is the recognition that place in some way relies upon the material condition of land. Elsewhere, Casey refers to how the activity of building occurs in a place and is reliant on "the lay of land," how taking away land "is to take away life," and how place is "landed."[85] He also refers to ground as the "undergirding support" for wilderness.[86] However, his discussion remains incomplete since it notes the integral relation between land and place but does not further investigate how land may be distinct in some significant way except as that which serves place.

In more recent work interested in broadening the notion of landscape and art, where Casey treats the importance of land, this primacy of place still dominates. For Casey, land is a liminal concept which mediates between the earth as "that which subtends human experience" and the world as "the communal and historical and linguistic domain of human speech and action."[87] And while he remarks with some force that the majority of Continental philosophers (including Heidegger) have neglected the importance of land, and while Casey employs land as a way of speaking more richly about the ontological nature of landscapes, there is still much missed in his discussion. Even if he restores some significance to land, as a liminal concept it remains subject to the role of place.[88] In this respect, Casey describes land as reliant on the specificity of place:

> [Land] is itself always singular: it is always just this land, located in this particular place and region and nowhere else. We are lucky to have it . . . not just in its sheer materiality (i.e., as soil or property), but in the phenomenological fact that it is the inner frame for all outgoing and ongoing perception, a basis for personal as well as public identities.[89]

But land is not reducible to place; it allows place to manifest. Nor is land a threshold to some other region or domain. It is land which gives itself in order for there to be anything like a specific place of natural beauty or a site for founding a village or town, farm, or commercial center. It is substantial and not liminal. So in contrast to Casey's view, I will argue in the next chapter that land is foundational as *hupokeimenon*. It requires us not to think of it as merely dependent on place but how it operates such that place can manifest.[90]

Like Casey, Malpas makes reference to land in relation to aboriginal conceptions of dwelling. And like Casey, there is a latent recognition that land is in some way fundamentally tied to the conception of place. Malpas remarks that there is a sort of substantiality of land that is not just a passive receptor of our building and dwelling activities; it also determines our activities in how we see land and location as being fit or unfit for certain activities.[91] However, the role of land seems little more than a metaphor or specific aspect of place. Malpas will thus identify place and ground as the same thing: "place . . . requires no such grounding of its own since it is ground."[92] Moreover, the ontological event of the disclosure of meaning presupposes the place "that gives space to beings."[93]

This suggests that land is not uniquely distinct from place, and it can be seen as a more concrete instance in which place has its influence. Malpas will therefore speak of "landscape" as a configuring of place on the land,[94] but he does not consider the role of land in this relation except as configured placially as a landscape. On this view, the philosophy of place performs the function of retrieving landscape from reductive notions where it might be merely an imaginative, static representation in our mind or in art.[95] There is perhaps another problem with the term "land" since it is used mostly in geographical science concerned with mapping locations and viewing these locations according to the homogenous conception of space.[96] The concept of land, simply put, does not allow us to go deep enough when understanding aspects of our situated manner of dwelling. Yet another limitation of the term exists in its elemental specificity; it cannot include water, or seascapes. Place, on the other hand, in referring to notions of locality and boundedness applies to both water and land.[97] Yet, as we will see in the next chapter, this claim about elemental specificity relies too heavily on an abstract—that is, an unlanded conception of locality. In the end, place itself is not possible unless the land makes itself available for something like building and cultivation. The place of the vineyard, or to conceive the sea as a place (wilderness), is not possible unless the land gives itself to us as the ground upon which this understanding can occur.

Let me be clear: The foregoing comments are not intended as rejections of the rich topoanalyses provided by Casey, Malpas, and others. And to say that I take land to be prior to place does not necessarily mean that I see their general views as incompatible with mine. It may very well be there is a difference of emphasis in view of the fact that what is thought is in need of clarification. Topoanalyses are, in this regard, interested primarily in showing how place forms a significant part of our identity and dwelling. My interest, on the other hand, is to assume an orientation in our questioning and thought that is no longer mired by the perspective of understanding ground as that which is *for* the human subject as the master of meaning. And Heidegger must therefore demonstrate how we are in some sense dependent on what precedes us, not just in a logical or general ontological sense, but concretely so.

Anticipating this shift, I should clarify that when using the terms I have sought to resituate in relation to land—that is, ground, place, and as we will see soon, earth—I will employ them in my own arguments as fundamentally presupposing this relation. So, for example, I will speak of place as significant, yet precisely insofar as this significance is owed to land in some sense.

5

The Being of Land

One of the guiding themes in the first part of this study was a tendency in economic thought to conceive land as natural material given merely for, and therefore subject to, human use. For Marx, land is nothing without the application of human labor, while underwriting the general capitalist economic framework is the idea that land lacks any distinctive features and can be treated as capital, which in turn requires it to be privately alienable. The aim of the previous chapter was to prepare a new way for thinking of land by showing, with reference to Heidegger's concern for givenness and ground, how our understanding and existence fundamentally rely on that which precedes us. I argued that because Heidegger considers ground in both ontological and material senses, he attempts to see this precedence as *hupokeimenon*, or the subject that underlies and provides for our grounded existence, or dwelling. However, Heidegger's treatment of the concept of ground seemed to fall short, and I identified a limitation in its inability to overturn the historical assumption since Descartes that the human being is the subject. Following from this, there are two problems that remain unresolved: How can we understand more fully the philosophical significance of the grounded nature of our existence? And how can this understanding succeed in the midst of a seemingly immovable modern conceptual prejudice which takes the human subject as most basic?

I will attempt to answer both questions by discussing *hupokeimenon* in relation to Heidegger's notion of earth and then to my reflections on land. This departure from the concept of ground enables us to understand how the philosophical meaning of our existence—or what Heidegger calls the truth of being—presupposes a relation to and involvement with earth. His treatment of earth elucidates how our dependence on a primordial source asks us to think of the cause of beings in a sense that decenters the role of the human as subject. Yet at the same time, I argue that this primordiality, so long as it remains a reflection on that which is supremely prior to us, falls short of thinking our relation to it more specifically and concretely. I note this risk in terms of a philosophical pietism, or what Ricoeur sees as the tendency of Heidegger's philosophy to take a short route to ontology and reside problematically in the poetic and "the seductions of the unarticulated and unexpressed."[1] My thesis, then, is to say that when land is taken as the foundation which is prerequisite to any act of human existence, it provides us with a way of conceiving an otherwise primordial notion of the givenness of existence in terms of a specific, concrete relation to the world in which we dwell. In Heideggerian parlance, I am insisting that in apprehending the "how of being itself," there is a "how to dwell" for human beings. As the basis of human activity and production, land allows us to recognize *how* we dwell—not only what we do on the land but with an awareness of our dependency on it. Land, by virtue of its visibility and ubiquity, is the basis for existence. In this respect, the inertia associated with the kind of solipsism pervasive in modern views of subjectivity, according to which philosophers attempt arduously and rigorously to build relations to the external world, is broken by a simple but nonetheless momentous shift: the center of gravity, as it were, transfers from us to what underlies us.

This chapter begins by resuming Heidegger's thought on ground as it is transformed in his notions of earth and poetic dwelling. I argue that earth allows Heidegger to express the asymmetrical relation between humans and that which precedes us in terms of a primordial material, whose original and indestructible nature is both the *source* of all that ontologically arises and the *limit* by which human activity is bounded. As source, it is not an abstract, metaphysical first cause or uncaused cause; rather, it is source perceived existentially and phenomenologically, as already there before we arrive and which in some sense gives our existence. As limit, earth's originality cannot be mastered since what springs from it, is subsumed by it. Heidegger understands this inevitability in terms of the finite life of entities and, more importantly, how the things that are revealed by earth must return to it in their demise (i.e., they are concealed by earth). As we will see, earth as both source and limit provokes the question of how we should exist appropriately, something that is captured by Heidegger's use of the term "poetic." I interpret poetic to mean an existence consciously aware of its bond to earth such that its mode of dwelling produces in accord with this bond. This productive dwelling, which draws on the Greek meaning of *phusis*, is *poiesis*. And so it is not just poetic in the sense of the poet who articulates this bond to earth in language, but is in the most basic sense productive.[2]

Moving beyond Heidegger, I note that his thought can be developed in a more specific, regional sense. This requires, nonetheless, understanding how earth can be conceived less primordially and more concretely in terms of what such a regional practice presupposes. I therefore discuss land as *hupokeimenon*, its original power to reveal and to conceal, and our dependence on this power.

Forgetfulness of Being

I stated in the previous chapter that Heidegger presumes that our current mode of understanding is pervaded by a forgetfulness. I explained how this oblivion manifests as absence and presence:[3] on the one hand, we lack an awareness of what should be present to thought; on the other hand, we preoccupy ourselves with those things that appear to matter most to us. Taken together, we think beings instead of being itself. There is, nonetheless, a bit more involved in this diagnosis. It is not simply a state of affairs; it is an active unfolding, a playing out of being through those beings (i.e., humans) who engage with and render reality through the work of their hands. In this sense, as the hermeneutical maxim goes, humans have not just a situation or an environment but a world in which the things in it are understood in relation to possibilities of being. As I have alleged, while the relation to ontological possibilities is one that Heidegger accepts as a basic existential feature of our existence, the problem with this feature, when caught up in a forgetfulness, is that it perpetuates and enhances our forgetting since our practices and relations become modes of articulating a framework born from this oblivion.

There are, suffice it to say, many different types of forgetfulness, which can vary from the attempt to escape pressing encounters with finitude, or what Jaspers refers to as "ultimate situations," to misconstruing fundamental relations to other humans and entities, or what gets grouped generally under the label "inauthenticity." One of the main foci of Heidegger's thought, as I have discussed, is a forgetfulness of the kind of precedence integral to givenness. Perpetuating and symptomatic of this forgetfulness is the language of metaphysics, whose expressly abstract nature draws our attention away from our relation to existence and, as it were, into the realm of eternal concepts in which the human mind is the ground and arbiter of knowledge.

In order to make the transition from ground to earth, let me recast this oblivion in terms of the representation of entities which I discussed earlier. In this case, I want to deal expressly with the "object nature" of this representation, which implies that an entity is taken as standing out in some decisive way; it is an ob-ject. To recall, Heidegger draws on the ancient Greek notion of entities as "standing there" in their placial and temporal context; this context should be well heeded. The contrast with the modern notion of object could not be starker in this sense since the modern view presumes that in order to be understood, entities have to be separated from their context as the object of our observation. This view is not passive but active in its attempt to extract or isolate those features which seem most relevant. In summary, the ob-ject nature of the modern mode of apprehending is "over against" because it views entities apart from the existential context in which they arise, where existential refers to an entity already being in a world and a place.[4] Or to put this assessment another way: the ob-ject view of entities ignores context in favor of a single cause, or that which is determined to have given rise to the entity, such as a gene or motive. The object is then nothing more than the effect of this cause.

Heidegger sees this predilection for single cause as especially modern[5] and notes that the Greek sense of an entity and its cause (*aition*) is understood as the entity being indebted to something else in its "existentially" given context. In other words, the ground of an entity is understood in manifold ways as the senses by which an entity can be understood to have its existence; it *occasions* the context for and the emergence of an entity.[6] There is not just one cause in this sense but many, such as the efficient, material, formal, and final causes.[7] A natural entity, like a rock or tree, can be understood in this sense as owing its existence to several relations because it relies on something antecedent to its very being in order to exist. Material cause is perhaps the most obvious insofar as a rock is constituted by what we identify according to categories like sedimentary, metamorphic, or igneous. These categories, to recall, are not absolute and comprise a frame of measurement by which we can know the entities we call rocks. In any case, the ancient Greek notion of cause is certainly not understood in the modern sense of attempting to locate a single cause to which an entity's existence can be attributed. Cause expresses rather a relation of dependency, which in turn sets limits on how the dependent entity can be.

These limitations are not flaws or detrimental deficiencies. The material sandstone limits a rock in a certain way that granite does not. The former is more permeable to water, for example, which makes it less suitable for climbing after a recent storm. Furthermore, this dependency is always something that can be experienced through observation. The final cause of a tree, which presumably is to reach a certain mature form we associate with its particular species, can be observed readily in an adult tree. In contrast, the modern emphasis on single cause wagers that whatever other contributing factors there might be in determining the being of entity, such factors are not as relevant. Perhaps they are even considered to be externalities that do not really participate in a thing's essence or nature. This tendency is prevalent in how some scientific accounts of causation isolate minute features invisible to the naked eye.[8] By implication, what appears to us as entities in being says nothing about the nature of these entities; one has to look behind the appearance.

One can in fact see that the contrast between the ancient Greek and modern parallels Heidegger's understanding of what separates the questions "how?" and "why?" The how, in attempting to discover the many senses in which an entity is, attempts to discern that entity as it is in its existential context. The why, because it takes the entity separate from its context, forms a representation of it according to those features vital to a frame of measurement that presupposes the isolation of these features. An instance of this arises in recent attempts to define aesthetic experience in terms of the frame of measurement called neuroscience, or what is the reduction of the experience of art to what can be measured by that science. Consider Heidegger's comments on a Greek statue:

> The statue of Apollo in the museum at Olympia we can indeed regard as an object of natural-scientific representation; we can calculate the physical weight of marble; we can investigate its chemical composition. But this objectifying thinking and speaking does not catch sight of the Apollo who shows forth his beauty and so appears as the visage of the god.[9]

What he notes in terms of the calculable, observable features are in essence no different from the observations made by a more sophisticated and technical form of observation that might arise in neuroscientific investigation. Both frames of measurement begin with the assumption that what it can measure accounts for what is most real in terms of an entity's cause. The scale used to weigh the marble has the same ontological relation to the statue as neuroscientific instruments used to observe the brain activity of the person who, for example, is looking at the statue as a work of art. Both regard the experience of the statue as residing not in our existential encounter with the work of art, but in some operation which must be calculated by means not available to the observer. In essence, the calculative approach is non-experienceable except as an activity of calculation.

Or, let us consider Heidegger's discussion of Nietzsche's question "What did we do when we unchained this earth from the sun?"[10] Heidegger notes the consequences of representing the sun as an entity at the center of the solar system made possible by astronomical calculation:

> The sun forms and delimits the field of vision [horizon] in which beings show themselves. . . . The earth as the residence of man is unchained from the sun. . . . The whole field of vision has been wiped away. . . . For man has risen up into the I-hood of the *ego cogito*. With this uprising all beings become objects. As what is objective, beings are swallowed up into the immanence of subjectivity. The horizon no longer illuminates itself.[11]

There are, of course, references to what I discussed in the previous chapter as the shift to the search for certainty, how this search is grounded in the self, and how this shift corresponds to the objectification of entities. What should also be noted is that the sun which appears existentially as the entity which rises and sets in relation to the horizon is, for astronomy, nonsense. Behind the appearance is the "real" being of the sun as our system's center. While Heidegger's point is not to reject the frame of measurement called astronomy, it is to say that one is deceived if one thinks this scientific way is the one and only way to describe the sun truthfully. Indeed, it cannot make sense of what it means for us to exist in the world; the existential encounter of the setting or rising sun is integral to the way we understand how to live—as an event to be enjoyed with another, as the indication of the end or beginning of the day, and so on. On this view, we never encounter the sun astronomically. That is to say, the truth of the astronomical representation of the sun has little involvement in how we understand our lives as a project to be lived and how we cope with and anticipate events.

To come full circle to the problem of the human when regarded as subject, the process of abstraction can only become dominant and used unawaringly when the human observer does not recognize that the entity in question discloses itself actively in its appearing, or "standing there." Heidegger thus says:

> But beings can be experienced as objects only where human beings have become subjects, those who experience their fundamental relation to beings as the objectification—understood as mastery—of what is encountered.[12]

His account may, nonetheless, seem somewhat unconvincing given the practical applicability of many frames of measurement that take entities as objects. Much of the debate about Heidegger's criticism of modernity has focused on what appears to be his pitting of an essentialist and nostalgic view of reality against a progressively technological one.[13] What I am noting, however, is how Heidegger is actually emphasizing what is crucial in this mastery—namely, the act of forgetting. In other words, evaluative claims about the mode or method of observation are secondary to a more fundamental issue. Methods may be problematic, but in order to see how they are so requires understanding the relation by which humans become engaged in these methods and disengaged from entities that are the objects observed by these methods. I want to argue in what follows that this required understanding involves a form of remembering what precedes us and doing so according to an entity that we experience every day. Heidegger thus turns to what will seem to be an anachronistic account of *aition* as earth. Metaphysical and calculative abstraction are in this sense turned on their head. The experience of being resides not in the purely conceptual or invisible but in the readily experienceable; so readily in fact that we tend to ignore it. As Raffoul notes, "the poverty of essence" does not overcome metaphysics by attempting to surmount it but "by climbing back down into the nearest of the near."[14] What can be nearer than the ground upon which we are rooted in and for this existence?

Earth as *Aition*

Any attempt to understand how Heidegger conceives earth as the *aition* of our being requires explaining the kind of dependence we have on it. In this section I do so in terms of the asymmetrical structure of existence. Heidegger conceives this asymmetry according to three features, or what I call earth's supremacy: (1) earth's relation to *phusis*; (2) how earth is determinative of human dwelling; and (3) as a more specific delineation of the previous point, how the sheltering nature of earth calls for our appropriate response to it. Earth is not just a material precondition of our being-in-the-world, but one that figures into every aspect of our being. It is the ever-present basis for the material, conceptual, and imaginative dimensions of our existence. Nonetheless, this is not to say we are readily aware of earth, and this is why Heidegger attempts to elucidate how its ubiquity constantly makes demands upon us by revealing our dependence on it.

Heidegger draws on the ancient Greek notion of *phusis* to indicate what earth entails as a primordial source constituting the being of things in general. Conventionally, *phusis* is often translated by the English word "nature," but in this sense it is too easily taken to be an external environment, that is, as an object representing a scene to which we retire on holiday, or as a resource we seek to exploit or conserve.[15] Indeed, while the ongoing processes of *phusis* are what we often associate with nature's cycle of life and death, Heidegger sees this circularity in an ontologically decisive way when noting the autonomy of *phusis* and therefore how this autonomy imposes itself upon us. Drawing on Aristotle, Heidegger understands *phusis* to be an ongoing process that gives rise to the beingness of beings (*ousia*) and allows these beings to stand "there" by themselves (*hupostasis*) and to lie present before us (*hupokeimenon*).[16] These three traits taken together constitute a process in which ontological donation figures as an original act. Natural entities can only be, stand, and lie before us if what occasions their existence is in some sense self-emergent and self-sufficient.

So given the essential priority that *phusis* has in relation to all that emerges in it, Heidegger's move to the concrete can be seen in his identification of earth as that which is the ground for *phusis*.

> The Greeks early called this emerging and rising in itself and in all things *phusis*. It clears and illuminates, also, that on which and in which man bases his dwelling. We call this ground the *earth*.[17]

As the basis for dwelling, earth participates in and provides the ground upon which the ongoing processes of *phusis* (or the cosmos in the ancient Greek understanding) can occur. And in modifying the ancient Greek thought by the identification of *phusis* with earth, Heidegger sees earth consequently as *hupokeimenon*. Consider the following passage:

> Only a minute fraction of what lies before us in this way has been laid down by man, and even then only with the aid of what was lying there before. The stones from which the house is built come from natural rock.[18]

"Natural rock" notes an aspect of earth which is seen by us as stone suitable for building. Earth is not just resource since in its materiality, in its concreteness, it reveals what existence can mean for us—that is, shelter and abode in a stone house. This meaning is played out through our building and dwelling which fashion our world. On this Joseph Fell observes: "Earth is not a category, nor is it advanced by Heidegger as a speculative ground. It is intended concretely, as an experienced place."[19]

There is a second sense in which *phusis* is primary. So-called natural entities arising from *phusis* emerge (are born or bloom) with no need of intervention from another source. In contrast, although a part of *phusis* insofar as we are "natural" beings, our mode of making is a derivative form of production. So while the processes of *phusis* and human production can be generally called *poiesis*, the latter has a narrow sense. It is thus specified as *techne*, by which things produced draw on or mimic the productive power of *phusis*. This is to say, while earth's givenness is self-producing and self-sustaining, human production (*techne*) fashions those things which are not so.[20] Earth is therefore ever-present as the subject of human activity.

The foregoing is not to say along with Marx that we rely on nature in a materialistic sense. One of the main differences between Marx and Heidegger is that for the former there is nothing beyond our engagement with and relation to material necessity (except perhaps a notion of *self-realization*). For Heidegger, the relation to the material precondition of existence is the point of contact through which a more fundamental relation to being is actualized. The relation to matter, nature, and the earth is one that is beholden to something beyond the necessities defining our biological and practical existence. Material is not transcended but participates in a more differentiated and complex mode of being via its use by humans in their work and activity.[21] Heidegger's concern is not therefore the precedence of earth as a resource for human activity but as source. He wants to elucidate how the status of earth as the material precondition governs our dwelling. For Marx, earth as resource entails no such governing process. And where for Marx the role of development is on the active side of the laborer, Heidegger stresses how any kind of development is bound to the supremacy of the earth.[22]

Indeed, this supremacy is highlighted not just by the original productive power to which earth gives grounds but how it limits us. This limiting account is to ensure that earth as *aition* is not misunderstood as a metaphysical principle which we can absolutely grasp in thought. Consider that Heidegger draws attention to how earth as original source is unfathomable, inexplicable, and therefore incapable of being mastered: "Earth thus shatters every attempt to penetrate into it."[23] It can be grasped only in its priority and precedence.[24] He highlights this impenetrability in relation to calculative thought which attempts to assume a mastery over that upon which we depend:

> It [earth] causes every merely calculating importunity upon it to turn into a destruction. This destruction may herald itself under the appearance of mastery and of progress in the form of the technical-scientific objectivation of nature, but this mastery nevertheless remains an impotence of will.[25]

Recalling my assessments of calculative thought, the significance of Heidegger's association of the "cause of beings" with earth lies in its account of how this cause is experienced in the fabric of existence; we encounter and engage with this *aition*. In his discussion of art, this engagement is expressed as "that into which the work sets itself back and which *causes* to come forth in this setting back of itself is what we called earth."[26] Because Heidegger uses the term "causes" in the sense of allowing,[27] the earth should be understood as allowing the work to arise in human activity so that it (the work) can set itself. But this applies also to so-called natural entities that do not require human activity since any emergence of an entity, natural or otherwise, depends on earth not only in drawing from it to get underway, but in relying on it to root itself and endure.

Yet these conditions of dependence, while enabling the existence of entities, have their limitations. As is usually the case for Heidegger, limitations are essentially positive in marking off boundaries,[28] and in this case what is bounded is our own subjectivity. Let us recall that *phusis* is that which loves to reveal and conceal itself.[29] Likewise, earth is that from which things arise and is that to which they return, or are sheltered: "The earth is spontaneous forthcoming of that which is continually self-secluding and to that extent sheltering and concealing."[30] The association of concealing and sheltering is a manner of expressing the double meaning of limit as marking off and yet being positive in some respect. So while Foltz notes sheltering is a way of supporting, by allowing earth to act as the ground in which something can take root,[31] there is something counterintuitive about Heidegger's use of the term which requires more consideration.

In fact, sheltering describes a dependence on earth constituted by law-like consequences. Earth's sheltering is a form of keeping the things of the world according to its self-producing nature. For something to be maintained in this self-producing nature is to subject it to the ongoing unfolding of *phusis* that we generally identify with the cycles of life and death. The revealing-concealing nature of earth means things arise and perish in order to arise again. In this sense, essential to earth's self-producing is contingency and impermanence, which allow it to maintain its cycle of life, the regeneration of flower from seed, and so on. Things must perish in order to persist in some way. It is the way earth is "marked out" (*dike*), as it were. Heidegger refers to this at one point as the "law" of earth which "strives to keep itself closed."[32] The sheltering nature of earth is thus both to allow it to be rendered productively and to instill in this rendering a certain kind of demise of what is produced in order that it can in some way continue and be renewed. So for earth to instill demise means that it makes innate to things a manner of perishing that in some sense brings about renewal.[33]

There are nonetheless nuances to the human dependence on earth that the examples of nonhuman, natural entities (like the tree or flower) cannot possibly convey. Given the derivation of human *techne* from *poiesis*, there is a unique manner in which we participate in perishing. This can be seen in how despite the ingenuity and skill involved in human producing, the entities we make are limited by their ultimate dependence on earth. They return to earth in some sense. As within the domain of human knowledge, where the human being is not the master of meaning, so too in the realm of production, the human being cannot gain mastery through its technics over the process of being itself (*phusis*).[34] Let us consider that if technics owe their existence to another principle aimed at the facilitation of our dwelling,[35] their principle is derivative, and as such, remains open to the question of how it relates to the more original earth. Are these technics appropriate to earth?[36] Or retrospectively, one might reflect on the consequences of a particular technic, like space flight. What this new mode of travel means, as Arendt notes, is that the human race is no longer bound to the earth, and the earth can in some sense be taken for granted.[37] Whatever the case, what I am calling the ontological limitation of human production and its products perpetually asks us to think on how we are dwelling in relation to earth. Only a form of dependence can provoke such a reflection, where in contrast, any notion that we are self-sufficient masters of existence or nature cannot really do so, at least not without some moments in which this mastery breaks down.

If my account of the shift from ground to earth is one made in favor of concretely understanding how it is we are dependent on the source of our being, then it remains questionable as to how far we are to assume the momentum of this thought. Is it enough simply to recognize how this dependence is involved in our use and relation to the material of the earth? Or should these modes of use and relation be conceived along the lines of specific human practices?

It seems that Heidegger appeals only in a general, even if substantial, way to the transformed mode of dwelling that takes into account the debt to earth. He refers to this poetic dwelling as a way of "founding": "The nature of poetry is . . . founding as bestowing, founding as grounding, and founding as beginning."[38] And he furthermore defines genuine founding as one which remembers its relation to earth. Its paragon is the poet who not only speaks the union between human dwelling and earth[39] but enacts a remembrance of earth in and through his or her activities, both of which Heidegger places under the term "conserving" (*Schonen*). Foltz clarifies that conserving, unlike preserving, "does not mean to refrain from using something or to set it aside, but to use it in such a way that harm is not inflicted upon it."[40]

If this is the case, then by reference to the poetic, it may also mean that Heidegger wants to move away from old metaphysical distinctions by lessening the importance of the categories of *theoria*, *praxis*, and *poiesis* insofar as he wants to conceive of a unity of thought and action as *poiesis*.[41] *Poeisis*, as poetic dwelling, would then refer to a unified mode of being, whose unity is primarily defined by action that remembers its relation to earth in its doing and evokes this relation for others in the ends it achieves or produces.[42] Joining action to the ability to remember through thought, Heidegger writes: "All the work of the hand is rooted in thinking. Therefore, thinking itself is man's simplest, and for that reason hardest, handiwork."[43] So dwelling poetically means living *productively* in remembrance of earth. Yet aside from Heidegger's own examples of the ancient, artistic, and the rustic, how can we envision this productive remembrance in the wider sphere of human activity? More critically expressed, does not the reference to poetic dwelling innately appeal to and encourage a self-enclosed sense of pietism which draws upon an individual already alienated from the ongoings of the world?

> Whether, and when, we may come to a turning point in our unpoetic dwelling is something we may expect to happen only if we remain heedful of the poetic. How and to what extent our doings can share in this turn we alone can prove, if we take the poetic seriously.[44]

While our response cannot reside in the application of the will to bring this turning point about, since this would rely upon the human subject of metaphysics, the overly cautious hesitancy to remain in a disposition of being heedful seems merely to be the application of the will toward another end—namely, inaction. Indeed, the risk of maintaining the primordial supremacy of earth may be the inability to ever think we are adequate to acting collectively and theoretically in relation to it.

Land as *Hupokeimenon*, or the Subject of Revealing

By designating land as *hupokeimenon*, the relationship between human beings and the earth is more specifically delimited, and therefore, we can gain a clearer understanding of how what is given elicits an appropriate response. In this section, I explore the extent to which land is the subject of revealing—that is, how it forms the basis upon which we relate to other entities and allows us to construct a world. I herein address concerns over the elementally specific character of land that seems to exclude air and water, which perhaps recalls a variety of criticisms—such as, economically speaking, the classical "mistake" of thinking land as fundamental to production and, phenomenologically, Luce Irigaray's allegation that Heidegger forgets air.[45] My response is not to attempt to lessen the degree by which land is fundamental, but rather to augment it. I want to argue that it is the subject from which we draw our understanding of relations to others.

Part of the difficulty in understanding the role of land lies in presuming that our being-landed describes a predicate of our manner of existence. We are bipedal as much as we are landed; whereas birds are both bipedal and landed but also winged and airborne. Perhaps in this sense we might refer to our grounded dwelling as simply a fact of our existence, where this fact is merely an accident or detail which should not be held over against other facts about other beings and their manner of existing. The problem with these claims is not their inaccuracy. To recall my discussion of measurement, they are specific frames through which entities can be grasped. So let me shift the terms of discussion. In a Heideggerian sense, another way of referring to our being-landed can be expressed in terms of existential facticity, where the finite structure of being itself and our occurring in being as human beings is simply the feature through which we have a sense of what it is to be, to dwell, to live. The facticity of being-landed is implicit in Heidegger's identification of dwelling with building on the earth:

> Building as dwelling, that is, as being on the earth, however, remains for man's everyday experience that which is from the outset "habitual"—we inhabit it, as our language says so beautifully: it is the *Gewohnte*. For this reason it recedes behind the manifold ways in which dwelling is accomplished, the activities of cultivation and construction.[46]

What is habitual is not just the ways in which we dwell through building, but our rootedness to the earth. That Heidegger does not explicitly discuss this rootedness, except in terms of building, perhaps indicates how our being-landed is habitual for him. Whatever the case may be, disclosing the significance behind this habit lies in seeing the richness in what it means to inhabit the earth, a richness which cannot simply stop at mentioning our relation to earth.

To support this claim, I want to describe being-landed not just as a feature of our existential facticity. I want to treat it as an *existentiale*, or as an essential feature of the way in which we understand. I will develop this argument in more detail in the following chapter. In this section I want merely to indicate how we are landed as a way of preparing for this more decisive turn. Schematically speaking, we think, imagine, wish, and strive as beings who live on the land. We speak of grounds (or reasons), horizons (or possibilities), foundations (or beginnings), rootedness (or deep bonds). Thus, not meant as a predicate describing a biological or merely physical feature of our existence, the description of being-landed is a condition through which things are revealed existentially to us. Neither earth nor ground sufficiently indicates this specificity. As Casey remarks, "Heidegger's earth is nowhere."[47] It can be said that ground and earth are generally phenomenological and require more descriptive determination since, to recall Foltz's reference to *zoe*, our kind of existence intensifies and augments the manner in which being appears. This intensification can be thought about at least in two ways. Land is the basis of existence. Consider that when I touch an entity, it is an entity as this stone, this book, this door, this person, this bench, this coin. Whatever the entity may be, its identity (its thisness) for me is gained through my contact with it on land. This contact involves both the specific materialization of this entity as a particular entity (it stands) and the situation in which my relationship to this entity is made possible, which subsequently is configured as place (it stands "there"). On the former: an entity draws its substance from land. On the latter: one gains access to entities only through dwelling on the land, alongside them.

The claim that land is the subject allowing for the materialization of entities is, in one sense, a truism as land can be seen in some way or another as giving rise to natural entities in growth and artificial entities in terms of material. In another sense, this claim seems tenuous with its presumption that land encompasses all natural entities. It is not element-sensitive and so indiscriminately forgets water, the air, and the sun. Nonetheless, this counterargument, at least from the perspective I offer, forgoes the specific locality from which we construe this distinction among elements and our relation to them. It may very well be that in addition to land there is both water and air, yet it is through our relation to land that other entities or aspects of nature are meaningful. Notice how our experience of the seeming ubiquity of the sun during the day is landed, or determined according to the ways land gives itself and the locations. Sunlight on the beach is different from the sunlight speckled by the mist of a waterfall or that appears within the chiaroscuro landscape of a forest. Or consider how the move in classical political economy to think land as standing for all of nature in fact means that while human production utilizes the sun and everything under it, such production is not actualized unless performed as an activity on land. Performance includes either the actual production or those activities that make use of what is produced. Land is the "upon which" of production and use.

In general, one can therefore say that the provision of land grants the specific productive activities; its general provision allows for differentiation in and through our existing. To be sure, human production is just one activity. Land provides the ground upon which various nexuses of relations can happen, those relations which Casey describes in terms of "arcs"[48] extending from the human body in a situated place. The fisherman therefore "lands" a fish according to a somewhat similar meaning as when a boat or ship is landed.[49] Indeed, the severe winter storms in southwest England in 2014 caused major fishing ports to be closed. It was not simply that the sea was too dangerous to navigate since there were lulls in the storm, but that the storm caused damage to ports and fishing boats, rendering them unusable. The sea was consequently inaccessible even when the sea itself had calmed. The landed space allowing for the transition to the sea was impassable; and hence so was the sea. These types of references are not arbitrary or accidental since they constitute a jointure between an activity taking place in or on a different elemental location and how it has its relevance to us in our activities on the land. We are more "located" and therefore reliant on the land than we might think; we perceive our relation to water and the sea from and with reference to our landed existence. To think otherwise is to forget the place from which we view our relation to other aspects of nature.

Turning to my second claim, that land provides access to entities through dwelling, I want to discuss the concept of ontological possibility, which is crucial to understanding how the potential we might ascribe to ourselves in terms of a project is enacted in the very place in which we can make a start. Heidegger says, for example, that "thereness" of place is "intensified as potentiality-to-be in its enactment and its being enacted. . . . Potentiality-to-be is the authentic phenomenon by which my Da-sein shows itself."[50] So where an evening meal has its potentiality-to-be as a celebration, the participants are not celebrants unless they recognize this potentiality. If they do, they act in certain ways to realize this potential—such as the opening of wine or champagne, the attempt to be convivial when one might otherwise be aloof, the selection of appropriate music for the occasion; all of these are enactments realized in the thereness of the celebration.

But more lies under the surface of thereness. When thereness is taken concretely, its reliance on land becomes more perceptible in terms of how land is used to found a location for an occasion—we till the soil, demolish a building site, or join a parade passing along the main thoroughfare. Land as the subject is *actual* potential-for-use. Its givenness is potential, not in the sense of never being actual but as that which remains actually present in allowing us to recognize our potential-for-being. In cases of use, the subject of land can be therefore understood as an active capacity, or in the ancient Greek, a *dunamis* for our own humanly conceived potentialities.[51] This is indeed one way of construing the emphasis Heidegger gives to our practicality and use of equipment: we see things in terms of potential uses for practical being-in-the-world,[52] and yet these potential uses involve some relation to understanding the potentialities provided by land. Economically expressed, as we saw earlier, this potential can take many forms as nature itself or in terms of human labor and capital which are, as we saw Knut Wicksell argue, reconfigurations of the productive capacity of land. Land is that entity upon which our activities can engage with other entities and thereby reveal a mode of individual and social existence. Of course, we tend to notice how important access to land is when obstacles impeding this access emerge: private property restrictions, detours, and inclement weather bring back to our attention how landed we are. Even to chat with someone in virtual space does not elide the provision of land from which I gain access to this space. Indeed, this space as virtual is in one sense physical and landed; its transmission over the air or through the ground requires land for its passage and for it to be received by landed beings.

Land as *Hupokeimenon*, or the Subject of Concealing

If concealment is the expression of the limitations of finitude according to which things that arise in being return to earth in their perishing, this passing away according to the ordinance of time is not absent a relation to land. If the facticity of being-landed is not simply a feature of our biological existence, then the meaning of land according to the conditions of finitude cannot be reduced to the observation that in our death we return to the earth in some form. Land is integral to the manner in which we come to terms with finitude and so cannot be simply a site on which our mortality comes to an end and returns to the material from which we arose. In this section I want to take up Heidegger's notion of concealment as sheltering in order to examine how land plays a role in a general historical unfolding of being itself and our human being. I should clarify here that in speaking of being itself and human being together, I am assuming an interpretation of Heidegger's thought in which although being itself is ontologically primary, a mutual dependence between the two exists. This mutuality can be expressed as the primary unity of being itself in differentiation through those beings who take the meaning of being to be its concern. In other words, though in and a part of being itself, we differentiate it through our activities of thought and building.[53]

To recall, I defined sheltering as the way earth allows itself to be rendered; and as a result of donating itself as substance and material, it instills a life limited according to the conditions of finitude and the dependence on earth. These conditions are those in which a certain law-like governance plays itself out, or what are the consequences arising from the ways we engage with being. We saw earlier how poetic dwelling is for Heidegger an existence that lives in appropriate relation to being and earth understood as *phusis* and ground. With land we can understand sheltering in terms of the kind of building and cultivation that might perpetuate remembrance of earth and the question of being.[54] Equally important, nonetheless, and perhaps more illustrative of my thesis, are negative instances where a form of land usage perpetuates our forgetting and so results in a disruption of sheltering. That is to say, because we have an inappropriate relation to land, its sheltering power is distorted. We are in some sense homeless.[55] Specifically, in what follows I will highlight how our current use of land underwrites a respective form of dwelling that forgets our dependence. Furthermore, this oblivion can be understood as homelessness in both the strict sense of not having a home and a figurative sense of a mode of existing that is unfit because it relates inappropriately to land.

If forgetting abandons the question of being itself for beings, then one would expect to find in a state of homelessness a type of objectification of land that ignores its manner of being. Land, in other words, would be represented in terms of certain predicates while ignoring how it is fundamentally the *hupokeimenon* for humankind. Some other representation of land would be placed before the ontological meaning of its being given; and because of this, whatever representation one entertained would determine how we relate to and use land. The most overt instance of this is the so-called land market, of which the housing market is derivative, where we treat land as asset and commodity. Heidegger comments:

> However hard and bitter, however hampering and threatening the lack of houses remains, the *real plight of dwelling* does not lie merely in a lack of houses. The real plight of dwelling is indeed older than the world wars with their destruction, older also than the increase of the earth's population and the condition of the industrial workers.[56]

Despite the post-1940s historical context, Heidegger sees specific problems like the lack of housing as symptomatic of the failure to understand what it means to dwell: "The real plight lies in this, that mortals ever search anew for the nature of dwelling, that they must *ever learn to dwell*."[57] Given that land is the subject underlying dwelling, the question of what it means to dwell can be interpolated as what it means to use land in such a way that these plights might not occur. So when John Stuart Mill remarked that "no man made the land. It is the original inheritance of the whole species," he had in mind the existing system of rights of ownership to land which have resulted in an illusory sense of the "sacredness of property."[58] Yet in order for his challenge to this system to be coherent, what Mill presupposed was the notion that the existence of land has precedence over the human community that arrives after it. That is to say, rights to landed property are conventional, or as Mill would say "expedient," and not natural. In other words, more significant in Mill's statement is its implicit ontological meaning: If land is given, and if we are reliant on its givenness and subsequent to it, how is that we should relate to its usage in our conventions?

Generally speaking, those predicates of land which appear to us as significant in this plight also obstruct our relation to land because they make those predicates seem more important than the nature of this relation. For example, scarcity of land is a predicate which appears foremost in the plight; and one might seek to remedy scarcity through something like a second home tax as opposed to asking what kind of relation to land we might be enacting such that there is this plight.[59] Or, we might argue that given the lack of availability or affordability of houses, we endeavor to create inexpensive housing. Yet this initiative elides what kind of land use is involved such that housing is problematic.

If this condition persists, an inverted world emerges wherein such predicates are abstracted from their context of givenness and seized in various ways through social conventions about ownership. Debates over the sufficiency and naturalness of these conventions often pit one individual's right to land against another's or even against public rights,[60] and the latter can include seeing land as an ipseity, or a subject with rights (i.e., the right of land against the human right to own it). These questions, in a Heideggerian sense, are trivial. By this I do not mean such matters should be ignored. As I indicated in chapter 3, much has been done in the field of legal philosophy with respect to challenging the status of land as private property. However, I do not want to soften the Heideggerian perspective since, as I stated at the outset of this study, what I am arguing is needed is a transformation of the way we conceive and relate to land. In this respect, disputing over rights of ownership presupposes land as an object of rights. It is an object precisely because of the advantages it provides and which subsequently subjects it to rival claims of use and ownership. For land to be omitted from the category of private property due to inconsistency of arguments is not sufficient because it still does not gain sight of the ontological nature of land. Put another way: for these debates to be coherent, specific predicates of land must be readily recognized. This recognition presupposes that land can be and should be described in this manner, which is to say as an object of rights, and nothing else besides. Ironically, then, the question of the meaning of land has been forgotten in debates about land. Debates about homelessness and our state of being figuratively homeless can then be said to coincide without accident.

Yet if land is, as I have claimed, the most fundamental subject, then Heidegger's insistence to think what it means to dwell cannot overlook it. If I am correct to suggest that we are unable to receive reflectively the givenness of land, then it seems likely that our use of land and the conventions defining it as an object will be problematic. That we cannot receive land as given means, in other words, that more remains to be done in the way of demonstrating our being-landed.

6

Excess and Gravity

There is an important feature of *existentiales* I have yet to discuss: an *existentiale* cannot be thematically grasped.[1] Because it persists as the condition of our being, we can never get entirely outside it in order to comprehend it. This does not preclude a productive understanding of it since the inability to gain a certain or final perspective is simply, as I discussed in chapter 4, a condition of our knowing that encourages our participation and further engagement with things. In this chapter I would like to account for the ways in which we can get a sense of our being-landed even if we cannot directly comprehend it. The phenomenological picture I want to paint would not be complete without seeing how land figures fundamentally in one's individual development. I employ Heidegger's notion of mineness to show that this development takes shape according to land's *excess* and *gravity*. By excess and gravity, land is formative of our dwelling.

Indeed, both terms capture what I envisage as a dynamic relation between humans and the land. Excess is that quality of land that we know *as* our possibilities for being. In other words, human possibility is an excess provided by land. Gravity accounts for the experience by which this ontological excess is felt and imagined as occurring on the land; it is a reflective and affectative experience taking shape in our habitation. I attempt to describe this experience in terms of gravity's attraction and demand.

Attraction is apparent in how imagined projects gain their force by being grounded; and by being grounded, they become practicable. Grounding excess is a matter of coming to a more concrete idea of actualization. To be, to actualize, to carry out . . . all of these are motivated by an excess through which we both aspire and risk in our dwelling and which was put so well by Albert Camus when he said, "a reason for living is also an excellent reason for dying."[2] Sisyphus, it cannot be forgotten, would not have his sense of momentary triumph without the situatedness of his existence afforded by the steep slope and the elemental boulder. Neither the reflective nor the affectative dimensions of apprehension have traction without imagining life as being lived on the land. To succeed or to fail is not finally an abstract possibility, but one that has sincerity because it is rooted in a specific ground of dwelling.

Demand is the ineluctable call we recognize in our relation to land—that in giving and grounding, land asks for something in return. I discuss this in terms of appropriateness: that recognizing the role of land demands an appropriate relation to land. While ethical questions pertaining to the conservation of nature may seem germane with respect to appropriateness,[3] herein I am interested primarily in anticipating the economic effects and how gravity calls for the appropriate usage of the surplus value called ground rent. As we will see in the next part, ground rent will provide the means by which we can appropriately make a return to the land.

In order to make good on my promise to show how our individual being is dependent on land, I begin with a clarification of the way the sense of one's individual being, or mineness, arises and how paradoxically despite this sense, one's existence is not one's own. Rather it is the excess of being itself that allows one to take hold of being as one's own. Before linking this role of excess to land, in the second section I distinguish my approach from Jean-Luc Marion's phenomenology. The fourth section then develops excess and mineness in relation to land. The final sections discuss the ways gravity sustains the sense of mineness according to an attraction to projects for being and a demand that asks us to dwell appropriately.

Beginning with Mineness

When explaining Heidegger's concept of Dasein, I referred to the sense of thereness which is "opened" through human engagement. In fact, our concern for what it means to be entails a kind of involvement that is not just reflective and inquisitive, but personal in such a way that we interiorize our experiences and encounters as we follow our thoughts and questions. So ontologically understood, our personal relation to being is predicated by our concern to respond to the question of the meaning of being, and it is through this manner of existing that our response allows us to gain a kind of ownership over our existence. That is to say, we appropriate our existence according to the responses we make in view of what it means to exist: this existence for oneself.

Heidegger encapsulates this personal dimension to Dasein by the concept of mineness (*Jemeinigkeit*). To recognize, grasp, and persist in a project is to appropriate an existence as one's own. We are thus our own possibility: "Dasein is mine to be in one way or another. Dasein has always made some sort of decision as to the way in which it is in each case mine."[4] By this movement of understanding one begins to emerge out of oneself in order to lay claim to an existence as being mine.[5] To understand something is thus to understand it according to one's own relation to and perspective of it. Yet while mineness involves an interiorization of what it means to be, it has also an exteriorizing momentum. Mineness, it turns out, is always involved in a relation to ends we project outside ourselves, as possibilities we would like to actualize: "That entity which in its being has this very being as an issue, comports itself towards its being as its ownmost possibility. In each case Dasein *is* its possibility."[6] Heidegger's use of "comporting" suggests that the recognition of a possibility already involves being drawn to it, and it is because of this event of being drawn to something beyond oneself (or what he calls "not yet")[7] that one is both within oneself and outside oneself. To recall his example from chapter 4 of moving within the lecture hall, in imagining the possibility of leaving the hall, I look toward the door from my position within the room and am already there in some sense, at the door.

As it stands, this account of mineness seems destined to culminate in some form of subjectivism or idealism. However, the great twist of Heidegger's phenomenology is to say that the existence that we have, and hence our sense of what is mine in and through existing, is not our own. So while *this* existence is for me, it is not my own. As Raffoul notes,

> Dasein's mineness . . . is conceived non-subjectively. The being of the being that I am is each time mine, owing to a call to which I have to respond, or correspond. Mineness thus can in no way be understood as a property belonging to a subject that is closed upon itself, or as what a subject posits by itself.[8]

Indeed, it is one of the features of an expressly *hermeneutic* phenomenology like Heidegger's to take into account different aspects of the facticity of our being when describing how it is we perceive, know, or understand. It decenters the human subject, and in this sense, subjects the human understanding to finite conditions of existence.[9] Raffoul thus clarifies that mineness should be understood according to the conditions of dependency because it is granted by being itself. In other words, if mineness arises because of our unique mode of being, which is concerned with what it means to exist, this unique mode is possible because being has given access to it. On a Heideggerian account, any ontological features constituting what it means to exist as a human being are in some way given by being itself. To recall from chapter 4, even questions relating to properties and causes of specific entities (why?) are derivative of a fundamental ontological givenness. Indeed, being itself individuates each particular Dasein on the basis of what it *gives* to each one of us:

> There lies in this "ownness" the most singular of singularities: no one can answer for this sending in my place. To be an individual means: my being is given to me as my own. I have this givenness of being to be; I must answer it and answer for it, which I can only do in the first person.[10]

Paradoxically, one's mineness is not really one's own. Dasein "has been brought into its 'there,' but not of its own accord."[11] And this is to say that what it means to be oneself is both to undertake projects which might actualize one's potentiality-to-be *and* to recognize that this undertaking is not due to one's own power or ability. One is not the origin of these actions just as one is not the origin of oneself.

Given this paradox, what appears on the side of human individual being as a kind of lack is, on the side of being in general, an abundance. Being gives to us, so that . . . Is this not a way saying there is an ontological excess to being itself that allows for human individuation? If mineness always presupposes a posing of the question about the meaning of being, this posing of the question is a form of recognizing what can potentially fulfill what is lacking. Comporting and projecting toward possibilities for being allow us to see ourselves as more than we are factually in any given state of affairs.[12] In other words, the kind of access that being gives to us in our thought about it is one that enables us to see what appears to us as something more, something excess. Ontological excess, it can be said, gives rise to an excess of human possibility.

Distinguishing Excess

Like my apologia in the introduction, this section is intended to address specific concerns about my use of phenomenology. In this case, it turns to the question of how my phenomenological approach makes use of excess in comparison to other phenomenologies. For the reader not interested in debates about such matters, this section can be passed over.

"Excess" is a term that is by no means a stranger to phenomenology. The conditions of the possibility for meaning rely on the manner in which an entity can be said to be given in excess of singular acts of perception. If it cannot, then our relation to external things falls prey to psychologism, that is, the reduction of meaning to the human mind. As Michael Dummett reminds us, the historical context in which modern phenomenology arose was marked by a fear of viewing thoughts as merely subjective and thus "private and incommunicable."[13] One way of combating this reduction is to argue that the entities we perceive have a non-reducible quality of appearance, or givenness. Ordinary instances are no exception; they provide the rule. Entities exist according to an excess of givenness.

Take for example the later thought of Edmund Husserl when discussing judgment and evidence. While the act of judging is usually understood as the agreement or correspondence between a judgment and a certain state of affairs, Husserl takes into account that judgments change based on the evidence presented.[14] Evidence is understood by Husserl to be the givenness of an entity in its appearing, and it is presupposed by the act of judging and is, in this sense, "pre-predicative": "That which is meant or, perchance, evidently viewed receives predicative expression."[15] And so even at the most basic level of explanation, one can detect this non-reducibility that exceeds our seemingly private thoughts about entities. Dummett notes:

> Husserl distinguished between the matter and the quality of any mental act, holding that acts that differed in quality might have their matter in common. . . . He is clear that a difference in the object referred to must imply a difference in the matter, but that there may be a difference between the matter of two acts, although they refer to the same object.[16]

There is no single determinate meaning of an entity at which we can arrive since we apprehend its givenness in one way at any particular time. Our measure of looking, as discussed in chapter 4, cannot contain the meaning of the entity under consideration. Yet this resistance is productive, precisely giving to the entity a fullness that is distinct and separate from our understanding. So despite the emphasis of Husserl's phenomenology on a transcendental consciousness and allegations that he never manages to overcome the isolation of the human mind (transcendental idealism), there is at the same time an emphasis on the givenness of entities, which in fact prevents intuition from being empty or solipsistic:

> Evidence denotes a universal primal phenomenon of intentional life . . . the quite preeminent mode of consciousness that consists in the self-appearance, the self-exhibiting, the self-giving, of an affair-complex (or state of affairs), a universality, a value, or other objectivity, in the final mode: "itself there," "immediately intuited"/"given originaliter."[17]

Consciousness is anchored to the world by virtue of the entity's originary givenness, and in this sense, by its excess that one can never begin without. "What is adequately self-given," comments Joseph Kockelmans, "can and must be taken as an absolute beginning . . . . Self-givenness in the absolute sense rules out any meaningful doubt."[18]

In Heidegger's thought, one way in which the excess of the givenness of entities appears can be described in terms of ontological difference. Ontological excess, in this view, includes Husserl's sense of "originaliter" insofar as beings give themselves originarily; yet it is the nature of this giving to conceal itself. Being gives itself to be seen as beings, yet as we saw earlier our inability to think being except in terms of beings means we are always involved in a limited and provisional understanding. Heidegger refers to these two qualities of giving and concealing as "concealing overwhelming."[19] Excess, it can be said, is the play of this concealing overwhelming of being which motivates human thought and constitutes the object of thought proper. It should be stressed, nonetheless, that this is only one way of understanding excess in Heidegger, and it is the way that Marion has read him (and phenomenology since Husserl) in order to offer his own version of excess, or the saturated phenomenon.

For Marion, phenomenology has remained ensnared by the human subject, failing to appreciate fully the givenness of entities because it relies on an operation of reduction issuing from the authority of human consciousness.[20] He observes that in Heidegger's early thought, the human mode of being must first be altered in order to participate authentically with beings; that is to say, Dasein results from a reduction that excludes certain traits and features:

> But it is still necessary that this Dasein is accomplished as such and therefore appropriates its unique manner of being and rids itself of an inappropriate way of being (that of the "They" who claim to understand themselves as if they were intra-worldly beings). Dasein must thus be itself reduced to itself. . . . The disappearance of all anthropological determinations (flesh, sexuality, ideology, and so on) . . . attests precisely to this modification of "man" into a Dasein, which recoils the reduction on its agent. The reduction thus always first reduces the one who operates it—and it is by this recoiling on itself that the phenomenological validity of each attempt at reduction is measured.[21]

In addition, Heidegger's emphasis on difference forgets that difference itself presupposes the appearing of the entity, and more to the point, of its *being given.* In other words, for Marion givenness is "pure" and precedes anything that we note in terms of its features of being, or beingness.[22] Indeed, the givenness of a thing is nonnegotiable and constitutes our experience of being-in-the-world. Marion considers, for example, how a tool—such as a screwdriver—imposes itself by confronting its user with a set of possibilities: "The tool imposes itself as a fait accompli because it imposes its possibilities on me as my own."[23] This fact of givenness is evident even more so when a tool is indeterminately understood, as in the case of an apprentice learning a skill:

> Because I am still unaware of its [the tool's] reified finalities, I must suspend my own; because I am not aware of "how it works," I must suspend every intention to avail myself of it, the time to "make myself accustomed to it."[24]

This means phenomena are saturated, and

> constitution encounters there an intuitive givenness that cannot be granted a univocal sense in return. It must be allowed, then, to overflow with many meanings, or an infinity of meanings, each equally legitimate and rigorous, without managing either to unify them or to organize them.[25]

Moreover, the excess of a phenomenon means that it is its own self, its own ipseity.[26] Marion's thesis, though heavily criticized for being un-Husserlian despite his claims to the opposite,[27] can be seen in some respects as a logical progression within phenomenology insofar as it chooses to play out the implications of excess. In other words, if entities give themselves in such a way as to always exceed our view of them, then one can assert more strongly that it is not, in the last analysis, the human who constitutes knowledge through acts of perception but the phenomena themselves. "The pure given giving itself depends, once reduced, only on itself. . . . Givenness therefore is measured only by its own standard, not by that of intuition."[28]

By maintaining the precedence of the "being given" that presupposes any other determination, Marion draws criticism for neglecting the hermeneutical structure of existence. Access to things is always mediated, no matter how many reductions of the entity one performs in order to see the thing as it appears concretely. His phenomenology therefore presupposes a hermeneutics of existence in which relations are already given in some specific, determinate way.[29] Having said this, what then might be at stake in the difference between being given and being-landed? In what manner is the excess of things given by land, that is, by virtue of our relation to land?

Because Marion is expressly concerned in a traditional Husserlian sense with describing how it is that it can be said that we can return to an understanding of the things themselves, the method of reduction is precisely the adherence to the assumption that bracketing discretely chosen features of existence attains a fundamental grasp of what is really real. Marion states, "Thus, givenness is deployed according to the direct *measure* of the reduction: the more the reduction is radicalized, the more givenness is deployed."[30] It is precisely the measurements employed in reduction that claim a monopoly over meaning. My aim is not so imperial. I wish merely to explain the conditions for the possibility of meaning beyond the common assumption that human beings face entities in a groundless, landless encounter. I make no claims to what comprises measurements or methods of reduction except to argue that we can apprehend the givenness of land in such a way that we can and should rethink the basis of our dwelling.

Consider how Marion's examples often provide detail about the mediate encounter with things, but rarely pay attention to the space in which this occurs and how it is grounded. Marion may appreciate the historical context of an encounter with the lecture hall in which he is speaking, but there is an emphasis on the givenness of that occasion as groundlessly abstract:

> Even this hall appears, in effect, according to the mode of the event. . . . Inasmuch as always already there, available for our entry and our use, this hall imposes itself on us as preexisting us, being without us, although being there for us, which therefore rises into our sight like an unexpected fact, unforeseeable, coming from an uncontrollable past.[31]

The hall as a phenomenon encountered may be saturated, but if it is, this description ignores its grounding and how this grounding may be responsible for our encounter with it. From where does it rise? And why is it finally linked to the expressly human—that is, historical consciousness of the past? In terms of its formal aesthetic qualities the lecture hall can be understood in terms of its materials and how the space within its walls and ceiling give shape through these materials, both within and outside the building housing it. What passage is given by the land as one moves from city street, to antechamber, to lecture hall?

There is a general problem inherent to phenomenology when it attempts to take things by themselves. What is a thing except that which has been identified within a context, a context whose structure of relations and meanings has allowed one to single out a particular entity that is to be reduced phenomenologically? In other words, it seems a sleight of method to insist that contextual relations can be bracketed in order to attend to the thing itself as it is and yet rely on those contextual relations to distinguish a method of reduction. The lecture hall is a lecture hall given the context of relations—the building, the occasion, the audience, the philosophical questions posed, and so on. The conditions for the possibility of meaning, in other words, are existential conditions in the fullest sense, filled in at rock bottom by our being-landed in a certain way. Excess does not obtain to entities *by themselves* but according to a context of relations.

If we remain with the idea that Heidegger is driving toward the concrete, we know that this relation to the excess of being is not abstract. I have discussed already how experiencing the "thereness" (the *da*) of our being requires a "there" that can be open to us. We do not impose thereness but gain access to it.[32] A potentiality-for-being—which is in each case mine—is possible only on the basis of an already given ground. Excess, as I will argue, originates from land.

Excess and the Place of Mineness

What then does it mean to envisage excess as originating from land? It means in some sense distinguishing how one's potentiality-for-being (mineness) is made possible by the land. My strategy for responding to this question is to redescribe the way in which the necessary relation we have to land is not simply physical or biological, but ontological. Because land gives the site upon which a project of being can be thought and schematized, we are dependent on it. There are two ways of describing this dependence, but before doing so let me remark generally that the imaginary case I employ is distinct from typical phenomenological examples that attempt to describe how the bareness of perception is involved in apprehending a fullness of meaning. This concern for meaning is not practical per se but theoretical in its attempt to show how there is meaning after all. In other words, seemingly practical examples—like Marion's lecture hall—are used as instances demonstrating the fullness of meaning. They are instances of the rule of givenness *originaliter.* They are integral to the structure of givenness itself, and no other entities besides perceiver and perceived need enter the analysis. Because meaning does not occur simply in a vacuum, my example intends to show how land is the fundamental ground for the manifestation of things and their meaning to us existentially. In what follows, I want to play on the meaning of land's necessity by showing, on the one hand, how it is necessary for our existence since it provides for us and, on the other hand, how this necessity leads to an excess we experience as possibility-for-being. So while land is always necessary, it is also always something more.

(a) Necessity as Access

First, let us consider that there is a necessity for land that can be readily understood in terms of *access.* Access to land is access to life (and as we will see below, access to being). If one were to imagine a ship being wrecked on a reef of an uninhabited island,[33] one would naturally assume that use of the island would flow freely among the survivors to meet their basic needs. But let us suppose that over the years, the marooned passengers and crew distributed the area of the entire island equally among themselves. If a second ship were to face a similar fate, its crew and passengers would unfortunately find themselves on an island fully occupied. Perhaps the newly wrecked survivors can appeal to a right to life which the inhabitants would find compelling. The easiest and fairest response to this appeal might be to divide the land once more so that each inhabitant, old and new, had a plot. Or would this be the easiest? Would the newcomers not have the right to life without access to land? Is not access to wages in the form of the products of their labor enough?

No. Labor still requires access to land, both in terms of the laboring process and a place for sojourning. And yet a reader inclined toward justification of private property by original acquisition might ask why.[34] Typically, when land is enclosed, or entirely owned, those without ownership may have a means to wages but end up paying a significant portion of those wages as a fee to gain access to the land. In the case of residence, this constraint is obvious in the fee paid to the landowner. With respect to employment, one need only notice that it is not the landless laborer who, requiring work, proposes the amount of wages, but rather it is the landlord, assuming he or she is the business owner, who has the leverage: "If you want to work, you will accept the wage I offer. Otherwise, you can go elsewhere."[35] Where is this elsewhere on an island where all the land is owned? Under such land enclosure, laborers have no leverage except to underbid their fellow laborers; they compete for the lowest wage they are willing to accept. On the other hand, if a laborer had access to land, the lowest wage would be determined by what the laborer is willing to accept *against* the effort required to work the available land. A laborer, in other words, would not tend to accept less than he or she might garner from working a plot of land him- or herself.[36] We thus arrive at the second form of necessity.

(b) Necessity as Privation

The compelling nature of access has a negative form—namely, *privation,* or the attempt to gain a significant control of access and therefore opportunity. If land is the source of livelihood, and if there are conventions allowing for ownership of land without limitations on the extent and duration of ownership, then what often follows is the practice of securing one's own livelihood by the least amount of effort possible, which is to own the source of livelihood of others and have them pay to access to this source by means of their own labor. As Adam Smith famously chides,

> The landlords . . . love to reap where they never sowed, and demand a rent even for [the land's] natural produce. . . . [The laborer] must then pay for the licence to gather [this produce]; and he must give up to the landlord a portion of what his labour either collects or produces.[37]

Evidence of the necessity of land presents itself in current practices intent on gaining control of this necessity through ownership. As observed in the previous chapter, the housing market is really, in this regard, the land market. In most cases, while the dwelling itself may be of some value, it is generally the value of land that constitutes the sale price. Buildings, by virtue of being rendered material, depreciate over time. Unless a community disappears or is severely reduced in population or prosperity, land maintains or increases its value even where buildings are not erected upon it. The housing market is therefore really a scheme by which current and prospective landowners attempt to profit by control of land through ownership. This control is exercised precisely in the sale price and, by extension, the expectation that the buyer can resell the land at a higher price to another. Those who are not owners are simply left to make payments continually to gain access to their livelihood; even the one who does not own the land outright but by mortgage still has a form of power in that he has grant of a title to land and can charge others for access. Privation of land is, in the Foucaldian sense, a discipline in which the land market goes beyond mere privation. It becomes an institution which, through the transactions of selling and buying, seems to have the right to assume its principle of ownership.[38]

To illustrate these points, let us return to the situation of the island of the shipwrecked where available land was problematic. Consider that the division of existing plots into smaller ones is not practicable and efficient for production (i.e., distributism). If this society allowed ground rent to be collected by the landowner, it would tend to have the concentration of ownership in a small segment of the population who are ready (i.e., having knowledge of how and why to own land) and able (i.e., having capital, authority, or power) to take hold of the land. In other words, there might be a distorted representation of the amount of unavailable land when a minority of the population own the majority of landholdings and are not penalized for withholding land from production (thus enabling them to speculate on the increase in value of owned but unused land). But even allowing that this were not the case, let us suppose that no land is available and is not the subject of monopoly or oligopoly. The land is enclosed but distributed to half of the inhabitants. Does it matter? The private collection of ground rent, as Smith rightly acknowledges, encourages landowners to lease the land to others so that these owners can collect rent without labor of their own. In such cases, the lease fee constitutes a large portion of the so-called cost of production; so-called because in this instance it does in fact seem to be a cost that needs to be paid *in order to produce* rather than a surplus value *deriving* from the quality of land being employed by labor. Taken from the profits of a business owner, wages will tend downwards. And laborers not having access to land find themselves again competing for the lowest wage they are willing to accept.[39]

(c) More than Necessity

Given the issues of access and privation, the language of necessity is nonetheless deceptive. The necessity of land is more than it appears since the fulfilment of basic needs tends to have in view ends beyond these needs. We do not just use land in the effort to sustain our metabolism; we cultivate the land in view of non-necessary values or the transformation of necessary ends so that they both fulfill needs and aspire toward higher values. We can even refuse to cultivate land—that is, refuse its necessity for our use, in order to conserve something we deem more significant than our immediate needs. So the analysis of land's necessity is but a partial step in understanding its significance. The imperative of recognizing land does not lie in its necessity alone since it is integral to so much more than brute sustainability. To the contrary, the perception of the necessity of land is magnified really and only by grasping the ontological nature of its excess. This is because if land's excess resides in providing for opportunities to actualize potentialities-for-being, and if these opportunities are integral to what it means to exist as a human, then grasping land means grasping how it is involved fundamentally as we exist as humans. There is thus never necessity alone, but a necessity that is subject to the excess of human possibility.

So excess of givenness, when understood from this ontological perspective, is the donation of the possibility-to-be—that is, the distinct possibility to be in one way and not another as it is projected by thought and in imagination. Yet the capability to participate in the excess is itself dependent on the space or location in which it can be imagined, again not in the abstract by itself, but in the context of dwelling. Amartya Sen refers to such spaces as "evaluative spaces" essential for realizing human capabilities. Emmanuel Levinas argues that transcendence for a possibility is therefore not simply negativity in Sartre's sense of the term. Rather, "Negativity presupposes a being established, placed in a site where he is at home; it is an economic fact, in the etymological sense of this adjective."[40] Jacques Derrida speaks of access to the physical landscape essential to grasping the nonphysical heights, bridges, barriers—and even the abyss itself—of existence and reason.[41] The excess of possibility, it can be said, is rooted in where one stands, and it is precisely in this standing-there that we gain a sense of what is involved in existing. *To be* means to carry out a manner of dwelling . . . for me, on this land.

It is, of course, by virtue of our concern for a potentiality-to-be that we see a "there" in which we can act and dwell in a certain manner. Through these acts and modes of dwelling, we disclose a unique existence.[42] We can take, for instance, the imaginative power of fiction which, as Ricoeur reminds us, reshapes reality. Films and stories that we enjoy for their ability to allow us to escape present worries and conditions are never merely entertainment but an escape to somewhere through the imaginative "nowhere" of the narrative. Yet to be nowhere, one must first be *there,* that is, situated in a location in which the mundaneness of one's everyday life can have contact with the imaginative world projected by the narrative. For example, the bench seat on the commuter train during rush hour acts as an intermediary place in which this nowhere can be encountered and the contact with one's surroundings can be momentarily suspended. Ricoeur states:

> The more imagination deviates from that which is called reality in ordinary language and vision, the more it approaches the heart of reality which is no longer the world of manipulable objects, but the world into which we have been thrown by birth and within which we try to orient ourselves by projecting our innermost possibilities upon it, in order to *dwell* there.[43]

Thus, in projecting oneself in some sense as being-in the world of that narrative, one imagines a different possibility for oneself in this world, this place, on this land for dwelling.

In this view, reversion to a chiasmus to stress the essential double role of land may not be too far-fetched. Because land grounds the conjunction between necessity and excess, one can say: land grounds the necessity of excess and the excess of necessity. The chiastic structure of life which land grounds can thus be described by a complementary relation. On the one hand, land is a necessary requirement for dwelling; it is never necessary *merely*, but necessary in order to do more than address basic needs. On the other hand, land gives an excess to our existence that is interpreted *as* necessary in the sense that the ontological possibility-to-be comprises a meaningful life.[44]

Have we now arrived at a position in this study where we can see one of the more compelling advantages of reading Heidegger's philosophy as a movement to the concrete? If mineness enables us to apprehend meaningful projects in existing, and if it originates from a source that is not ourselves (that is, not our own), then understanding this paradox in terms of our being-landed enables us to see how human existence is not only contextualized but in some profound sense bound to this context in a form of philosophical allegiance. Yet, there are further implications that give more definition to this allegiance. Land precedes our existence and is not ours; yet, it is the place in which excess is experienced as mine to be lived. This suggests that mineness, in not being able to withdraw simply within one's sense of self-identity, must be pulled out of itself only as one's existence becomes more one's own.

Gravity as Attraction

We can understand the expressly personalizing effect of land's excess in terms of attraction. Yet what kind of attraction would this gravity be? If one were to take Simone Weil's characterization of gravity as paradigmatic in meaning, the facticity of our being bound to earthly forces would be understood negatively as an obstacle or limitation. In contrast to grace, or transcendence, gravity is for Weil a form of bondage which directs our energies according to base virtues. Weil's employment of the metaphor is particularly apt since she does not want to speak only about attraction but also about the increased strength of this force the closer one is to its source. Base virtues make it exceptionally more difficult for us to attain higher modes of action, such as love, primarily because when one is ensnared by gravity, one's perspective is largely unable to move beyond the sphere of the influence of base wants.[45] Yet gravity is not purely negative; it is necessary. Transcendence is not possible unless there is already the downward attraction to the base. But the negativity of Weil's definition is not what I wish to focus on as hypothetically paradigmatic.

Weil's characterization of gravity involves mostly the relation between people and what is, as it were, above them. This gravity, in other words, is conceived along the lines of not really pertaining to our being-landed. It is therefore a gravity of intersubjective relation, of human beings in relation to a love that might ultimately reconcile the problems with difference while at the same time maintaining difference.[46] Alluring as this proposition is, it minimalizes and thus neglects other aspects of our existence that may contribute to grasping and moving beyond our limitations. The same may be said of Marion who, as one would expect, defines the force of gravity as that which emanates from the phenomenon of an entity giving itself as itself.[47] For Marion, the encounter with the givenness of phenomena—that is, the third reduction—occurs always at the ground zero of perception, which is to say no ground at all. This is because it involves nothing more than the relation of oneself to the saturated phenomena.

It is curious that both these representations of gravity occur in a landless world, and to this extent, one can ask how the intensity of the attraction that Weil and Marion identify is inadequate. Identifying gravity with the ability of entities to be what they are, Casey argues that gravitational attraction gathers according to places which in turn allow things to take "a stand in the world"; in their effort to remain upright, things gain "constancy of form and shape."[48] Casey has in mind both metaphorical and scientific senses of the term, but of course the meaning of gravity should not necessarily be subordinated to the scientific worldview. Gravity is not primarily supposed to be apprehended scientifically. When expressed as a general law of attraction to which all things are subject, as Heidegger points out, one talks circumspectively in such a way that no longer has existential meaning for us.[49]

Rather, we experience gravity as an intense feeling and thought of belonging to the land because its force of attraction draws us into dwelling, or on Casey's view allows us to take a stand. To be me, I must take a stand; to be visible to others beyond merely "myself." So the standing that takes place for us is an attraction to belonging and dwelling, a heaviness precisely because the question and burden of what it means to be accompanies our entry into and persisting in the world. By gravity we experience our rootedness in existing and can take up a position or a locality in existing; and far from weighing me down as a hindrance to my dwelling, it is, on the contrary, the sole presupposition allowing me to make my way, by rooting me in a world. Yet, attraction is not fully choate in terms of heaviness and standing. Attraction also provides a sense of measure in which the projects we imagine according to excess can arise in relation to other things and persons. It affords me a view to life—the landscape of life and death, as Derrida calls it.[50]

Heidegger describes this view in terms of the measure between earth and the heavens. And unlike the specific frames of measurement we employ to analyze entities (per chapter 4), this kind can be said to be ontological in the sense that what is measured is human dwelling according to the standards of its finitude and its potentiality-for-being. Indeed, specific frames of measurement attempting to reckon with finitude in discrete ways—that is, gain access to beings—presuppose this more fundamental kind of measuring.

> Man measures out his dwelling, his stay on the earth beneath the sky. . . . Man's dwelling depends on an upward-looking measure-taking of the dimension, in which the sky belongs just as much as earth.[51]

In one sense, sky can be taken as the possibility-for-being; it is earth that not only makes the sky visible since it provides a standpoint but also allows the sky to take shape in terms of projects and actions. A possibility-of-being is viewed as occurring concretely as this life, on this ground. Recognizing the essential relation between the view to human potential-for-being and our rootedness, Heidegger states, "Man's taking measure in the dimension dealt out to him brings dwelling into its ground plan."[52] But how should we understand Heidegger's emphasis on ground plan? Is the term "ground" used merely to describe something accidental about the plan, or is the plan essentially what it is because it is defined as being related to ground?

The ground of existence, to recall, cannot be displaced somewhere else—neither in transcendence (e.g., God or the ego) nor in the things themselves. Taken concretely, ground is itself the foundation determining the remit in which excess and gravity appear. A plan in tandem with ground is then a way of describing how our projects take into account, or view, how we are grounded in a certain way and a sense of measure involving how this way of being grounded should be carried out. More specifically, a plan would take into account the measure in which we recognize land for what it is in its givenness and how we then should become discretely involved with it in its use. In other words, the view afforded by land is a view *from* land (as subject) and a view *of* land (as subject). What would it mean to hold both views together in our thought and action, to maintain a sense of measure?

Gravity as Demand

Understood as a force of attraction, the pull of gravity has certain demands not accurately conceived if thought solely along the lines of physical compulsion. The attraction toward a heavier mass extended in space is one of determination in a strong sense; it can only be avoided by the intervention of an equally strong or stronger force. Yet redescribing this context in terms of being-landed means that we do not resist the attraction to the base by any intervention, from ourselves or another. In a way, we settle on (as opposed to struggle with) the base. That is to say, we attempt to understand the context of attraction with its ground in view. I want to argue that this view, by virtue of tending to the ground that underlies it, cannot but help recognize that its possibility is owed to the ground. So in being-landed, attraction occurs as a compelling view in which what we witness cannot be so easily ignored. To get a sense of this, I want to develop Heidegger's notion of guilt (*Schuld*) more concretely.

Heidegger, of course, does not intend guilt as a moral concept. It is a manner of being capable of recognizing that to which one is indebted and that by this debt one's actions have certain demands placed upon it. To be guilty is precisely absent of its normal moral meaning in which one recognizes fault for the intention and/or consequence of an action or thought. As ontological, being-guilty is not a property of our being but the condition of our existence, that is, a mode or *existentiale* through which we live. Thus distinct from the ethical sense of guilt, which involves a lack or failure to do something properly, the ontological sense follows from the recognition that one is not the origin of one's being thrown into existence. Raffoul endorses this ontological reading brought to the fore by Ricoeur in *Oneself as Another*:

> Dasein is delivered over (*überantwortet*) to its own Being in order for Dasein "to be" it, that is, Dasein is delivered over to the responsibility (*Verantwortung*) for its own being, that is, having to answer (*Antwort*) for its own being. Being-guilty should then be understood as constitutive of the very possibility of the self. . . . It is the very possibility of selfhood, being-guilty cannot be reduced to a particular modality thereof. *It is as guilty that I am.*[53]

Raffoul thus clarifies that guilt involves a lack, or nullity, that makes one aware of one's own dependence on something other than oneself:

> The "nullity" lies in the fact of not being the basis of one's own being, of being thrown into existence; the "guilt" lies in the fact that I must

> make myself the origin or basis of this existence of which I am not the origin.[54]

But what effect does this lack, this nullity have?

Where the moral concept has its remedy in a form of atonement for a lack or transgression, the ontological concept has its remedy in reorienting the manner in which we engage with being. There is no single action that can redeem one from guilt since to address that for which one is guilty often involves a transformation of understanding, a so-called rehabilitation or peripeteia in which life is lived differently. Thus, Stephen Crowell clarifies that being-guilty is an *existentiale* through which we take responsibility for a manner of existing.[55]

Assuming that *existentiales* can participate together and eliding any discussion of a hierarchy,[56] the meaning of being-guilty with respect to being-landed becomes a sense of guilt for existing on the land. Heidegger is careful to diminish the possibility of seeing the constitution of being-guilty as an injunction from the outside, where something like a debt is imposed upon us. The impetus is in fact on the side of human being insofar as it is due to its manner of caring that the debt is recognized.[57] This is because we recognize the conditions of our existence *as they are given* existentially and not as something imposed upon us. So while ontologically speaking ground is first in its originality, the human recognition of its originality requires the development of a self who can raise the question of the meaning of its existence. Indeed, recognizing one's guilt is not blocked by mineness but requires it.[58]

With respect to land, this means that its demand is recognizable only due to the view we have of its ground. To see that the view *from* the land is also one that is *of* the land is therefore a manner of admitting land into our understanding of existence. To admit land is a way of admitting guilt for our existence on the land.

But, of course, the question of the meaning of existence does not directly lead to or entail a view that can grasp its dependency on land. So how is it that one can say in existence we become aware of our guilt of being-landed? If the move toward the concrete can be seen as a move toward a more specific form of existential relation, in which guilt manifests according to specific existential relations and not just general ontological ones, then guilt is known according to the ways in which our uses of land have certain consequences.

I have mentioned previously that this existential use-consequence relation is most evident in terms of the land market, or the state of affairs where landless beings are required to give a significant portion of their blood and sweat in order to have access to land. This state of affairs is underwritten by a conception of land as alienable, which we saw in chapter 3 was historically preceded by the conventions of private property deriving in part from modern natural law theory. But it is not the inappropriatness of the convention of private property in land I want to stress, but how it participates in and therefore encourages an ontological misrelation that is instantiated in our dwelling. While the housing market and its bubbles are symptomatic of this misrelation, the problem with relying too heavily on the cogency of such historical events lies in counterclaims to what actually has caused recessions. We rely on other arguments, like empirical ones, and lose sight of the philosophical thread. So, for example, if we once thought that after the 2008 recession the viability of a free market and those formulae economists relied upon were no longer amenable, opponents might simply claim to the contrary: data shows that the market was not free enough. Taking this into consideration, let us then highlight the philosophical dimension by generalizing how the gravity of land can lead to a misrelation to its excess.

Georges Bataille offers a persuasive diagnosis of the modern economy in terms of excess as "an accursed share." Deriving from a basic biological need to grow and perpetuate the survival of oneself and one's species, human labor is no different than that of plants and animals which expend energies for the same purposes. But this expenditure for humans, as Arendt has noted well, takes on a different form in how it reshapes material in order to break with necessity. Human labor (*animal laborans*) is human work (*homo faber*), in this sense; by making with the hands we can store and produce in abundance such that we are no longer beholden to necessary tasks. Work allows us to be free from perpetual toil; we are at work in order to be at leisure, as Aristotle famously put it. The durability and objectivity of things made by human labor provide a stability that allows us separation from the persistent demands of nature. By durability, we can step out of the ever-changing flow of the Heraclitean river.[59]

Yet stepping out of the flow and demand of nature means, for Bataille, that humans become involved in a flow and demand at a different level. Referring to this as "the general movement of the economy,"[60] Bataille notes that the problem is not with the capacity for productive power but consumption:

> The living organism, in a situation determined by the play of energy on the surface of the globe, ordinarily receives more energy than is necessary for maintaining life; the excess energy (wealth) can be used for the growth of a system (e.g., an organism); if the system can no longer grow, or if the excess cannot be completely absorbed in its growth, it

> must necessarily be lost without profit; it must be spent, willingly or not, gloriously or catastrophically.[61]

In short, we are stuck with an excess that we cannot consume easily or naturally, and so we turn to other means of spending the excess. But this problem is not of the same intensity for humans as it is for other organisms. While nonhuman organisms may overpopulate and overproduce in some fashion, humans alone can produce according to storing surplus—that is, the accumulation of wealth in commodity form.[62] As discussed above, one of the ways of storing this surplus is to control the means of livelihood by capturing the land according to conventions of private ownership. If Bataille's thesis is correct—if excess energy is problematic precisely when an organism can no longer expend it—then we might see how controlling the excess given by land has become synonymous with the modern economy.

There is one more point to mention about Bataille's thesis before departing from it. He argues that the misrelation to excess is decisive and pervasive once it starts. He refers to this in terms of a pressure which expresses itself in the need for extension and which has effects of producing luxury or dearth.[63] We know that when identified as the means to produce excess, there is a desire to control land. Part of the desire, as an exponential effect, is to take the surplus (or its equity, which would be the same) generated by one's landed holding and reinvest it in the land market in order to secure a large slice of the pie. A crash in this market results when more investment goes into land and less into wages and when the land market slows down because no one is willing to or cannot pay the price for land. Speculative investments then begin to fold when those borrowing money to secure their place in the land market cannot afford their mortgage and loan payments. Why? Because wages have decreased or remained stagnant. In Bataille's words, this is catastrophe preceded by the glorious living of land speculators.

Bataille is pessimistic about our ability to cope with surplus, reducing the human relation to it in terms of an inevitable biology that takes on a variety of historical expressions—for example, the excess of the human victim taken by sacrifice in the Aztec civilization and the squandering of the excess in potlatch. The supervenience of an ethics, or what would be the attempt to subsume the economy under ethical precepts, is merely symptomatic of this biological relation. For example, the Reformation disdain of worldly possessions and wealth was essentially an ethic attempting to dissolve the excess according to notions of good faith and vocation.[64] Yet a curse tends to have a remedy, and in this case such a pharmakon might reside in breaking the way in which excess is understood.

Let us return to Heidegger's notion of being guilty. In his later thought, guilt is arguably reconceived in terms of memory which gives thanks to an origin. While not identical, I would nonetheless like to assume their interrelation in order to make the connection between being-guilty and being-landed. There is no Dasein that is not already guilty for an existence it did not author; and there are no acts of speaking and thinking that are not already responding to something demanding to be recollected. Both look back toward an origin that does not arise from the human being alone; Dasein toward being thrown into the world, memory toward being itself. Consider when Heidegger says, "To appropriate a past means to come to know oneself as indebted to that past."[65]

To describe guilt and memory as a form of becoming appropriate to that which precedes oneself is a way of accounting for the manner in which both decenter oneself. Guilt and memory are manners of distancing oneself from what is most familiar in order to move nearer to what requires to be heeded or thought. As such, they bring into view what it means to have an appropriate relation to things we attempt to appropriate in our understanding. "Memory initially signifies man's inner disposition and devotion," writes Heidegger, and he adds elsewhere that memory, in giving thanks, recognizes those things which we do not have ourselves.[66] The mode of being-guilty is similarly speaking a mode of dwelling that is constantly intended toward that which is not one's own.

It is, of course, land that is subject, and understanding its gravity by way of the detour through guilt and memory allows us to see how a view that is both from land and of land is a way of appropriating the latter into the former. That is to say, our view from land becomes appropriate by recalling land. So when Heidegger remarks, "Appropriation has the peculiar property of bringing man into his own. . . . Thus appropriated, man belongs to Appropriation" it must be thought along with his comment a few lines later: "We can admittedly succeed in this only when we have previously gained insight into the origin of space in the properties peculiar to site and have thought them adequately."[67] Have we thought these properties adequately? If, as I have argued, these properties are ones relating to access to life, which in turn reveal a more fundamental access to being, then simultaneous being-guilty and being-landed seems to drive towards a concrete response in which we not only dwell, but do so in a way that gives back to land. To recall, if guilt involves a constant mode of engagement (and not a single act or event), responding to the nullity at the basis of one's own being is played out in one's mode of existing. But how can we return to land in a way that expresses a gratitude for its surface (*super-facere*, or that which allows for human doing and making)? To answer this question, which implies a specific, concrete practice or practices, let me turn to a common criticism of my attempt to develop a sense of practical action from Heidegger's ontology. In proposing a move toward the concrete, have I reified being?

In his critical review of Raffoul's book, Steven Crowell expresses "little fondness" for those interpretations that attribute an agency to being (i.e., being gives).[68] He argues that it ontifies being (e.g., reifies or objectifies being),[69] and indeed, this accusation would apply to my argument (i.e., land is subject; land gives). Crowell further states that such interpretations diminish the importance of ontological difference; in other words, they opt for the ontic in attempting to resolve difference. In my case, the difference is resolved in an economy that gives back to land. Consequently, there is no longer being itself or even beings, but a kind of voluntarism in view of land. There are two possible replies. First, the strong appeal to ontological difference itself relies on ontifying difference as a concept determinative of interpreting the range of ontological meanings and possibilities. This rebuttal is not merely rhetorical because in doing so, such critics fail to see how their *application* of difference involves an agency expressed under the aegis of critique. This agency is not positive in its edicts (i.e., being gives), but negative in what it prohibits (i.e., being does not give what you think it does). To the contrary, as I discussed in chapter 4, difference in Heidegger names an essential relation which, while it cannot be overcome, is there to remind us of the *Seinsfrage* and our fragility of understanding. On this view, projects are wagers; they are undertaken despite risks. Difference demands of us to realize that these wagers are not only contingent but ways of letting something more primordial lie before us. Second, ontifying and concretizing are not the same. In contradistinction to the ontification of being, I envisage in my thesis on land a way in which the difference matters concretely (to reify and concretize are not the same). Ontological difference has existential implications which require thinking the human condition not just in terms of possibility but of what this possibility means in terms of an existence that cannot omit its dependency on land. This dependency, moreover, is not just existential if existence itself is constituted by many regions of engagement. I will thus speak of how difference implies a certain economic practice of taxation. The final division of this book is dedicated to explicating the viability of this concrete relation to difference.

Part 3

The Economic Turn

7

Correlating Land

Before moving to the expressly practical and prescriptive conclusions of this study, the economic relevance of the foregoing phenomenological claims needs some substantiation. The aim of this chapter is to show how land is the subject (*hupokeimenon*) of economic activity and thus transforms common economic meanings. By drawing on key aspects of the phenomenological analysis and correlating them with economic concepts, I will examine the limitations of assumptions relating to agency and production and how their meanings can be broadened when seen discretely in terms of our being-landed.

The correlations I propose can be mapped at three levels, where each level pertains to distinct domains of our being-in-the-world—namely, that of subject being (land), individual being, and communal being. The progression to each level expresses land's increasing and nuanced involvement in economic activity. It is increasing because the more economic activity develops, the more land figures as foundational. It is nuanced because by virtue of being a development it involves differentiation through activity which, as we will see, obscures the relation to the foundation.

	Phenomenology	Middle Term	Economics
land	subject	originality	naturalness
individual	mineness	motivation	self-interest
communal	commerce	capacity	advantage for individuals

The first level encompasses the phenomenological originality of land as subject and how it corresponds to the economic designation of land as natural origin. The middle term common to both sides is thus "originality." Because the notion of natural origin is insufficient, phenomenology provides a different tack for conceiving our economic relation to land. This in turn prevents it from a typical kind of reduction prevalent in economic modeling, which I discuss in relation to ecological economics.

The second level examines how a general economic agency originates from the land via its relation to commodities. The middle term at this level is "motivation," or that according to which the self is driven to be and to act. The phenomenological sense of mineness, discussed in chapter 6, will allow us to contextualize traditional assumptions of economic self-interest and broaden the notion of motivation. To engage in actions like production and use of commodities is to participate in *the effort to be* that underwrites the sense of who one is.

The third level looks beyond individual agency toward the communal effects of being-landed. I explore the dynamic relation by which the subjectivity of land allows the production and use of commodities to be communally significant. I explain this in terms of the capacity of commodities, or what is implied in the general economic term "stock," as that which is in store for potential use for the community. Thus, the middle term here is "capacity." For economics, capacity is the advantage of commodity use for plural individuals. Phenomenology transforms this relation by defining capacity as the potential for communal being and development, or what I argue to be the meaning of "commerce."

The chapter concludes by returning to the conceptions of production and land after the correlations have been drawn. This then allows me to respond critically to Veblen's prioritization of technical knowledge raised in chapter 1.

Correlation 1: The Originality of Land as Subject

What is the economic relevance of the phenomenological account of land as subject? It changes the ground upon which economics defines its central terms. To demonstrate this, I want to begin with a consideration of an economic school of thought that might at first seem to be an ally to my argument. By contrasting subtle yet key differences, I hope to show how the phenomenology proposed offers a decisive turn.

In chapter 3, I briefly alluded to ecological economics as an alternative, reconstructive theory which arguably adopts the central importance of land I have so far discussed. Indeed, when recalling how critics dismissed any special consideration for land owing to its natural status, it may seem that an ecological approach would provide a response since it emphasizes the primacy of nature and land within the context of reacting to neoclassical economics.[1] Yet despite the degree to which ecological approaches agree about the importance of land, an ambiguity appears in their description of land. There are two, interrelated critical points I would like to raise in view of this description.

The first concerns whether or not the conception of land as resource is really adequate to emphasizing the preeminent role of land. Consider, for example, the following:

> Land remains the primary source of energy and mass that compose our food and fiber. This explains why the agriculture and forestry sectors of an economy are land-intensive. Land also remains a primary factor of production in all other economic sectors where it provides mainly space. Third, the most important interaction between humans and other biological communities is the competition for land.[2]

Land is not only central to agriculture but to any activity requiring space. However, despite describing land as "source," this passage does not go so far as to say what the implications of this meaning of land are. It merely highlights how land is integral to the kinds of economies we have. What results from this is a failure to express in economic form how the necessity of land might not only mean we treat it as a fundamental concept but as one determinative of other economic concepts. Contrary to this, the most telling feature in this passage is how the necessity of land is a focus of competition, or what in fact means the subjugation of the concept to land to other economic terms and meanings. Ecological economics thus examines how "modelling this competition is fundamental to conducting integrated analyses of ecological-economic activities."[3] In other words, land figures in the ecosystem as the provider of services and natural capital, and a revised economic model might therefore intend to show how a natural power source can be managed more effectively in terms of social and environmental sustainability.[4] But does not the idiom of source, despite how importantly we perceive it, really translate into a new attitude that might take seriously the role of land? Or is land reduced to the role of fulfilling an economic equation, which would mean in the end that the importance of the meaning of land is expressible only by its internal language of economic calculus?[5] What can this form of calculation really demonstrate for our understanding? It seems to me that what remains despite the demonstration by the mathematical form is a conception of land as only a store that sustains all life on the planet.[6] That is to say, the idiom of power source really describes land as resource. Is this enough?

One reply is to say that it is enough insofar as ecological economics makes cogent the very real threat of dire consequences that mistreat the environment, especially the fictions about elasticity and constant provision of energy which conventional economics often assume. However, from a strictly phenomenological point of view this approach fails to see nature as source except in a narrow sense of something to be sustained in order to maintain life—a kind of economy for Plato's city of pigs.

I think the weakness of this position can be more fully exposed when considering my second point. While admirable in one respect, the ecological concern reduces to a kind of biological determination, which tends to exclude larger philosophical questions about human existence. This problem is evident when considering how its description of land is couched within a specific attitude that relies on fear and punishment. The short form of this states that should we ignore land in economic production, what will result is an unsustainable relation to nature. But there is more to this short form that I want to express in relation to the mechanism it employs.

Ricoeur discusses the problematic use of fear in his critique of religion when acknowledging how atheism of the Nietzschean and Freudian varieties rightly points out the absurdity and destructiveness of the kind of responsibility generated by fear. He speaks of this in terms of the binary relation between "accusation and consolation."[7] Accusation is not only blame, but blame attached to punishment—"Look what has happened due to your actions." Consolation results from taking action in obeisance of this fear. It is framed positively—"You have acted rightly, so here is your reward." The problem for Ricoeur is the limitation this binary imposes. It prevents a mature involvement in existence since we are forever caught like children in a web of fear and reward.[8] In other words, because our motivations for existing are reduced to this form, larger philosophical questions remain irrelevant or inaccessible.

Within the ecological scheme, accusation and consolation are really reductions of human existence to a merely biological level—the cycle of life and death, whose highest aim can be expressed only in terms of the perpetuation of this cycle, whether individually or at the level of species being. Its punishment is of course extinction of the species being or nature as a whole. I think a Nietzschean response is a valid one here as it claims that both human beings and nature have been misconceived. It is not simply that there is more to human existence than sustainability, but there is more to nature as a whole.[9] The creative vitality of life has been reduced to a mundane perpetuation of existence in favor of nothing. Sustainability of the environment may be a necessary feature of our being-in-the-world but it is not its foundation. Moreover, to make it so would be a decision based on bad faith. Why?

Let us consider Hannah Arendt's analysis of a view toward life that knows only the perpetuation of its existence. She argues that strictly speaking if self-preservation were genuinely the primary concern, one would know life only as a series of moments in which one was presented with different means or threats to life as singular decisions but not from a perspective that could make sense of these confrontations at a metabiological level. Arendt clarifies that this type of concern is not the same thing as an anticipation of death since death is a concept of which one becomes aware and anxious according to the manner in which an already existing social world allows it to be a concern.[10] Yet, of course, we exist in the social world, and it is this world that makes something like sustainability an issue. To eliminate this contradiction, the assumption that land is merely and only important for economic activity needs to be corrected.

The phenomenology I have proposed begins with a fuller account of land. To recall from chapter 6, land gives access not just to life but to being—that is, where existing involves raising questions about what it means to exist. To utilize phenomenology thus means that certain primary conceptions define the remit of the economic model rather than conform to its terms—in the instance of ecology, how competition for and use of land can be sustainable. Different types of models might then emerge because they begin with a different representation of life. The reasons for not reducing land to capital or labor, and moreover, for taking it to be more than just a natural entity for which we compete, place economics in view of something that exceeds its assumptions about what is meaningful for the flourishing of economic activity. As Düppe puts this matter when noting a certain irony of the field, "The discipline of economics is determined by the commitment to a language that stems from a theory no economist actually believes in."[11] Of course, this irony is not trivial. The failure to attempt to correlate economic terms with a wider philosophical understanding means its narrowness, to draw on Marx's term once again, *reproduces* itself in our daily lives. Having said this, the reader might wonder how land as subject might in fact change the way competition for land persists. I address this question in the next chapter.

Correlation 2: The Motivation Arising from Being-Landed

The correlation affects what it means to be an acting economic agent in two ways. First, when understood in terms of material provision, the originality of land figures as a unique kind of productive debt. The excess of land gives the conditions and material to be transformed by labor. Second, as we saw in chapter 6, land is the origin of one's philosophical reflection insofar as it occasions the sense of mineness through which one has one's mode of being. When applied to economic production, this origin suggests that commodity production and use has a much broader and deeper foundation than the traditional notion of economic self-interest. Commodities, as I will argue, are involved in an exercise of ontological possibilities for being.

(a) Productive Debt

Let us recall yet again Knut Wicksell's characterization of capital goods as basically entities of stored up labor and land. On his account, the notion of a precapitalist society absent of complex technological developments shows us that production is predicated on a basic relation in which labor and land figure as the two main factors of production. Labor may be active, but it relies on the passivity of land which occasions its use. Passivity is, as we have seen in chapter 1, a deceptive descriptor since in the case of land it accounts for its precedence. It is passive because it does not need to be produced by another or draw upon something outside. On this Henry George remarks,

> Production, as a term of political economy, means a drawing forth by man; a bringing into existence by the power of man. It does not mean creation, the proper sense of which is the bringing into existence by a power superior to that of man.
>
> . . .
>
> Man is not a creator; he has no power of originating things, of making something out of nothing. He is a producer; that is to say a changer, who brings forth by altering what already is.[12]

To this limitation of human power, there is of course more. George adds that human production is not only limited in the abstract sense of being categorically different from creation, but that existentially, as it were, human production is limited in another sense in how it is dependent on an other:

> All his production has as its substratum what he finds already in the world; what exists irrespective of him. This substratum or nexus, the natural or passive factor, on which and by which the human or active factor of production acts, is in the terminology of political economy called land.[13]

So in a certain sense, the limitations of human production are those imposed by the theoretical limitations of economic method. This is true insofar as economics, in not being able to comment on the derivative capacity of human production, no longer treats it. Land remains original to the extent that we always require it, but this does not mean we have to recognize it. When George comments that land "exists irrespective" of us, its independence can be an obstacle to our understanding. Because land exists regardless of what we do or think, economists can take this to be an alibi according to which they can simply disregard or pass over its originality. Thus economics can focus and has focused primarily on the human element, whether in terms of labor power or a psychology of decision-making.

But let us resist this attitude. We can do so by seeing how land is linked to ontological possibility even in its economic role. It achieves this through existentially setting the conditions for production which in turn allows commodities to be employed in our existential projects.

(b) Mineness and Commodities

What does it mean to produce a commodity?[14] At the purely physical level, there is the application of labor and capital in order to bring about an entity that serves a purpose without which that purpose could not be easily met, if at all. The attachment of the commodity to purpose is conventionally seen as the point at which value emerges, unless one holds dogmatically to a substance theory of value in which the actual entity can be said to intrinsically possess a value. Whether it is socially necessary labor-time, utility, or a general notion of the subjective projection of worth, that a commodity can be used for some end figures significantly into economic accounts of value-creation, or why one decides to labor in the first instance.

So the idea of commodity production cannot be separated from questions of commodity use. Without making too much of the significance of etymological analysis, it is still worthwhile considering the fundamental meanings of terms used to describe the results of production. "Wealth," "commodity," and "goods" all have a root meaning involving well-being, benefit, or advantage. It is quite easy to assume that these meanings primarily refer to economic well-being, where to have wealth or goods is to have valuable assets. If economics is primarily concerned with value, the production of commodities can only be thought according to what it takes to be a measure of value. This holds true for classical as well as neoclassical theory. The social activity of production can thus be explained, for example as William Jevons does, by utility:

> Utility only exists when there is on the one side the person wanting, and on the other the thing wanted . . . Just as the gravitating force of a material body depends not alone on the mass of that body, but upon

> the masses and relative positions and distances of the surrounding material bodies, so utility is an attraction between a wanting being and what is wanted.[15]

Despite the difference in explanatory devices, Jevons's account is similar to aspects of classical thought that describe economic motivation in terms of desire and self-interest. Value is therefore always something that is already familiar and indeed given, even if potentially, in terms of a basic desiring.

Because these assumptions are tied to a limited understanding of human action and existence, they easily if not naturally reduce to defining economic value as it matters to the individual alone, or self-interest. Though it is not true to say that economics maintains a strong sense of psychological egoism, which in a certain sense is beyond its remit since this position calls for a substantial philosophical anthropology, it is nonetheless correct to say that the use of self-interest to describe economic motivation comes part and parcel with its notion of value and how such value is detached from key aspects of human existence. On this front, both Smith and Mill offer specific accounts of human motivation and do not claim that "this is how humans are in essence." George is thus well in the right when he qualifies, "Political economy has a duty and a province of its own. It is not and cannot be a science of everything."[16] Yet this does not exonerate economics. If the effort to be is what underwrites economic production, the terms "wealth," "commodity," and "goods" must bear some trace of their larger remit and application. Indeed, to provide benefit or advantage is to add something more to the given state of affairs. One way of saving this trace is to read the terms in relation to the meaning of excess discussed in chapter 6. The benefit and advantage of commodities are excess of self-interest because they are addressed to the effort to be and presuppose a relation to others (and to land!) so that this effort can be thought and enacted. Still another way of saving this trace is in terms of gravity. The attraction of which Jevons speaks does not exist only between two abstract entities—"the person wanting" and "the thing wanted"—but by virtue of those projects toward which we gravitate and which are the prerequisite for any desire to use a commodity. This larger existential context should not be overlooked. Let us therefore see it in more detail by degrees.

In a previous book I examined the products of work within an ontological context—that is, work things as entities and not commodities.[17] I want here to reiterate my argument and supplement it in relation to the economic sphere. Agreeing with a general Marxist analysis, I described the entity produced by work in terms of objective formation, which in turn has a stabilizing effect for both the individual and the world. For the former, the formation of entities allows for the development of identity—to see oneself in the work, to come to know oneself in the laboring process. For the latter, as we have seen Arendt emphasize, the world arises as a stable and durable milieu in which we can relate to others and have projects of being that break with the mundane biological cycle of life and death. Through work we gain a separation in which we are no longer simply natural. Departing from Marx, I argued that things of work have a significant ontological status distinct from human self-consciousness and actualization. This status may ultimately bear on human concerns, but things of work do so primarily by virtue of their own manner of being.

I referred to this as the metaphorical, or figurative, nature of work. Drawing on Ricoeur's theory of metaphor, I argued that the necessary and formative dimension of work is akin to a literal level of meaning. For Ricoeur, it is the apparent contradiction of literal meanings that drives metaphor to predicate new meaning. So, for example, even in mundane cases where one might say "Man is a wolf," the contradiction between literal meanings occurs when we know that one entity cannot be identical to another entity. We are asked to arrive at a new meaning by seeing "man" in some sense as a "wolf." Taking Ricoeur's theory analogously, I described the necessary level of work as inherently contradicting in a broad sense according to the way it renders what is already given materially *into* something else. Out of this transformation arises not just an object for a use, but a thing whose manner of being outruns any specific use. Things of work participate integrally in our self-understanding, or what I have referred to in this study as mineness. Not just self-consciousness, but contrary to Marx, a project in which human self-consciousness may be but just one aspect as opposed to its center. This movement away from the material constitution of self-consciousness is apparent in how work itself is never simply about fulfilling necessity, notwithstanding pecuniary need, but is always something more without transcending this necessity.

It would be quite tempting to argue that when reduced to the economic realm, this power of work is diluted or distorted. The cycles of production and consumption in the modern market economy result in things of work that are poor in quality or satisfy superficial desires. I would not dismiss this point since it describes a current malaise consequent, at least for me, on the lack of awareness of the points I have raised in this present book. Yet, there is an opportunity to see the commodity in a new light. This involves linking the metaphorical nature of work with the prevalence given to land. The metaphorical is but another way to describe the excess of land, that is, how the possibilities of existence become figured into commodity form. Saving the commodity from the vicious circle of consumption, where the activity becomes an end in itself, means in part saving the idea of the self who takes an interest in purchasing and using things.

If phenomenology is our starting point, commodities form the stuff of the larger movement of existence in the general effort to be. The narrow notion of economic self-interest (I do not want to pretend it does not exist at some level) can therefore be seen as a kind of personalization of the effort to be: to see oneself in and through the use of commodities—that is, in the first person. Even a deplorable instance of this, where one might witness, for example, a person obsessing about an expensive new car and how it will express a sense of their status and identity, is at the ontological level an expression of the desire to be. Such instances go wrong when one believes that one's ownmost potential for being is in the satisfaction of ends relating to the possession of specific commodities. As Aristotle would aver, such confusion mistakes the accumulation of commodities for an end in itself. There is, of course, much that needs to be threshed out in view of agent intentionality and exactly how commodities enable and shape this intentionality—can commodities be said to have their own kind of intentionality?[18] For my limited purposes, we need only see how the commodity is not as banal as we might tend to think. Self-interested use of commodities describes not the basic motivation of economic activity but its aberration when not related to questions about existence. We can see this more dignified role of the commodity more clearly at the communal level.

Correlation 3: Communal Capacity and Commerce

The beneficial nature of commodities at the level of individual being is expressed at the communal level in terms of the *stock* of commodities. Individual production and use of commodities always presuppose the communal infrastructure in which specific types of labor and uses of commodities are possible. However, economics tends to see this phenomenon in terms of the production of wealth and its distribution as it is determined by individual rational agency. Even the term "social capital" does not escape this assumption entirely when its meaning is reduced to a context or structure as a setting for individual agency.[19] Nonetheless, for whatever arguments that can be made for the significance of the prerequisite of social structures, relations, and values, there is a distinct problem with commodities. The materiality of commodities is inseparable from its marketability since its being produced derives from an anticipation of how, as an object, the commodity will be desired by an agent. Commodities are in this sense the antithetical context according to which the concept of social capital has gained prominence, since the latter designates the means and ends by which individuals achieve some use or advantage according to a collective existence and intangible goods.

So the conventional economic view of commodities is fundamentally predicated on an atomism of society, where goods are defined mostly by individual benefit. Society may exist and may be required for such benefit, just as Smith's butcher requires the baker, and so on, and the marketplace in order to trade for his own benefit; yet, society itself is essentially driven by the engine of the economy running on the desires and decisions of individuals.

But what then of the *stock* of commodities? Is it merely a store of commodities available for individuals to use? The phenomenological correlation of motivation in the previous section suggests this cannot be the case. This is because the motivation for producing and using commodities is not derived from self-interest but from a more fundamental ontological desire to be. This clarification not only breaks with traditional assumptions about economic agency but also makes unlikely and untenable the assumption that the economy is built from the atomistic level of the individual. It is unlikely because the desire to be cannot be achieved in isolation and presupposes a relation to others. It is untenable because self-interest in the weak or strong form would then be parasitic upon this ontological fact of our being.

So how then can the ontological nature of commodities be understood at the communal level? On my view, the stock of commodities cannot just be a numerical increase of goods available for a greater quantity of individuals. If it were, the increase in capacity would be reducible to individual advantage and the provision of stock would be valorized for this purpose (e.g., the emphasis on gross domestic product). So if capital goods are stored up labor and land, the increase in the stock of commodities can be understood as what I referred to as stored-up capacity. Commodities, in Heideggerian parlance, *stand-there* as things to be used. They are not present-at-hand as mere objects but, by virtue of their being produced for specific ends, reveal their capacity to do something. The clock that tells time, the saw that cuts wood, the umbrella that provides shelter from the rain. Stock is therefore not simply a store of goods but the display of potentials for what is possible. The mode of being of the commodity is one of an excess according to which other ends are possible.

Assuming for the moment that the provision of this stock is not distorted by numerical excess or deficiency of supply, whether caused by contingent forces or the intentions of speculators, it appears that the basis of the community well-being requires to some degree the presence of such stock. This can be seen when commodities, in providing the capacity for use, allow members of a community to address any given situation calling for a particular capacity. Circulation of stock is thus a circulation of capacity for individuals within a community to act. Moreover, the effect of increased capacity need not be envisioned solely in terms of directly aiding or benefiting the community, as with instances of obligations arising from social capital. Here the stock of commodities is distinct: it expands communal capacity according to a commerce in which individuals who can see more in terms of their own possibility allow others to see more in terms of theirs. This way of describing commerce entails the wider dissemination, not of exchange value, but primarily the encounter with things of work that might transform our understanding of the potential-to-be. It means, in other words, enlarging a general capacity for being that expands given the spread of commodities.[20]

Indeed, the understanding of commodities as providing a capacity can be said to be its ontological meaning. Consider the following passages from *Being and Time*. First, Heidegger observes how things produced in work act as a nexus through which we gain access to the world. Even at its most basic level of material constitution,

> the work to be produced is not merely usable for something. The production itself is a using *of* something for something. In the work there is also a reference or assignment to "materials": the work is dependent on leather, thread, nails, and the like. Leather, moreover is produced from hides. These are taken from animals, which someone else raised. . . . So in the environment certain entities become accessible which are always ready-to-hand, but which, in themselves, do not need to be produced.[21]

Things of work enable a kind of stable access by which relations to the world and indeed others can be figured and take place:

> Here the world is encountered in the work in which wearers and users live, a world which is at the same time our world. The work taken care of in each case is not only at hand in the domestic world of the workshop, but rather in the *public world*.[22]

It is perhaps true that the public world for Heidegger is largely permeated by fallenness and inauthenticity, but it is also true that this condition is resultant upon a more primary ontological feature of *giving access.* That it may be fallen is only possible because it has the opportunity not to be so.[23] Hence,

> Along with the public world, the *surrounding world of nature* is discovered and accessible to everyone. In taking care of things, nature is discovered as having some definite direction on paths, streets, bridges, and buildings.[24]

And this phenomenon is by no means an exception to the larger sphere of the public world in which commerce occurs. Indeed, one can extend Heidegger's account to commodities:

> This constitutive reference is by no means lacking when wares are produced by the dozen; it is only undefined, pointing to the random and the average. Thus not only beings which are at hand are encountered in the work but also beings with the kind of being Da-sein for whom what is produced becomes handy in its taking care.[25]

When things of work are available on a large scale ("produced by the dozen"), this availability is undefined in the sense that they are generally present for purchase—that is, as a commodity. Heidegger's reference to randomness and averageness can be understood in the light of the marketplace which offers such wares, perhaps catering to the lowest common denominator in taste and quality. But apart from this, there is still in the commodity an ontological force in which care permeates and extends since it is through such things that we are able to be handy, or practical, in our projects. Commodities, it can be said, provide for a commerce of care.[26]

Is this ontological assessment of commodities so far from political economy? Perhaps we can read the production of wealth in commodity form in a new way. Let us consider the foregoing ontological account in correlation with Henry George's observations about the capacity of commodities:

> By the storage of labor, which is involved in the production of wealth, it becomes possible for man to change the time in which a given exertion shall be utilized in the satisfaction of desire, thus greatly increasing the sum of satisfactions which a given exertion may procure. And by the using of wealth as capital, which is the calling of past exertion to the service of present exertion, he is enabled to concentrate exertion upon a given point, at a given time, to call in, as it were, forces of nature which far transcend in their power those which nature has put at his use

> in the human frame. . . . By turning his labor into capital in the form of a bow, he may exert in one instant the force that can be accumulated during longer intervals of time; and finally, as a result of many transmutations of labor into capital, he can exert in the rifle chemical forces more potent than any of the forces of which the energies of his own body give him command.[27]

While the passage above is focused on the relations between wealth in commodity form to what a user is able to achieve, George's view can be said to be similar to Heidegger's insofar as the commodity occasions, or gives access, to the realization of capacity and indeed requires and draws on other existing commodities and workers. In some sense, Heidegger's disdainful comments may express the sense in which the public world falls short of fully appreciating what and how it is structured in relation to understanding our existence. Yet at the same time, it is the necessary part of the world in which humans can individually and collectively belong together. This is because projects involving possibilities of our being may not be common to or shared among all individuals, but through these projects the commodity is a common point of reference. It is both available to all as an enabler of capacity and gives to the community a greater potential to be when new commodities emerge from the constant projects of work.

Returning to Land

We have come a long way in seeing how the originality of land has its economic permutations in something that might seem quite distant and distinct from it—that is, the commodity. Where is land in all the activity that has formed and constituted the world, of the realizations of projects, and the proliferation of goods available to the being of the community? It has, of course, gone nowhere. It has always been the subject providing the ground and source upon which the production and use of commodities can take place. More importantly, as I argued in chapter 5, being-landed is the condition of our human existence such that land provides the physical and imaginative schema by which we are led into activities of production. Commodities are made *for* some use and end. In this sense, the capacities provisioned by commodities are ultimately owed to the givenness of land. I will pursue this argument further in relation to Veblen in the next section. At the moment, I want to treat the reasons why the fundamental role of land can be forgotten despite its primacy. In fact, these reasons will help contextualize the insufficiency of Veblen's account.

The typical starting point for the critical view motivating a phenomenological analysis is what we take for granted in some kind of attitude. The typical rendering of this diagnosis within phenomenology is to say that one form of understanding operates to the extent that other forms of more reflective and philosophical understanding are ignored. Heidegger, when referring to the former as everydayness, refers specifically to the ways in which our everyday familiarity with time—for example, clock time, schedules, calendars, and so on—inhibits, but does not prohibit, the recognition of those questions addressed to our finitude which everyday time cannot sufficiently admit. Hence, finitude and death remain sources of anxiety for the everyday attitude. Yet it is precisely because the everyday can evoke anxiety that it has a positive role. By way of its affectative evocation, it provokes reflection.

Heidegger's analysis need not be limited to temporality and death. It can be applied to anything designated as fundamental to our existence. This is because Heidegger's view is predicated on a tension in which what can be termed the foreground of our understanding (i.e., the everyday world) is what allows us to encounter more significant meanings. We gain access to deeper meanings via the everyday, and this is only because the everyday is itself a species of what is fundamental.[28]

There are of course many levels to Heidegger's analysis, but let us here recall a theme discussed earlier in chapters 4 and 5—forgetting. Our so-called everyday understanding is one of forgetting the role and importance of land. Moreover, the decisive feature of this understanding is that its contents and concerns tend to reinforce and perpetuate its oblivion. What characterizes the familiar meanings in our day-to-day existence, and what therefore blocks access to deeper questions, is the degree to which our everyday life tends to orient toward things in a particular way. In short, we tend to see things themselves in terms of simple practical relations without recognizing how in fact such things are mediating and determining our understanding. To see an entity like a tool merely as a means to achieve an end misses something important for Heidegger.

In *Being and Time,* he uses the term "ontic" to describe a way of apprehending entities in a limited way as mere objects. When seeing a thing ontically, we thus tend to see it only in terms of certain features and properties in the service of our own ends. And this way of seeing fails to meditate on deeper questions about the being of the thing: "That which is *ontically* so familiar in the way Dasein has been factically interpreted that we never pay any heed to it, hides enigma after enigma existential-ontologically."[29] Essentially, on my reading of *Being and Time,* the enigma is ultimately how things disclose temporality and a sense of thereness, which may or may not link up to questions concerning finitude.[30]

It is perhaps no surprise that one can find in the thought of Henry George observations readily correlating with this phenomenological account. Indeed, complementary to Heidegger's analysis of everydayness are seemingly innocuous statements by George. First, he notes the fundamental role of land. Any variations of our habitat "require not only a preliminary but recurring use of the solid surface of the earth, [and] it is to that solid surface that our material existence and material production are confined."[31] He then comments on how this role is rarely something we bear in mind:

> But a fundamental perception is not always a first perception. . . . Perception is by contrast. What we always perceive neither attracts attention nor excites memory until brought into contrast with non-perception.[32]

It would be hasty to deem George's point as little more than an observation about the manner in which things we passively perceive gain significance when juxtaposed to a contrasting event or encounter. Particularly if we draw on comments he makes with regard to the modes of production of wealth, we find a more detailed account of why this failure to perceive land occurs. In short, because efforts of human production are engaged in such a way, as Heidegger has shown, that they focus on specific ends irrespective of larger questions and problems, they tend to forget their basic reliance on land. And in doing so, it means that our modes of production, as they perpetuate an oblivion about the importance of land as a factor of production, can result in an economic contradiction: Laborers, concerned mainly with their own skill or trade, face situations in which, without having access to land, they cannot labor for themselves.[33]

George refers to three modes of production. He describes the first level as "adapting," which involves a type of production "mechanical in its nature, and consist[ing] in the change of place, form, condition or combination of what is already in existence."[34] This mode is the most basic since it consists in transforming what is given by nature and made accessible by land. Examples include fishing, hunting, mining, manufacturing, transporting, and various services in which we use existing means to obtain a product. It is important to note that this mode, while being basic, is not similar in purpose to the accounts of Grotius, Pufendorf, and Locke that appeal to a state of nature as a foundation upon which each extrapolates the basis for more advanced societies. Adapting is basic because at any level of social, industrial, and technological development this activity is limited to a simple form of relation—that is, use of existing material.

In this sense, the manufacture of simple tools from base elements is no different than the construction of mobile media devices from elements. While sophisticated in composition and design, they are adapted from existing material. George's distinction draws on the making-creation pairing mentioned earlier—humans cannot create since they require material. The power of adapting, George clarifies, even if extended infinitely "would not enable him to manufacture a single wheat-grain that would sprout."[35] To be sure, radical innovations in techno-science still rely on already given and existing material.

When human work participates directly in the production of things, drawing on the forces of nature, George refers to this as "growing":

> In this man utilizes the vital or reproductive force of nature to aid him in the producing of wealth. By obtaining vegetables, cuttings or seeds, and planting them; by capturing animals and breeding them, we are not merely enabled to produce vegetables or animals in greater quantity than Nature spontaneously offers them to our taking, but, in many cases, to improve their quality of adaptability for our uses.[36]

Hence in this mode we do not merely use what is given by nature, we attempt to use the "vital and generative"[37] forces of nature. While farming is an obvious instance, it can also include scientific attempts to engineer genes, to clone species, or even the in-vitro genesis of organic material. Though George does not say so, it is at this level that the relation to land becomes more explicit since instead of simply drawing on existing and given natural entities, we settle a plot of land in order to concentrate production. After all, farmland is Ricardo's prime example demonstrating the doctrine of ground rent.

The third mode is specific to the human being since it no longer draws *directly* on, though it presupposes, nature as origin. Instead its focus is the activity of the human community. It is the production of wealth through exchange:

> That it is by and through his disposition and power to exchange, in which man essentially differs from all other animals that human advance goes on, I shall hereafter show. Yet not merely is it through exchange that the utilization in production of the highest powers both of the human factor and the natural factor becomes possible, but it seems to me that in itself exchange brings about a perceptible increase in the sum of wealth, and that even if we could ignore the manner in which it extends the power of the other two modes of production, this constitutes it, in itself, a third mode of production.[38]

Exchange is expressly conventional, as opposed to natural. It not only relies on forms of agreement between trading individuals but in most instances a currency upon which trading parties can agree has value, often as a promissory note. Exchange presupposes the establishment and sufficiency of the other modes since without them there would be nothing to exchange. Moreover, because of its distinction and role at the social level, it occupies a place where it can affect the prior modes of adapting and growing. Exchange often becomes the focus of the attempt to control the modes it presupposes through certain strategies of exchange, or what are the activities of speculators trying to take hold of certain segments of the market.

If George is describing the manner in which modes of production rely on nature, how is it that these modes, while requiring land, obfuscate this fundamental relation? The answer lies largely in the structure of the three modes of production. Because the first two modes are basic, because they engage directly with nature, they constitute the foundation upon which other human activities can develop. Yet what occurs at each level is an increase in reflective and practical momentum away from this foundation. That is to say, while we always require land, the specific forms of relation to land at each level tends to lead us in our reflections away from a recognition of this relation. Since each mode expresses a higher degree of complexity—nature used, nature imitated, nature as the basis for an "artificial" form of wealth production—the origin providing for these activities becomes less recognizable. Land in this sense gives itself so something other can take place. Yet this also means that we can become enthralled with the things we produce and use, or what can be called a glancing away from the origin and basis of our existence to something like a horizon of possibilities. Thus there is a conceptual transformation: we see the source *as* specific futural possibilities. Land, while the foundation of production, becomes the too familiar ground upon which we think intensively on other ends.

Veblen in View of Ontology

To recall, Veblen argues that the use of land and hence its perceived value are not possible without a preexisting technical knowledge. He gives precedence to the immaterial over the material. George offers the opposite position when giving precedence to land. Who is right and who is wrong? Each seems committed to a position that cannot be compromised or mediated—what has priority, human or land? As I noted, complicating this matter is George's appeal to natural law, a rhetoric which may seem uncompelling to the modern reader. But we have come a long way since the initial discussion of Veblen in chapter 1, and I think we are in a better position to appreciate the ontological commitments in George's thought. Indeed, George's conception of land can be seen as unambiguously ontological when he argues that "while the fundamental quality of land is that of furnishing to men a place on which they may stand or move, or rest things on, this is not the quality first noticed."[39] For George this fundamental role is demonstrated in a thought experiment when he asks, "Take away from man all that is contributed by external nature, all that belongs to the external factor land, and you have, what?"[40] Take away land, and there is no remainder. No matter how reflectively spontaneous, even *homo economicus* cannot produce ex nihilo.

To bolster this way of reading George, one can, as I have done, graft George's position on to the more explicit ontological claims that Heidegger makes. In view of Veblen's thesis, this would be tantamount to arguing that while there must be the fore-structured, technological knowledge of the world in order for human beings to act in any capacity, world does not precede the original position maintained by earth and, as I argued by extension, land. Karl Polanyi puts the general case vividly:

> [Land] invests man's life with stability; it is the site of his habitation; it is a condition of his physical safety; it is the landscape and the seasons. We might as well imagine his being born without hands and feet as carrying on his life without land. And yet to separate land from man and to organize society in such a way as to satisfy the requirements of a real-estate market was a vital part of the utopian concept of a market economy.[41]

So the kinds of technological knowledge of which Veblen speaks are ontologically derivative of our condition of being-landed and are added on to this condition as a way to change or transform it. As I mentioned in chapter 1 in relation to Schabas's account of the development of economic thought, Veblen's view is typically economic insofar as it brackets fundamental philosophical meanings it unawaringly presupposes or refuses to acknowledge. Instead of the economy being embedded in phenomenological conditions of existence, existence itself is embedded in the economic system.[42]

But if ontology has the first word, it does not have the last. The economic correlations examined in the previous sections were attempts to see how an ontology of land participated at the economic level. The move to the economic may be a turn, but it is not one that constitutes a break. It is the attempt to see how land as subject informs economic production. This does not mean that humans are merely vessels through which land acts. Because land is in the position of subject, it grants the possibilities for human action. So the way humans engage and use land involves an active participation which translates land's originality through these engagements and uses. If we allow Veblen's thesis on human knowledge to remain humbly within an economic remit, then it can be seen as no longer making claims about the nature of reality but of the manner in which human knowledge is essential to economic production, that is, an activity which is derivative of land's provision.

There are crucial implications of this view which I will develop in the next chapter. For now, let me conclude by saying Veblen's thesis should be understood as a recognition of what occurs when humans encounter and become involved in an especially human way with land. That is to say, human involvement does not remove or diminish land's ontological priority but results in a unique expression of its excess in and through the human manner of being, essential to which is the kind of technological knowledge Veblen describes.

8

Dilemma of the Excess: Rent and Taxation

The foregoing account of the ways land is involved and indeed presupposed by economic activity would be unsatisfactory if it did not imply or yield specific prescriptions consistent with its conclusions. Elucidating such practices would certainly offer some distinctions by which similar-spirited attempts to critique and reenvisage the economy are made. For example, post-structural criticisms of capitalism tend not to offer positive reform, often alleging the entire system is irredeemably flawed due to assumptions about human subjectivity and the commensurability of values.[1] Ecological approaches, as we saw, prioritize land's importance, yet without a sufficient grasp of how and why we should do so beyond the threat of dire environmental consequences. Even if ecological economics proposes a normative measure similar to what will be expressed in this chapter, it does so from a different ground which, in the end, fails to recognize the basis of our dependence on land as ontologically constitutive of our existence. This is the difference between land conceived as source and resource; land as subject and natural object.

Succinctly put, the taxation of ground rent is the specific economic practice that can affirm land as subject. To see how this proposal is consistent with my phenomenological thesis, I begin with a discussion of the manner in which land's excess places a certain type of demand on us. I examined this demand generally in chapter 6 by way of the concept of gravity—that is, how our dependence on land results in a kind of force we must acknowledge and to which we are asked to make an appropriate response. In this chapter I will refer to this gravity in terms of the dilemma which land presents to us by virtue of its excess and consequent production of ground rent. To see this dilemma is decisive. It goes entirely against the grain of that philosophical imaginary of privation I depicted in chapter 3, and practically, as we shall see, it affirms a categorically different mode of land usage and possession.

The first section of this chapter explores how excess arises as ground rent and the dilemma this presents with respect to how we might claim this excess and apply it. Because the economic use of land is a specific kind of engagement, I explain that excess appears according to these parameters, which I describe according to the category "finite." Given that ground rent is an expression of the excess of land, I then consider in the next section the rationale for the taxation of ground rent. I conclude with separate sections discussing four key logistical matters—ownership, estimation of the tax, its collection, and implications for understanding the economic concepts of scarcity and competition.

The Excess of Land as Ground Rent

If the phenomenological object of analysis involves the emergence of meaning in our encounter with entities, then the economic correlate to this dimension is the production of value in our use of entities. Each term respectively occupies the center around which human activities are oriented. For phenomenology, it is the intentional relation toward things in view of understanding; for economics, it is the laboring and exchanging acts in view of value production. Thus, the previous chapter mapped value production in terms of existential projects requiring the traditionally conceived main component of an economy—that is, the commodity. Yet we also saw how land is essential for the production and use of commodities. Its excess can be perceived in how it grants the events, to use Henry George's parlance, of adapting, growing, and exchanging. The production of commodities and the provision of services are situated in specific places, as specific relations to land. Its grant of the excess of possibilities for being, in other words, manifests according to its *finite* qualities and varied conditions and, of course, how we become involved with such qualities and conditions in economic production.

Understanding how finite qualities are central to our perception of land and its potential uses is essential. It is because of its expression in finite qualities that something like excess can take its most expressed form. Finiteness by its nature provides a specific type of contact and encounter, localized according to specific features. Hence excess is perceptible for humans when the finite features of the land can be seen as yielding certain possibilities for being. That is to say, we see in our engagement with land's features new opportunities and ventures. This suggests that our being-landed is an involvement with land's being-finite. Or, if one prefers, the relation can be expressed as a double negative: the finite conditions of land (i.e., its scarcity and variable qualities) and our finite uses converge as a way of participating existentially in land's excess.

Noting this relation admits a further advance in the correlation. Excess occurs not only in the production and use of commodities in our existential projects. In addition, the human use of land allows for a special type of excess since it involves inevitably at some point comparative uses of land. Land is not only used to produce, but in instances where there is marginal land, to recall Ricardo, there arises a surplus in production due to advantages that superior plots of land provide. This way of describing the excess is, as the reader will have no doubt anticipated, a way of accounting for ground rent. Land's excess correlated economically is ground rent as surplus value. Let us recall Henry George's own formulation of this phenomenon: "The rent of land is determined by the *excess* of its produce over that which the same application can secure from the least productive land in use."[2] This means that if excess is expressed finitely, then it does not disappear but seeks further determination in a remainder—a remainder that itself is finite in form, or what is economic value. What remains is a surplus after the completion of the specific, finite projects undertaken in production. Put more within economic terminology: ground rent is the value, excess the returns to labor and capital.

In summary of the above, the correlation of land's excess can be understood at two levels simultaneously: (1) fundamentally as the grant of possibility for being in production (as discussed in chapter 7); and (2) in terms of advantages bestowed under specific finite, landed conditions for production. These conditions often involve land's scarcity and the competition for its ownership which this scarcity fuels. In what follows, I want to provide some *indication* of how the phenomenological account I have proposed recontextualizes our understanding of scarcity and competition, or what is a so-called groundwork for their redefinition. My strategy here is to show how our current understanding of land, by way of these concepts, anticipates the rationale for a tax on ground rent. After discussing the details of this tax, we will then be in a better position by the conclusion of this chapter to see how the tax in fact corrects our understanding of scarcity and competition; that is, they are transformed.

Scarcity and competition in fact go hand-in-hand, and the standard criticism of them focuses on the failure of economics to move away from negative assumptions about the nature of all things economic. Stephen Marglin voices a strong refusal to accept such terms:

> The idea of unlimited wants, and its corollary of universal scarcity, is fundamental to economics. Indeed, every mainstream text with which I am acquainted defines economics as the study of how scarce resources are allocated unlimited ends. But the real issue of unlimited wants is not whether people want more, other things being equal; it is instead whether this desire for more [i.e., competition] is allowed free play in the economy.[3]

Other thinkers, beginning with notions of grace and gift, attempt to rethink an economy based not upon agonistic tension but upon giving and donation.[4] Both views, the expressly critical and the reconstructive, offer much-needed perspectives on ways to rethink our economic situation apart from scarcity and competition. For my part, I want to redefine these notions from the perspective of land's subjectivity.

To say, as I have, that excess appears through finite features is to say also that excess appears in some sense through scarcity. This is because specific finite features are those which pertain to certain advantages for production that cannot be found everywhere. However, understanding the relation of excess to the finite is complicated by the so-called empirical fact about scarcity. This fact usually involves the observation that land and nature are finitely limited by area and what they can provide. Thus with growth of the population, competition for land and natural resources becomes much more intense. However, this empirical fact should not be taken as necessarily accurate. In particular, it should not be confused with the assertion that the world is overpopulated per se and by implication that there is not enough land available to meet the needs of the current population. It is important to bear in mind that scarcity is often perspectival,[5] and that the real problem may be in our interpretation of a current state of affairs.

If this is case, then the perception of scarcity is based on the availability of land, not in nature, but as perceived within the framework of social practices. In other words, scarcity is represented (or reproduced) through social practices. Where land is abundant and yet limited in access by a few members of the population, the availability of resources will not meet the requirements of the majority.[6] Thus overpopulation can itself appear to be an empirical "fact" due to the way access to a finite entity is limited or controlled. Indeed, recalling the island of the shipwrecked from chapter 6, if one person owned the entire island and could enforce this ownership, any remaining number of people, be it one or one hundred, would find themselves in a world that was overpopulated—that is, in a world unable to meet the needs of subsistence. Or consider how in a land-enclosed society, the incentive of landowners is to increase the value of their land. Population concentration in urban areas often appears in two guises—density and expansion. By "density" I mean the vertical increase of people in a given area. Privatization of ground rent encourages to a large degree vertical development so that more people can be housed in a given area and thus more rent can be captured per plot. By "expansion" I mean the horizontal increase of people settling in outlying areas. The implementation of a property tax (or a tax on real improvements) encourages horizontal expansion where land is available. This is because the incentive is to pay less tax for adding to a site and instead to develop a new plot of land.[7]

In both instances, the population of the urban center is concentrated such that the overall effect is an increase in land values. To be sure, in the instance of horizontal expansion there is a lag in the land market until speculators and realtors can assure themselves of interest in the available, outlying land. It goes without saying that urban centers provide more opportunity for wage earning. And while this opportunity is paramount to those seeking a living, it cannot be ignored how wages are not unrelated to land value. Notice how without wages, there is no one to pay the rent. Wages can be said to determine the accessibility of land to the extent that the rental market will keep its rates as a high as possible so long as laborers can manage rental payments.[8] And laborers barely able to meet subsistence find the easiest way to meet these payments is by sharing the cost of renting with others. So while wages are important, they are accepted on the basis of being able to meet the cost of having access to land. Population growth, whether by increase in density or by expansion, is determined by wages at one level but more totally by access to land.[9]

I mention these points not to dismiss concerns about population growth but to bring to our attention yet another way in which the phenomenology of land may provide a different, constructive perspective. Scarcity of land is not the problem per se but how we relate to it in terms of use and ownership. This way of describing the problem does not make it any less grave since scarcity is still experienced. Yet it does allow a different diagnosis. The experience of scarcity results from the land being made less available, that is, held out of use for production. As we saw in chapter 1, the potential for future rents translates directly into the desire to own a particular plot of land. As we saw in chapter 6, the seasoned speculator knows very well that the less land is made available in a vicinity, the more the value of land will generally rise. So capturing future rents leads ironically to keeping the land from those uses that might produce these rents. George notes the physical and psychological effects well when discussing how an inimical pressure is put on those seeking to use land that ultimately perpetuates itself. He considers an example of a farmer seeking land:

> [The margin of cultivation] is forced so much farther than he otherwise need have gone, by the speculation which is holding these unused lands in expectation of increased value in the future. And when he settles, he will, in his turn, take up, if he can, more land than he can use, in the belief that it will soon become valuable; and so those who follow him

> are again forced farther on than the necessities of production require, carrying the margin of production to still less productive, because still more remote points.[10]

The fierce permutations of competition are, of course, part and parcel of this relation to scarcity. Competition need not be an all-out confrontation. It can take the guise of market frenzies, of ideologies in which benefit is presented as a limited opportunity that requires financial sacrifice (e.g., a high-interest loan), or perhaps the ambiguous instance when a large retail chain first claims it has bought vast amounts of land with a view to future expansion but then decides to build houses on these plots for profit.[11] Needless to say, for most the prospect of owning land is the competitive game in which borrowing against future wages is its ante.

Yet, what if excess were not alienable? How would this affect our relation to scarcity and how might it transform the notion of competition? One might be tempted to think that prohibiting private ownership of land and its finite features is the only option. This is not necessarily the case. Because excess commutes into value form, one need only prohibit the private consumption of this value.

The Excess of Land as a Source of Taxation

Before discussing what I mean by "tax" more specifically, I want to begin with what I think is a key assumption in its conception. Anything referred to as a tax means that whatever is the subject of this tax is recognized as belonging to the public. Thus debates over taxes usually take issue with what is rightfully public or private. So in saying ground rent is a source of taxation, I am saying it should be seen as belonging to the public. At first glance, this thesis may seem inconsistent with my claims that land is ontologically prior to human dwelling. But in recalling my attempt to mediate Veblen's thesis on the role of human knowledge, the importance of the distinction between the ontological and the economic becomes apparent. It is this: ground rent can be seen to belong to the public at the economic level. This does not make obsolete the phenomenological thesis about the subjectivity of land.

The previous section has examined how the excess of land manifests in and through its finite features, and moreover, how these finite features give rise to ground rent, and here is the key to my mediation of Veblen's thesis, *when the human community recognizes these features in terms of specific projects and possibilities.* So while the originality of land's grant for possibilities of being remains foundational, we see at the human level of activity a manner of engaging with this grant such that it takes on what I have been calling ever-differentiated finite forms. Indeed, it is the correlation between phenomenology and economics that allows us to do so. Where at the phenomenological level excess is the grant of land, at the economic level excess is translated into ground rent by way of human involvement. The originality of land still remains; it has simply come into relation with another, and by virtue of this, expressed itself uniquely according to this relation as ground rent.

There are at least two consequences of this unique translation. The first is really a clarification of how the human community, and not human individuals, is required in the production of ground rent. This point only emphasizes Veblen's argument about the role of technological knowledge as historically and communally constructed. Notice the prevalence of common stock that Veblen sees as enabling individuals to pursue their own projects:

> As the common stock of technological knowledge increases in volume, range, and efficiency, the material equipment whereby this knowledge of ways and means is put into effect grows greater, more considerable relatively to the capacity of the individual.[12]

As that which results from the application of this knowledge to land, ground rent is no exception. George thus argues in distinction to the original position that land occupies in his theory,

> Consider what rent is. . . . It is due to nothing that the land owners have done. It represents a value created by the whole community. . . . Rent, the creation of the whole community, necessarily belongs to the whole community.[13]

To reiterate, we see the advantage of the correlative thesis in that it can maintain, on the one hand, claims to land's ontological priority; and on the other hand, the essential role of human knowledge and action in translating land's excess into finite value form.

The second consequence involves the designation of the human community as that which must take accountability for the kind of excess it has brought about, or what I envisage as being fulfilled when seeing ground rent as a tax. The tax serves a decisive role in addressing a philosophical problem concerning the translation of excess into finite value form. This is simply to point out that the finite form (as finite) cannot be commuted back into its original state. It is materially impossible to return the surplus value to its source because it has taken expression in value form. Yet given that ground rent arises from the relation of the community to land, it is entirely consistent to say that public deliberation can identify the ways in which the application of the value form can be invested. In other words, taxation of ground rent offers a finite way in which the finite value form might be returned in some sense to its source. And it can then be said the dilemma of the excess is this: the community that benefits from land's excess then assumes the responsibility of best using the excess in view of the original relation to land.

This view assumes quite a substantial link between a tax and public deliberation as well as the capacity of public deliberation to recognize the source of its viability. So let me say more about my assumptions. I do not accept the view that taxes are per se a form of confiscation, as right-libertarian thinkers would aver.[14] Influenced primarily by the work of Liam Murphy, Thomas Nagel, Jeremy Waldron, and Lewis Hyde on the matter of ownership and what might be rightfully one's own,[15] I cannot conceive of a community in which some form of debt to the past accomplishments of others is absent. A tax (direct or indirect) is, on this view, a way of accounting for this debt. It asks of individuals and groups in a community to recognize that their livelihood has been made possible by the work of others. Tax expresses a practical relation: the idea that individuals can persist in existence by themselves without the benefit of an already given social structure is an impossibility. As we have seen, the force of my phenomenological claims is that the given social structures are really indebted to land, and therefore, that the "first" tax should attempt to account for this. The finite expression of excess in terms of ground rent provides precisely a manner of acknowledging this debt.

To get a sense of why, let us contrast a tax on ground rent with the negative conception of tax as penalty or confiscation. Putting aside questions of what constitutes entitlement and desert, most taxes practiced today tend to act like penalties: income tax is a direct penalty for working; property tax is an indirect penalty for making improvements; sales tax is an indirect penalty for purchasing. In view of these problems, George formulates a hypothesis:

> The best tax by which public revenues can be raised is evidently that which will closest conform to the following conditions:
>
> 1. That it bear as lightly as possible upon production—so as least to check the increase of the general fund from which taxes must be paid and the community maintained.
> 2. That it be easily and cheaply collected, and fall as directly as may be upon the ultimate payers—so as to take from the people as little as possible in addition to what it yields the government.

3. That it be certain—so as to give the least opportunity for tyranny or corruption on the part of officials, and the least temptation to law-breaking and evasion on the part of the taxpayers.
4. That it bear equally—so as to give no citizen an advantage or put any at a disadvantage, as compared with others.[16]

As the reader will have no doubt anticipated, a tax on ground rent meets these conditions.

This is because (1) ground rent is not the outcome of labor but of some perceived or actual advantage provided by land; so its collection does not affect the actual production of value, or the returns to labor and capital. Moreover, the fact that it can be reinvested into the community means it can help the development of the general polity. (2) The amount of land one uses cannot be hidden since use of land is held by title as a matter of public record. (3) Assuming the previous point to be correct, the paths by which corruption can conceal itself on balance sheets and ledgers are limited. And (4), if the surplus arises from land, taxing it is not a penalty except for the landowner, and even this point is disputable (I will address this in a later section). A tax on ground rent is, in George's analysis, not a penalty at all.[17] It is a manner of accounting for the source that makes possible our human existence and how this source manifests in and through our relation to it. Tideman argues that it is perhaps misleading to characterize the collection of ground rent as a tax since ground rent is a distinct value that originally has no possessive tie to laborer or landlord.[18] But despite this cogent point, the advantage of describing it as a tax has an advantage. It is overtly linked to the public realm in the form of revenue for investment.

I admit that I am assuming that by default for something to be a source of public investment entails public participation in a deliberative capacity. Following Arendt's account of speech as that which comprises the public realm—"With word and deed we insert ourselves into the human world"[19]—I am assuming that the public arena of debate is one in which deliberation informs the investment of public funds. If the tax on ground rent were genuinely linked to an appreciation of land, I believe a variety of public institutions and governments could flourish.[20] What I think to be the more philosophically problematic issue is why a tax of this kind would invoke public interest and dialogue to the degree that there would exist the cohesion and communication—dare I say commerce?—that Arendt keenly notes.

If ground rent is defined as a surplus arising from land and the human interaction with it, a tax on it would then be a kind of inheritance resulting from the human inhabitation of the land. Tax would take on a symbolic dimension expressing a debt that might call to mind further reflection on the source that has provided for us. Furthermore, the link to deliberation would involve the possible recognition that inheritance should be used to return the value to its source by perpetuating a manner of inhabiting that remembers its relation to the source. To recall Foltz's clarification of *Schohnen* in Heidegger's thought,[21] the tax allows a community to conserve (keep) itself and the land. The essential point is the recognition that the use of funds is more than strictly economic. Philip Goodchild speaks of this in terms of what he describes as the economic problem of attention and credit:

> How is wealth, the benefits accrued through cooperation achieved through the pledging of flesh and blood to be distributed? What is worthy of credit and investment, in other words: the pledging of time, attention and devotion or the pledging of flesh and blood?[22]

Economic production involves more than its models can account for in terms of time and value because production is always a function of how a community can persist in its effort and desire to be, or what Goodchild captures vividly by the terms "flesh and blood." With the stakes of attention and credit raised to that of expressing a debt to land and the community, matters of investment assume a philosophical depth and public breadth that I think would be infectious. Its gravity, in other words, would attract by virtue of involving the allure of an excess to be spent and not a necessity compelling participation by threat or fiat. Arendt therefore observes,

> This insertion [into the public realm] is not forced upon us by necessity, like labor, and it is not prompted by utility, like work. It may be stimulated by the presence of others whose company we may wish to join, but it is never conditioned by them; its impulse springs from the beginning which came into the world when we were born and to which we respond by beginning something new on our own initiative.[23]

As a concern for pubic deliberation, the tax on ground rent might then act as a source for new beginnings for others, and the subjectivity of land can be said to persist.

Unfortunately, criticisms concerning the practical viability of a tax on ground rent have successfully curtailed further consideration of its philosophical meanings. I hope that this study, by beginning with the philosophical, has at least shown practical criticisms to be limited insofar as they assume a meaning of land that is highly questionable. In any event, practical questions do need to be addressed. And on this matter,

George has been misunderstood on several fronts. As these issues inevitably concern economic analyses, I cannot competently discuss their substance. And others have already done so.[24] So in the next three sections, I want to treat general questions relating to ownership of land, estimation of the tax, and collection of the tax.

What Does This Mean for Ownership of Land?

I will leave aside distinctions involving legal conceptions of ownership and speak instead of a general view of what might be entailed in our use of land. On the one hand, a tax on ground rent does not entail a system in which there is no individual ownership of land. On the other hand, neither does it mean that the typical convention of private ownership prevails. What arises is a substantial conceptual clarification: land can be privately *possessed* but not owned, if ownership involves exclusive rights to title, use, and profit in perpetuity. Possession is a temporary right of use with its duration restricted by the fee of access one pays. Tideman clarifies: "Like rental, a system of private possession of land involves an obligation to make regular payments to the government for the use of land."[25] Perpetuity of use is allowed so long as a rental fee is paid. This rental fee, as one might guess, is the tax on ground rent. Let us see the ramifications of this in more detail.

If a fee is required for use of land, this means use acts as the main determining factor. One would not pay a fee if one did not intend to use the land, whether one were a potential user or one to whom land might be transferred. In some significant respect the tax on ground rent forces a person using the land to make a decision as to whether he or she will continue to do so. The incentive is to use land for production because one will be liable for the tax on ground rent regardless of use or nonuse. (In cases of land used for residence, the fee paid would have to be covered by one's earnings or pension.) Nonuse of land is a cost one must be willing to pay. For example, for the farmer who lets the land lie fallow, nonuse of land often figures into the farmer's calculations of production over all his or her lands according to an extended period of time in which crops can be rotated. Indeed, similar uses of land in the vicinity would arguably take this into account in the determination of ground rent. Imagine adjacent land so rich that it need not lie fallow. Its rent would be much greater than its inferior neighbor. In contrast to current conventions of landownership, this type of property right is often referred to under the general term "usufruct."[26]

Nonetheless, proponents of ownership argue on moral grounds that a tax on ground rent disadvantages landowners. Plots of land were originally bought with exclusivity and perpetuity of title in mind, and to take this away, even if by democratic changes in the law, is to cause financial loss and perhaps, in some rare instances, to take away a sole means of livelihood. There is a short and a long reply to this objection.

The short reply emphasizes the clarification that land is not confiscated, just the surplus value it generates. If landowners object to this reply because the title to land includes ownership of this profit, then their initial argument should be modified to say that a tax on ground rent disadvantages landowners where the intention to own land is with a view to capturing a surplus value they do not create. This admission weakens their appeal unless they attempt to invoke neoclassical idioms, to recall Gaffney, and claim ground rent to really be like the returns to capital. But this study, I hope, has made this claim unconvincing.

The long reply involves a moral counterargument showing how landowning results in a form of slavery. As mentioned above, the disadvantage claimed by landowners is a right to profit created by others. But this is not all. As I indicated in chapter 6, because exclusivity of ownership denies access to land, and because speculation on land values often involves withholding land from use in order to increase its value, the livelihood of others is held hostage by landowners seeking to gain from withholding land from use. George is therefore not shy in his rhetoric:

> If chattel slavery be unjust, then is private property in land unjust. For let the circumstances be what they may—the ownership of land will always give the ownership of men, to a degree measured by the necessity (real or artificial) for the use of land. This is but a statement in different form of the law of rent.[27]

We have seen just as much if our example of the island of the shipwreck is accurate. George is so firm on this point that he argues against compensation to landowners, since in effect this would be compensating them for a recognized evil. It would also mean paying them the future rents from public funds, which is to say that the public would pay for their compensation by means of taxation.[28] Other economists, such as Fred Foldvary, have proposed a graduated transition to a ground rent tax to allow for landowners to adjust.[29] Whatever the case may be, the matter is undeniably complex and involves more than moral and economic issues; for it raises questions about historically sedimented practices and the role that collective forgiveness plays in issues of distributive justice, something that Aristotle names in a single word, *epeikeia.*

Let me conclude this section by making clear how this notion of possession correlates with the phenomenological domain. Just as the sense of one's own existence (mineness) was shown not to be one's own, so the possession of land is understood as being possible because land gives itself. Both mineness and possession are therefore not claims to ownership, but a manner of relinquishing a privative attitude: to lose oneself in order to be more.

How Is the Tax Estimated?

Simply put, the taxed amount is estimated as the ground rent of a plot of *unimproved* land—that is, land less the improvements made to it—or what is the estimated future surplus generated by unimproved land were it to be put into use.[30] As I have discussed, the estimation of ground rent is really how we see the value of land. To pay a fee for access to land is to estimate that future returns will meet or exceed its value. Hence, the identity between ground rent and land value has its basis in the desire to obtain access to land. Notice how this distinction breaks with typical assumptions that improvements made to land entitle the laborer to its ownership. Such capital improvements can be effectively bracketed out when determining the ground rent. While improvements affect land used for agriculture but not manufacturing, urban development, and residential construction, the essential point is that land value is itself distinct and separate from the value of improvements. This is not to say, of course, that there are no instances in which this distinction is complicated. For example, restrictions placed upon improvements—such as historical conservation—may cause the value of land to decrease since there is not much flexibility in how that land can be used.[31]

Much is debated, even by economists in favor of a ground rent tax, as to how to estimate ground rent in terms of unimproved land value. One of the common allegations is that the distinction between land and improvements is not calculable with any certainty. But I am not sure how or why it needs to be unless one persists under the illusion that economics is in some sense a pure science providing a certainty of values.[32] In lieu of this, there is an existing practice in which land values are determined, and that of course is used in the real estate market. Values are based upon speculation as to what potential buyers will pay to gain access to a plot of land. This value only need be adjusted to account for the land less its improvements. Foldvary argues that

> professional real estate appraisers routinely separate a site's ground value and the improvement's value. This separation is typically required

> for fire insurance. Banks for mortgages also commonly require it. These parties estimate site value as a residual after the replacement cost of buildings, adjusted for depreciation. This process is combined with computerized contour mapping of site value per square meter, based on actual land-sale and lease data. The computerized mapping works to smooth out the assessments, and can be done to emphasize long-term trends rather than year-by-year fluctuations in land values (as is done today with the assessment of property-tax).[33]

This process of evaluation has the merit of being flexible according to increases or decreases in the need and desire for land. But it also brings to light how an existing community can increase the value of unimproved land. In other words, it would be a mistake to think "unimproved" refers to a plot of land as it might exist in a state of nature. It simply means a plot as it exists in situ historically. So a bare piece of land may increase in value because the surrounding land is developed into a neighborhood with desirable services and amenities. Its value may also go up because years later the type of people forming the neighborhood give it a certain social prestige.

Let us then assume the tax can be estimated. Would it be a sufficient source of public revenue? It is important to bear in mind a distinction. Proponents of a "single tax" are those who claim only one kind of tax is necessary to levy on the public. George was in fact a proponent of a tax on ground rent as a single tax because he thought it would be a sufficient form of public revenue by itself given its lack of significant transaction costs, its resistance to corruption, and its potential beneficial effects on social and economic development.[34] Tideman argues that a tax on ground rent would likely not be sufficient by itself but would nonetheless be a significant source of funding.[35] It could certainly be substituted for direct forms of taxation which tend to be felt the hardest by individuals. Whatever the case may be, a tax on ground rent does not entail an argument that it be the only form of taxation.

Another version of the sufficiency question draws on the obsolescence of the doctrine of ground rent in a technologically advancing society. Critics often point out that the doctrine of ground rent was formulated at a time when the economy depended largely on agriculture. As I noted in chapter 1, ground rent applies to all lands, whether used in agriculture, manufacturing, or residence. A more recent reformulation of this challenge involves virtual transactions where the bulk of the provision of services and products occurs via the Internet or has to do increasingly with immaterial goods mediated by the Internet. However, as long as we remain fundamentally dependent on land under finite conditions, ground rent will always emerge. Jürgen Backhaus therefore argues that the variety of networks (i.e., mobile communication, transportation, utilities) require access to land in order for them to be operative and cannot be exempted from the type of land-based economic system George describes.[36]

Also, it cannot be forgotten that eventually the returns to production are returns to forms of dwelling on the land. One may gain one's livelihood through something like Internet gambling, perhaps betting on nonmaterial transactions or events; however, these earnings do not remain virtual. They are used and invested. The more wealth returns to a community in the form of spending, the more lucrative landed businesses become. As I argued above, this results in the increase of land values used for other activities. It may eventually return to the gambler's home or even the land the gambling provider uses to conduct its business. Does the professional trading in the derivatives market not wish to buy property, perhaps in exclusive areas? seek an increase to his or her standard of living? in short, seek new possibilities for dwelling on the land?

How Is the Tax Collected?

The issue of collection is often raised by critics who prefer a less centralized government or those misunderstanding that George's theory necessitates the nationalization of land. Quite simply put, the collection of the tax would involve a public agency but to a degree less complex than current home revenue agencies. It is important to bear in mind that the transaction costs normally associated with the collection of money for the public is likely to be much lower. This has mainly to do with the object of the tax. As George points out above, the amount of land one is using cannot be concealed, and there is only need for the estimation of the value of the land itself, not records of years of income, sales, and other associated transactions.

Scarcity and Competition Revisited

I suggested from the outset that the phenomenological account of land is necessary because conceptual prejudices have prevented us from understanding the genuine ontological basis of the economy. This means as well that various economic terms and their meanings might be distorted. If conventional economic thought sees scarcity as a fact of our existence, the correlation between phenomenology and economics has attempted instead to see how excess manifests finitely such that our relation to these finite conditions is determined by how we perceive scarcity. This is to say that what appears limited is not. And in some sense, the condition of scarcity is excess *being* finite.

To recount the comments in the groundwork provided in the first section of this chapter: the essence of finiteness is not a condition of lack but a productive absence. What is absent but the unqualified presence of abundance, of land that can produce without qualification to its features? What then is required of us but to see how the conditions of land's finite manifestation can be used such that its excess can be affirmed? It is the role of gravity to ensure that we feel the force of our dependence on land, and this, as Heidegger's thought has helped us to see, involves responding in an appropriate fashion. One can thus say that our relation to the excess, to land's abundant provision, is mediated by the finite.

We can now return full circle to the claim that scarcity is often interpretive. The interpretive aspect now figures fundamentally, not simply to emphasize the perspectival constituency of it, but to show how the perception of scarcity is a prompt, or perhaps even a provocation. It asks us to question whether our current relation to things has caused the emergence of scarcity. Does our current practice of allowing ground rent to be claimed privately create an inaccessibility of land? We can answer this by turning to the manner in which competition manifests in relation to this practice.

Because the incentive to own land to make a profit from its value becomes economically counterproductive, the tax on ground rent means that competition for land, whether in calculated and deliberate attempts at speculation or in the efforts to get on the property ladder, would cease to exist. Land would no longer be a commodity, no longer an asset, no longer an item whose purpose was to pass on to others for a profit. For however much land one wanted to grab, there would be a cost as long as ground rent was generated. It is true, of course, that as far as laboring is concerned, not everyone needs to possess their own plot and instead can work for another who does. This, however, does not diminish the fact that in the majority of businesses under the current system of ownership, the fee paid to have access to the land is a substantial cost. There are thus two potential, beneficial effects of the tax to note. First, because a tax on ground rent reduces competition for ownership of land, it reduces the artificially high values of land (caused by a misrelation to scarcity). Second, this means profit and wages would be higher.

To recall from chapter 6, in a system where land is privately owned, any return to wages and profits tends to increase rents and land values. The more one earns, the more the speculator will be tempted to raise prices. As long as someone is willing to pay the higher price, the landlord need not lower rents. Hence, even in recessions, land values remain high under the expectation that there is someone still willing and able to pay the prices set. George therefore observes, "The confident expectation of increased prices [of land] produces, to a greater or lesser extent, the effects of a combination among landholders, and tends to the withholding of land from use."[37] Recall that because most governments do not penalize landowners for unused or vacant land (and just the opposite, for making improvements to the land, or what is a property tax), landowners are not adversely affected by recessions. Production in a recession typically remains low, yet if unused or vacant land is available only at a high cost, the overall inaccessibility of land in a region only increases the demand for it. Land values can then remain artificially high.

But can a case be made that "free market competition" can compensate in some way for the problems of private ownership that I have indicated? Tideman points out that competition for land in a free market often results in a "winner's curse"[38] where one obtains land at a price that exceeds its actual value. This is because competition often involves purchasing without perfect knowledge. With land, this knowledge usually fails to account for the sufficiency of its future returns. Hence, one might be tempted to take out a high-interest loan to buy a plot of land and later lack the financial resources to maintain payments. Competition of this sort may provide lucrative investments for individuals for a while, but its inevitable result is a collapse of the land market when a significant percentage of purchasers cannot make good on their loan payments. Suffice it to say, competition of this kind is not possible under a tax on ground rent because there is no gain to be made from speculating on a value that cannot be privately consumed. And what remains but the excess—that is, to invoke Arendt once more, the plurality of individuals can be articulated as a new beginning. We should then not fear excess as a form of economic surplus we can spend only through means of competition and violence, as Bataille might have us believe, but as a value expressive of what is given by the ongoing event when both land and a community come together. What is this event of coming together if not a manner of being appropriated by land, an event made possible by the simultaneous splendor of its excess and the force of its gravity?

Conclusion

What Land in View?

> The sun waits for no man and was sinking lower and lower. "Oh," he wondered, "have I blundered, trying to take too much?"
>
> —Pahom, from Tolstoy's story "How Much Land Does a Man Need?"[1]

We return to Pahom. His last thoughts indicate a recognition of his plight, but to what extent? In the introduction I stated that Tolstoy's story was not about over-acquisitiveness, but about our misunderstanding of land as a source of life and of how our practices of land use develop from this misunderstanding. Consequently, Pahom's problem cannot be one of merely taking too much. It is the presumption that land can be acquired in order to own it and its ground rent exclusively. In other words, the problem is acquisitiveness of land as such.

Thus more strongly, if one is to adhere to this reading of the story, it means that even if Pahom had taken less land, his demise would be inevitable—perhaps not on that day, but soon enough. Is this reading still tenable? The ending to the story is not equivocal. It is important to note that Pahom's last thoughts are prompted by the threat of death—"have I blundered, trying to take too much?" Pahom therefore seeks to understand what might have prevented his situation. But any alternate ending that might avoid his demise would be impossible, yet not because having been given another chance he would have failed to take less land. Rather, the impossibility persists precisely because those conventions encouraging and justifying the acquisition of land as an acceptable means to livelihood result in social practices that create life-and-death situations. I have attempted to argue why this relation is so in terms of the kind of fundamental access that land provides and how privation of this access, which occurs mostly by captivation of land's ground rent, is inimical to our individual and social being. So even if Pahom would have acquired less land, in any possible world where landowning is a convention of exclusive ownership, tragic consequences would inevitably arise—whether these are in the form of economic recession, social strain, individual incapacitization, or privation of land from others.

So Pahom's tragedy is marked not by the measure of land he has taken but by the reversal of a relationship: land as the source of life becomes the source of death. This coincidence comes to final expression the moment Pahom dies, which is also the moment the elder, who proposed the contest, thinks he has succeeded. "Oh, well done!" exclaimed the elder. "That's a lot of land you've earned yourself!"[2]

So we return to land. I have argued that a view of land that appropriately recognizes its subjectivity, as opposed to its being an object, can only be established according to philosophical thought. And it is, more precisely speaking, phenomenology that allows us to take land and human existence together in order to see how the latter is ontologically and existentially dependent on the former. Yet while philosophical investigation may provide the conceptual means by which we can think our possibilities for being in new ways, the state of our practical existence is often what blocks such changes from being fully actualized, that is, as part of the life-world. Fore-structures, disciplines of power, modes of production, mundane reiteration, bad faith, loss of capabilities . . . attest to a kind of preeminence that the practical plane of existence has over the profoundest philosophical insights. There are perhaps many different, effective ways to confront or resist whatever distortions are occurring on the practical plane. By means of correlating, and not reducing, economics to phenomenology, I have proposed that rethinking the way ground rent operates and should be collected and consumed provides a way of remembering, on this plane, what it means to be subject to land. If life, existentially conceived, relies on the reproduction of those conditions allowing us to be, what mode of our existence can reproduce life, can reproduce those existential conditions we take as given?

That something like economic production cannot be thought according to a type of memory that attempts to constantly recall the basis for existing, attests to an incoherence that is not so easily blamed on the impermeable boundaries of professional and theoretical specializations. Nor do I think one can argue the world is too complex to expect a coincidence between existential meanings and economic values. I have attempted to show how this incoherence exists by virtue of the ways in which we misconceive land. In closing, I want to say there is a simplicity to the philosophical and economic theses I have proposed, a simplicity whose strength lies in how it connects the seemingly complex nature of economic activity to a basic observation and wager about our manner of existing that can be observed by anyone. And while I wish to avow the cogency and coherence of my arguments according to the limits of the study I have set, there can be little doubt that the questions arising consequent to my claims will be of those kinds seeking to provide further verification and debate according to professional and theoretical specialisms.

But those questions, far from being a distraction, are a start; and one that is entirely different from the one Pahom undertakes. It is, I would like to believe, an opening onto a new terrain of philosophical inquiry that returns us to the land as much as it calls on other disciplines, fields, and forms of life to think the significance of our being-landed in many ways.

Notes

Introduction

1. Leo Tolstoy, *How Much Land*, 97.

2. Tolstoy's interest in land reform and the economics of Henry George are well known. See, for example, Kenneth Wenzer, *An Anthology of Tolstoy's Spiritual Economics.*

3. J. S. Mill, *Principles of Political Economy*, 412. See David Ricardo, *Principles of Political Economy*, 45–57.

4. Robert Heilbroner, *The Worldly Philosophers*, 191.

5. Stephen Kresge and Leif Wenar, *Hayek on Hayek*, 63. For a discussion of Hayek's misunderstanding of Henry George, see Fred Harrison, *Ricardo's Law*, 236–37.

6. Paul Krugman, *The Accidental Theorist*, 114 and 115, respectively.

7. Amartya Sen, *Commodities and Capabilities*, 3: "What is objectionable in the economic theorizing that identifies widely different concepts of self-interest, motivations, etc., is not that fact of simplification itself, but the particular simplification chosen, which has the effect of taking a very narrow view of human beings."

8. R. G. Collingwood, "Economics as a Philosophical Science," 162. For the logical priority of presuppositions, see Collingwood, *An Essay in Metaphysics*, 21–48.

9. Martin Heidegger, "On the Essence of Ground," in *Pathmarks*, 105.

10. Michael Foucault, *The Order of Things*; and Philip Mirowski, *More Heat Than Light.*

11. Friedrich Nietzsche, *Untimely Meditations*, 75.

12. Foucault, *The Order of Things*, xxiii.

13. Kenneth Westphal, "Do Kant's Principles Justify Property or Usufruct?" §1.5.

14. Heidegger, *The Basic Problems of Phenomenology*, 130.

15. Paul Ricoeur, *Hermeneutics and Human Sciences*, 117. By the phrase "critical interpretation," I mean to capture the entire arc of interpretation of which Ricoeur speaks in order to provide hermeneutics with a critical function vis-à-vis the critique of ideology; ibid., 91–100.

16. Heidegger, *Being and Time*, §6. References to *Being and Time*, when referring to page numbers, will indicate the pagination of the English translation followed by the pagination in the 7th German edition in italics. The Macquarrie and Robinson translation is used unless otherwise indicated.

17. Ricoeur, *Hermeneutics and the Human Sciences,* 114.

18. Although outside the remit of my approach, Ricoeur also shows how phenomenology presupposes hermeneutics—namely, that any phenomenological investigation is also a mode of interpretation. Ricoeur, *Hermeneutics and the Human Sciences,* 114.

19. See, for example, Bruce Foltz, *Inhabiting the Earth,* 118–19.

20. Phenomenology can be understood as making wagers about being and reality in order to understand it anew. It may be that the different foci of other approaches are not mutually exclusive. I deal with the question of rivalry briefly in chapter 4 when discussing the topoanalyses of Edward Casey and Jeff Malpas.

21. Todd Mei, "An Economic Turn: A Hermeneutical Reinterpretation of Political Economy."

22. Paul Ricoeur, *Oneself as Another,* 22.

23. See, for example, Pierre Bourdieu's study of "symbolic capital" or Stephen Marglin's analysis of the historical development of land enclosure. The desire to control landed property presupposes the notion that such kind of property is a form of wealth; Bourdieu, *Outline of a Theory of Practice,* 174–75; and Marglin, *The Dismal Science,* 299–307. Hannah Arendt shows how this was absent in ancient times, and there was certainly the recognition that private property was not possible without the public realm; Arendt, *The Human Condition,* 61–68.

24. Todd Mei, "Economy of the Gift."

25. See, for instance, Jacques Derrida, *Given Time.* The most common criticism of gift exchange is that it creates an expectation of a counter-gift, thereby placing the recipient of the "first" gift under an obligation *and* ultimately creating an expectation of a return gift that undermines any benevolent intention of the donor. Following Ricoeur and Marcel Hénaff, I agree that an appropriate subjectivity of donation and reception can involve recognizing a gift and, within the language of phenomenology, allowing what is donated to break through or rupture our subjectivity and perception of the everyday. Gift is not only possible, but transformative.

26. Jeff Malpas, *Heidegger's Topology*; and François Raffoul, *Heidegger and the Subject.*

27. See, for example, Joanna Hodge, *Heidegger and Ethics,* 108: "The difference between Heidegger's diagnosis and the modern analytical view is that Heidegger diagnoses an end and abandonment of philosophy at work in the emergence of a split between a subjectivism, as a foundation for knowledge, and an objectivism about what there is. Human beings as subjects, becoming the foundation for knowledge, is for Heidegger a mark of the end of philosophy."

28. Hubert Dreyfus and Harrison Hall, "Introduction" to *Heidegger: A Critical Reader,* 4–5.

29. Robert Scharff, "Rorty and Analytic Heideggerian Epistemology," 498. To be sure, Scharff's criticism of the analytic-Heideggerian position is more nuanced than the complaints expressed above.

30. Scharff, "Rorty and Analytic Heideggerian Epistemology," 495.

31. See, for example, Hubert Dreyfus, "Can There Be a Better Source of

Meaning than Everyday Practices?" I do not think Dreyfus's attempt is successful. See Todd Mei, "Heidegger in the Machine."

32. My thanks to Robert Scharff for discussing matters hermeneutical with me over the years.

33. Till Düppe, *The Making of the Economy.*

34. For more on my reading of Heidegger and metaphysics, see Todd Mei, "Heidegger and the Appropriation of Metaphysics." The case for understanding overcoming metaphysics as a manner of appropriation has been stated well by Raffoul, *Heidegger and the Subject,* 138–39.

35. Tolstoy, *How Much Land,* 110.

36. See, for instance, Plato, *Republic,* 10.595b. While not mentioning *adunamia,* the lack of capacity is a constant theme in the *Republic* and is linked to the start of the dialogue when Socrates is held against his own power and asked to respond competently to philosophical questions. For more on this, see John Sallis, *Being and Logos,* 312–29.

Chapter 1

1. See also Michel Foucault, *Archaeology of Knowledge,* 129–30.

2. See especially his assessment of more recent economic theories which try to avoid formalism; Düppe, *The Making of the Economy,* 183–205. See also Serhat Kologlugil, "Michel Foucault's Archaeology of Knowledge," 19–20; and Guus Dix, "Ricardo's Discursive Demarcations."

3. For a history of theories of rent, see Jayati Ghosh, "Differential and Absolute Rent"; and Nicolaus Tideman, "The Economics of Efficient Taxes on Land," 105–21.

4. For example, Foucault confuses rent as a fee and rent as a surplus when arguing that "ground rent is the effect, not of a prolific nature, but of avarice of the land"; Foucault, *The Order of Things,* 281. As I argue in the next chapter, rent does not result from land monopoly; it would obtain given the conditions Ricardo cites regardless of private or collective ownership. As I will argue below, Margaret Schabas (this chapter, note 48) also seems to be involved in this confusion.

5. See, respectively, Guy Routh, *The Origin of Economic Ideas,* 38, 63–68, 71–72.

6. Jürg Niehans, *A History of Economic Theory,* 104–5. Henry George observes that according to John McCulloch the doctrine of rent was first stated by James Anderson in 1777 and later by Edward West, Thomas Malthus, and Ricardo. See George, *Progress and Poverty,* 168; see also Jürg Niehans, *A History of Economic Theory,* 77; and Keith Tribe, *Land, Labour and Economic Discourse,* 119. It is certainly present in Petty, *A Treatise of Taxes and Contributions,* 24–25: "I say, that when this man hath subducted his seed out of the proceed of his Harvest, and also, what himself hath both eaten and given to others in exchange for Clothes, and other Natural necessaries; that the remainder of Corn, is the natural and true Rent of the Land for that year; and the medium of seven years, or rather of so many years

as makes up the Cycle, within which Dearths and Plenties make their revolution, doth give the ordinary Rent of the Land in Corn."

7. Tribe, *Land, Labour and Economic Discourse.* This discontinuity is not strictly chronological as feudal practices overlap with the classical period.

8. Tribe, *Land, Labour and Economic Discourse,* 145.

9. Ibid., 26, 113.

10. Marglin, *The Dismal Science,* 81–87.

11. Tribe, *Land, Labour and Economic Discourse,* 58–59. See also Max Weber, *The Protestant Ethic,* 59.

12. In view of rational choice and its representation of the human being, see Elizabeth Anderson, *Value in Ethics.*

13. Compare Karl Polanyi, *The Great Transformation,* and Gunnar Myrdal, *The Political Element.*

14. Tribe, *Land, Labour and Economic Discourse,* 81–82.

15. Dotan Leshem, "Oikonomia Redefined," 44. For more on Aristotle's economic thinking and how it differs from modern conceptions of use and exchange, see Todd Mei, "The Pre-eminence of Use."

16. Tribe, *Land, Labour and Economic Discourse,* 55–56.

17. Ibid., 61–64.

18. Ibid., 72–73.

19. Ibid., 59.

20. Ibid., 78.

21. Ibid., 99.

22. Although Tribe does not explicitly allude to self-creation, I take liberty in linking his project with Foucault's thinking on self-creation as a work of art. See Foucault, *Dits et écrits,* as quoted in Gary Gutting, *Thinking the Impossible,* 72.

23. Foucault, *The Order of Things,* 384; see also Michel Foucault, *Society Must Be Defended,* 10.

24. Foucault, *The Order of Things,* 385.

25. Michel Foucault, *Essential Works,* 248, as quoted in Gutting, *Thinking the Impossible,* 34.

26. Tribe, *Land, Labour and Economic Discourse,* 160. Compare Jacques Rancière, *Dissensus,* 92.

27. Foucault, "About the Beginning of the Hermeneutics of the Self," 181, as quoted in Jeremy Carrette, *Religion and Critical Psychology,* 28.

28. This reservation has been also expressed from a different methodological perspective. See, for instance, Harriet Friedmann, "Household Production."

29. Tribe, *Land, Labour and Economic Discourse,* 113 and 159, respectively.

30. Peter Benson and Stuart Kirsch, "Capitalism and the Politics of Resignation," 460.

31. Tribe, *Land, Labour and Economic Discourse,* 160.

32. Foucault, *The Order of Things,* xxiii.

33. Gutting notes how this changes in the texts of the 1970s with Foucault's interest in "an ethics of self-creation"; Gutting, *Thinking the Impossible,* 141–44.

34. Alasdair MacIntyre, *Three Rival Versions,* 55. I am here assuming that

archaeology and genealogy share in the problem MacIntyre identifies despite their differences.

35. MacIntyre, *Three Rival Versions*, 55. Axel Honneth makes a similar criticism, calling genealogy a "parasitical critical procedure, since it lives by presupposing a normative justification that it does not itself try to give"; Honneth, *Pathologies of Reason*, 48.

36. If Tribe holds to the idea that feudalism is bound up with a political and juridical hierarchy, the way in which mercantilism marries this hierarchy with economic profit acts as a possible counterexample. Perhaps mercantilism is a transition between the feudal and the classical. But this would be odd to assert since the classical thinkers saw themselves as breaking decisively from mercantilist errors and its ethos of selfish gain—the latter being the very thing for which classical economy is criticized. Compare Robert B. Eckelund and Robert D. Tollison, *Mercantilism as a Rent-Seeking Society*, 18–25.

37. See, for example, Adam Smith, *The Wealth of Nations*, 1:153.

38. Tribe, *Land, Labour and Economic Discourse*, 117.

39. Margaret Schabas therefore notes that unlike Malthus, Ricardo was much more interested in capital accumulation and profit rates in relation to the fertility of the earth; Schabas, *The Natural Origins of Economics*, 118.

40. See also Tribe, *Land, Labour and Economic Discourse*, 66.

41. See Smith, *The Wealth of Nations*, II:463.

42. Tribe, *Land, Labour and Economic Discourse*, 113.

43. For more on the breakdown of the synthesis between nature, the human being, and God, see Louis Dupré, *Passage to Modernity*.

44. Schabas, *The Natural Origins of Economics*, 41.

45. Mirowski, *More Heat Than Light*, 132.

46. Jacob Viner, *The Role of Providence in the Social Order*, 78–82; and Gunnar Myrdal, *The Political Element*, 5–6.

47. This is not to say I assume an argument against theories of natural law. Perhaps through a new critical development of natural law (see Francis Peddle, "Distributism and Marginal Productivity"), my position can be further argued. But my purpose here is only to note how the notion of gift is involved in classical thought. I will take issue in chapter 3 with the modern natural law tradition. More broadly speaking, I think any attempt to return to natural law and economics would require taking into account post-structural challenges aiming at the discursive formations of what is in fact natural versus artificial; see Dix, "Ricardo's Discursive Demarcations."

48. In this respect, my thesis is more specific than Schabas's. When substantive conceptions of nature are examined, she notes how thinkers rely on varying meanings, such as nature understood as providing immutable laws, as a providential force, or as gift. In claiming a more specific thesis, I am not assuming Schabas would agree with my argument. Certainly, there is a point of contention over the place I give to rent and my interpretation of Ricardo. Schabas appears to confuse the production of rent with the institution by which it is collected by the landlord. She sees Ricardo himself viewing rent as artificial, a meaning she does

not clarify; Schabas, *The Natural Origins of Economics,* 114–15. Use of this term seems to indicate two meanings: first, that rent is not consistent with the natural state of economic production; and second, that as artificial it is in some sense contrary and therefore unjust. However, Schabas's claim seems inconsistent; the use of inferior land in Ricardo's model is not artificial but the result of natural and actual scarcity. On my reading, Ricardo notes rent as a genuine economic phenomenon (or law) and is critical of the practice where a landlord takes rent as a fee for access to land. Taking into account a wide variety of debates, see Nancy Churchman's clarification on this matter; "David Ricardo on Public Policy," 142.

49. See also Schabas on Malthus's view of the natural causes of disasters like famine; Schabas, *The Natural Origins of Economics,* 108.

50. Henry George, *Progress and Poverty,* 38.

51. Thomas Malthus, *The Nature and Progress of Rent,* 28–29.

52. Nicholas Baudeau as quoted in Schabas, *The Natural Origins of Economics,* 45.

53. Du Pont as quoted in Weulersse as quoted in Schabas, *The Natural Origins of Economics,* 48.

54. Schabas, *The Natural Origins of Economics,* 90; see also Karl Olivecrona, "Locke's Theory of Appropriation."

55. George, *The Science of Political Economy,* 166.

56. See, for example, Smith's brief comments on the development of private property; Smith, *The Wealth of Nations,* 1:167–68.

57. Schabas, *The Natural Origins of Economics,* 114; on Ricardo's lack of emphasis on individual agency, see 119.

58. Ricardo, *Principles of Political Economy,* 52 n.1.

59. Ricardo, *Principles of Political Economy,* 48. For an analysis of the nature of Ricardo's modeling and its empirical and numerical basis, see Mary Morgan, *The World in the Model,* 56–63.

60. Ricardo, *Principles of Political Economy,* 47.

61. George, *Progress and Poverty,* 168; compare Schabas, *The Natural Origins of Economics,* 47.

62. Myrdal, *The Political Element,* 63, writes on Ricardo: "Land and rent are excluded from the theory of costs and exchange value by the assumption that the exchange value of corn is determined at the margin of cultivation where no rent is paid."

63. George, *The Science of Political Economy,* 151–52. Compare Tribe, *Land, Labour and Economic Discourse,* 85, 94.

64. Jean-Baptiste Say, *A Treatise on Political Economy,* 31.

65. Smith, *The Wealth of Nations,* I:269. See also Mill, *Principles of Political Economy,* 55: the notion that "nature lends more assistance to human endeavors in agriculture, than in manufactures" was "held by the French *Economists,* and from which Adam Smith was not free, arose from a misconception of the nature of rent."

66. Smith, *The Wealth of Nations,* 2:462, as quoted in Tribe, *Land, Labour and Economic Discourse,* 102.

67. Smith, *The Wealth of Nations*, I:268.

68. Smith, *The Wealth of Nations*, 2:463, as quoted in Ricardo, *Principles of Political Economy*, 51 n.1.

69. Richard Cantillon, *Essai sur la nature du commerce en general*, 36.

70. Mirowski, *More Heat Than Light*, 159 and 168.

71. Routh, *The Origin of Economic Ideas*, 72.

72. Smith, *The Wealth of Nations*, 1:218–19 and 4:273. See also Tribe, *Land, Labour and Economic Discourse*, 119.

73. Malthus, *The Nature and Progress of Rent*, 14–15.

74. Ricardo, *Principles of Political Economy*, 51–52, n.1.

75. Schabas, *The Natural Origins of Economics*, 121, refers to J. R. McCulloch, who dissolves the distinction between productive and unproductive use of land.

76. George, *Progress and Poverty*, 169.

77. Ibid., 170.

78. Mill, *Principles of Political Economy*, 451.

79. George, *Progress and Poverty*, 166.

80. George, *The Science of Political Economy*, 495–503.

81. Mason Gaffney, "The Role of Ground Rent," 64.

82. Peddle, "Distributism and Marginal Productivity," 318

83. Thorstein Veblen, "On the Nature of Capital," 518.

84. Ibid., 522.

85. Neil Niman, "Henry George and the Development of Thorstein Veblen's Theory of Capital"; and James Horner, "Seeking Institutionalist Signposts."

86. See Marc-André Gagnon, "Capital, Power and Knowledge According to Thorstein Veblen," 594.

87. Veblen, "On the Nature of Capital," 524. See also Thorstein Veblen, *Absentee Ownership*, 139–40.

88. Veblen, "On the Nature of Capital," 530.

89. Niman, "Henry George and the Development of Thorstein Veblen's Theory of Capital."

90. George, *Progress and Poverty*, 163.

91. Horner, "Seeking Institutionalist Signposts," 248–49.

92. George, *The Science of Political Economy*, 56 and 68.

93. Ibid., 77.

94. Ricoeur, to my knowledge, does not use the phrase exactly. He refers to an autonomy dependent on heteronomy; Ricoeur, *Oneself as Another*, 275. Boyd Blundell uses the phrase in his study of Ricoeur; *Detour and Return*, 121.

95. George, *The Science of Political Economy*, 88.

96. The incident is reported in James Thompson: "Buildings Destroyed after Rate Relief Abolished." Compare Fred Harrison on the Harry Hyams-Centre Point debacle in London; Harrison, *Power in the Land*, 84–85.

97. I exaggerate, of course. What is excluded by models is not just an issue that only approaches like genealogy and archaeology can discern. The broader issue is how models function in relation to scientific thinking and representation.

98. Collingwood, *An Essay on Metaphysics*.

Chapter 2

1. See, for example, John Bellamy Foster, *Marx's Ecology*; Luiz Barbosa, "Theories in Environmental Sociology," 28; and Jean-Paul Deléage, "Eco-Marxist Critique of Political Economy," 48, as discussed in Brett Clark and John Bellamy Foster, "Marx's Ecology in the 21st Century," 148.

2. Clark and Foster, "Marx's Ecology in the 21st Century," 166–67.

3. Paul Burkett, *Marx and Nature*, 80.

4. Paul Samuelson, "Wages and Interest," 911; compare John Milios, Dimitri Dimoulis, and George Economakis, *Karl Marx and the Classics*, 14–15; Dick Bryan, "'Natural' and 'Improved' Land in Marx's Theory of Rent," 176; and Niehans, *A History of Economic Thought*, 145. G. S. L. Tucker sees Marx as drawing more on Ricardo's method than his content, though at the same time, Marx is more "abstract" and "empirical" than Ricardo; Tucker, "Ricardo and Marx," 268–67.

5. Karl Marx and Friedrich Engels, *Collected Works*, 38:258–62, as discussed in M. C. Howard and J. E. King, "Marx, Jones, Rodbertus and the Theory of Absolute Rent," 70–83. For an analysis of Marx's relation to Smith and Ricardo prior to 1851, see Michael Evans, "Karl Marx's First Confrontations with Political Economy," 115–52.

6. David Harvey, *The Limits of Capital*, 331; compare Marx, *Capital*, 3:881.

7. Ben Fine, "On Marx's Theory of Agricultural Rent," 251; and Bryan, "'Natural' and 'Improved' Land in Marx's Theory of Rent."

8. For an overview and critical analysis of Marx and rent, see Miguel Ramirez, "Marx's Theory of Ground Rent," 71–91. Mark Blaug notes without ambiguity, "Marx's theory of absolute rent has no validity except in terms of his theory of surplus value and the resulting necessity of transforming value into prices"; Blaug, *Economic Theory in Retrospect*, 299.

9. Neoclassical commentators have implicitly done the same. See, for example, Niehans, *A History of Economic Theory*, 140–55; Samuelson, "Wages and Interest," 299. On the relation between Marx and Keynes, see Donald Winch, *Economics and Policy*, 32–33, 346–47. For a sympathetic approach to Marx, see Pat Sloan, *Marx and the Orthodox Economists*.

10. Marx, *Capital*, 3:752, where land stands for all of nature.

11. Dupré, *The Philosophical Foundations of Marxism*, 223, emphasis in original; see also Louis Dupré, *Marx's Social Critique of Culture*, 165. For my assessment of nature and necessity, see Todd Mei, *Heidegger, Work, and Being*, 15–31. This reduction therefore has ramifications in relation to how human beings can engage in a mode of existence beyond necessity, a problem relating to Marx's intention to link freedom to necessary labor without describing this freedom in terms of theoretical (i.e., nonideological) content.

12. This means Marx cannot be accused of a blind form of anthropocentrism. Much recent commentary on Marx and nature has attempted to show him to be environmentally sensitive. See, for example, Lixin Han, "Marxism and Ecology: Marx's Theory of Labour Process Revisited"; and Foster, *Marx's Ecology*.

13. Marx, *Capital*, 1:284, 638. Fowkes renders "der allgemeine Gegenstand der menschlichen Arbeit" as "the universal material for human labour."

14. Karl Marx, *Grundrisse*, 488–90.

15. Harvey, *The Limits of Capital*, 335, quoting Marx.

16. Foster, *Marx's Ecology*, 168; see also Burkett, *Marx and Nature*, 76.

17. Karl Marx, *Economic and Philosophical Manuscripts*, 107–08; emphasis in original.

18. Marx, *Capital*, 1:129.

19. Ibid., 1:126.

20. Marx, *Grundrisse*, 490. Burkett's defense of Marx against critics, who not only fail to mark the distinction between use-value and exchange value but also ignore how use-value can arise without labor ("primary appropriation" as in hunting and gathering), misses still the degree to which nature is marginalized in status; Burkett, *Marx and Nature*, 104–05.

21. Karl Marx and Friedrich Engels, *The German Ideology*, 42–43, 49.

22. Marx and Engels, *The German Ideology*, 63. I explore this in more detail in Todd Mei, *Heidegger, Work, and Being*, 26–27; Mei, "An Economic Turn," 316–19. In short, if one looks at Marx's translations of classical sources on land, one can detect his move to reduce nature to mere matter. Guglielmo Carchedi argues for the development of a Marxist theory of knowledge which can incorporate both the material and mental dimensions of production; Carchedi, *Beyond the Crisis*, 183. This thesis would seemingly overcome the problem with objectification I discuss. However, I see no reason to think Carchedi's argument is anything but a development beyond Marx's thought.

23. Marx, *Grundrisse*, 453–54; italics omitted. For the role of *Grundrisse* as an intermediary between the early and late Marx, see John E. Elliott, "The *Grundrisse* as Social Theory."

24. Marx, *Capital*, 3:772, 756.

25. Ibid., 3:752, 515. In the Fernbach translation, "sich selbst verwertenden Wert" is translated as "self-valorizing."

26. Ibid., 1:129.

27. See, for instance, Dupré, *Marx's Social Critique of Culture*, 177; Milios, Dimoulis, and Economakis, *Karl Marx and the Classics*, 18; Ernest Mandel, *Marxist Economic Theory*, 705; and Ben Fine and Alfredo Saad-Filho, *Marx's "Capital,"* 16.

28. Mirowski, *More Heat Than Light*, 180. See especially Marx where he speaks of the conservation and transference of value; Marx, *Capital*, 1:307.

29. Mirowski, *More Heat Than Light*, 182. For a summary of some of the complexities involved in assessing Marx's relation to classical value theory, see Gary Browning and Andrew Kilmister, *Critical and Post-Critical Political Economy*, 41–44.

30. Marx, *Capital*, 3:780–81.

31. Ibid., 1:317.

32. Ibid., 3:781.

33. Ibid., 3:782.

34. Ibid., 3:787. For a negative example involving how capital improvements are confused with natural fertility, see Marx, *Capital*, 3:813.

35. Ibid., 3:782; see also 3:880–81.

36. Capital is reliant on Marx's labor theory of value. Neoclassical theory

limits its conception of land as capital to the observation of how it *behaves* like capital irrespective of how its value has been generated.

37. Marx, *Capital,* 3:784.

38. Ibid., 3:756–57.

39. Harvey, *The Limits of Capital,* 337. Bryan notes an internal inconsistency when Marx attempts to collapse the distinction between natural advantage and artificial capital improvements; Bryan, "'Natural' and 'Improved' Land in Marx's Theory of Rent." In giving prevalence to labor as the creator of value, Marx marginalizes the role of land by grouping it with the material labor uses for production—that is, capital. That this move anticipates in some manner the neoclassical decision to reduce land to capital is arguable in retrospect. See Bryan, "'Natural' and 'Improved' Land in Marx's Theory of Rent," 180.

40. Marx, *Capital,* 3:786.

41. Ibid., 3:786.

42. Ibid., 3:782.

43. Ibid., 3:787.

44. Harvey, *The Limits of Capital,* 336.

45. Marx, *Capital,* 3:755. See, for example, Milios, Dimoulis, and Economakis, *Karl Marx and the Classics,* 132; and Ben Fine, "On Marx's Theory of Agricultural Rent," 249–51.

46. Marx, *Capital,* 3:755–56.

47. Ricardo, *Principles of Political Economy,* 23.

48. Ricardo, *Principles of Political Economy,* 50; and Miguel Ramirez, "Marx's Theory of Ground Rent," 73. For Ricardo's reliance on market price and how this contrasts with Marx, see Scott Meikle, "Quality and Quantity in Economics," 259.

49. George Stigler, "Ricardo and the 93% Labor Theory of Value," 366.

50. Ricardo, *Principles of Political Economy,* 279.

51. See, for example, Harvey, *The Limits of Capital,* 353–54; Fine, "On Marx's Theory of Agricultural Rent," 251; and Ramirez, "Marx's Theory of Ground Rent," 73.

52. Marx, *Capital,* 3:775. It is convenient for non-Marxists to assume the equivalence between rent and land value because they do not see a problem with both being described as exchange value. Myrdal does not see rent as equivalent to exchange value; Myrdal, *The Political Element,* 63.

53. Though Ricardo would never agree, these products are essentially the wages of labor. George argues against conventional classical thinking that wages are a cost of production; George, *Progress and Poverty,* 50–70. His theory was mathematically formalized by Philip Wicksteed; see Mason Gaffney, Fred Harrison, and Kris Feder, *The Corruption of Economics,* 64.

54. Marx, *Grundrisse,* 558.

55. Marx, *Capital,* 3:885; see also 3:889.

56. J. K. Galbraith, *The Affluent Society,* 28.

57. Marx and Engels, *Collected Works,* 41:381, as quoted in Howard and King, "Marx, Jones, Rodbertus and the Theory of Absolute Rent," 77.

58. Ricardo, *Principles of Political Economy,* 280.

59. Ibid., 279.

60. Marx, *Capital*, 3:882.

61. Ibid., 3:883–84.

62. Ibid., 3:813.

63. Ricardo, *Principles of Political Economy*, 54–57. It is worth noting that Ricardo refers to the first instance in terms of an advance that allows for a decrease in the application of capital. So a better manure, for example, would mean less use of machines to turn the soil. While his terms are not without ambiguity, both the manure and the machines are capital, as they are for Marx; *Capital*, 3:756. Ricardo seems to imply that given both types of capital, employment of the improved manure and the withdrawal of the machines reduce the cost of production.

64. Ricardo, *Principles of Political Economy*, 56.

65. Harrison, *Ricardo's Law*, 39.

66. See also Marx, *Capital*, 3:775.

Chapter 3

1. Vilfredo Pareto, *Manual of Political Economy*, 321; and Blaug, *Economic Theory in Retrospect*, 86, respectively. For a survey of economic history and attitudes toward land as a factor of production, see Christopher Ryan, "Land as a Factor of Production."

2. See Jeremy Waldron, *The Right to Private Property*, and Waldron, *The Rule of Law*; Stephen Munzer, *A Theory of Property*; and Alan Ryan, *Property*. All three have offered persuasive philosophical and legal arguments against notions of private ownership based on the right to perpetuity. All three apply their theories to problems with landownership, either directly or when turning to case law. In this chapter, I am not so much interested in a general theory of property and its application to land as much as in how land is conceived as capital on the basis of it being classified as private property.

3. *The Philosophical Imaginary* is the title of Michèle LeDoeuff's book. She uses the term differently than I intend since she is interested in the kinds of images that pervade the history of philosophy yet go unnoticed by philosophers because their task is conceived as a pure form of thought without a significant role for images in the substantial constitution of this thought. I want to adopt her general mode of inquiry which attempts to discern latent and subdued meanings ("affectivities") that sustain "the effort of philosophic production and the system of presuppositions which govern the distinction between the thinkable and unthinkable"; LeDoeuff, *The Philosophical Imaginary*, 19.

4. Charles Taylor, for example, speaks of the "social imaginary"; Taylor, *A Secular Age*, 173.

5. Mei, *Heidegger, Work, and Being*, 95–106.

6. C. B. Macpherson, *The Political Theory of Possessive Individualism.*

7. See, for example, Geoff Kennedy, "Capitalism, Contextualisation and *The Political Theory of Possessive Individualism.*"

8. For those interested in hermeneutics, I am here appealing both to the autonomy of the text and the historical responsibility this autonomy implies for

us. So if a text projects meaning beyond the intentions of its author and the original audience, it also, by way of having this historical autonomy, generates an interpretive burden—how we understand a text has ramifications.

9. Karl Polanyi, *The Great Transformation.* Having said this, I realize there are arguments demonstrating the theological foundations (explicit and implicit) in economic thinking. See, for example, Johannes Thumfart, "On Grotius's *Mare Liberum*"; Robert Nelson, *Economics as Religion*; and, more generally, John Milbank, *Theology and Social Theory.*

10. For more on this, see Mei, "Economy of the Gift."

11. Hugo Grotius, *The Freedom of the Seas* [*Mare liberum*], 1 and 5, respectively.

12. Hugo Grotius, *The Rights of War and Peace* [*De jure belli ac pacis libri tres*], II.2.ii, 420. When appropriate for some texts of Grotius, Pufendorf, and Locke, I indicate the citation as follows: book number (capitalized Roman numeral), chapter (Arabic numeral), section (lowercase Roman numeral), and page number of the edition I am using (Arabic numeral).

13. Stephen Buckle, *Natural Law,* 10–16, 35–52; and concisely John Salter, "Adam Smith and the Grotian Theory of Property," 9–12.

14. Grotius, *The Freedom of the Seas* [*Mare liberum*], 24.

15. Grotius, *The Rights of War and Peace* [*De jure belli ac pacis libri tres*], II.2.i, 420.

16. Buckle, *Natural Law,* 36–37.

17. Grotius, *The Freedom of the Seas* [*Mare liberum*], 1–2.

18. Compare Grotius, *The Rights of War and Peace* [*De jure belli ac pacis libri tres*], I.1.xii, 159.

19. Grotius, *The Rights of War and Peace* [*De jure belli ac pacis libri tres*], I.Prologue.vii, 84–85; see also the role of reason in Buckle, *Natural Law,* 24–25.

20. My use of the term (obviously distinct from Rudolf Carnap's usage) follows from how Blaug uses the term in contrast to falsification; *The Methodology of Economics,* 51. On Grotius's motives, see Jan Paul Heering, *Hugo Grotius as Apologist,* 20–21, 64–92; Thumfart, "On Grotius's *Mare Liberum*"; and Knud Haakonssen, *Natural Law and Moral Philosophy,* 29–30.

21. Buckle, *Natural Law,* 106.

22. Marcelo de Araujo, "Hugo Grotius, Moral Scepticism," 163.

23. Grotius, *The Rights of War and Peace* [*De jure belli ac pacis libri tres*], II.2.ii, 421.

24. Grotius, *The Freedom of the Seas* [*Mare liberum*], 25.

25. This is, in part, Henry George's argument for land reform in *Social Problems.*

26. Buckle, *Natural Law,* 37–39. He notes later that in the natural law tradition it was Hutcheson who equates private property with scarcity; Buckle, *Natural Law,* 225.

27. Araujo provides a detailed account of this in terms of self-interest qualified by the natural laws of "Let no one inflict injury upon his fellow" and "Let no one seize possession of that which has been taken into possession of another"; "Hugo Grotius, Moral Scepticism," 158.

28. Grotius, *The Rights of War and Peace* [*De jure belli ac pacis libri tres*], I.Prologue.xii, 91.

29. Ibid., II.2.ii, 423–27. See also Thumfart, "On Grotius's Mare Liberum," 78–79.

30. J. B. Schneewind, *The Invention of Autonomy*, 73.

31. Grotius, *The Rights of War and Peace* [*De jure belli ac pacis libri tres*], II.2.ii, 427.

32. Samuel Pufendorf, *The Whole Duty of Man*, I.3.vii, 55–56.

33. Ibid., II.1.ix, 171.

34. Buckle, *Natural Law*, 80.

35. Samuel Pufendorf, *Of the Law of Nature and Nations*, IV.4.iv, 364.

36. Ibid., IV.4.iv, 364.

37. Buckle, *Natural Law*, 79. Pufendorf follows the terminology inherited from Grotius—where perfect and imperfect rights refer to "moral qualities" that are respectively a "faculty" and an "aptitude"; see Grotius, *The Rights of War and Peace* [*De jure belli ac pacis libri tres*], I.1.iv, 138; see also Schneewind, *The Invention of Autonomy*, 79.

38. Haakonssen, *Natural Law and Moral Philosophy*, 38, 42–43.

39. Richard Tuck, *Natural Rights Theories*, 160.

40. For more on this distinction, see Schneewind, *The Invention of Autonomy*, 119–23.

41. Pufendorf, *Of the Law of Nature and Nations*, IV.4.i, 361.

42. Schneewind, *The Invention of Autonomy*, 122.

43. Pufendorf, *Of the Law of Nature and Nations*, I.1.vi–vii, 4.

44. Pufendorf, *Of the Law of Nature and Nations*, IV.4.4, 365.

45. Pufendorf, *The Whole Duty of Man*, I.3.xii, 58. Schneewind accounts for this in terms of Pufendorf's voluntarism: "Reason shows us God's most general instructions. The rest is up to us"; Schneewind, *The Invention of Autonomy*, 140.

46. Haakonssen, *Natural Law and Moral Philosophy*, 43.

47. Pufendorf, *The Whole Duty of Man*, I.3.ix, 56.

48. Pufendorf, *Of the Law of Nature and Nations*, IV.4.iv, 364–65.

49. Waldron, *The Right to Private Property*, 150, italics in original.

50. John Locke, *Two Treatises of Government*, II.5.xxvii, 216.

51. Although he comments, "Nature willed . . . that other [things] through industry and labor of each man become his own" and "possession of immovable [implies] either the erection of buildings or some determination of boundaries," labor does not figure strongly in his account; Grotius, *The Freedom of the Seas* [*Mare liberum*], 2 and 25–26, respectively.

52. Buckle, *Natural Law*, 101.

53. Locke, *Two Treatises of Government*, II.5.xxix, 218. See also Waldron, *The Right to Private Property*, 151.

54. Locke, *An Essay Concerning Human Understanding*, I.2.21, 68–69.

55. Ibid., I.3.13, 83.

56. Pufendorf, *The Whole Duty of Man*, I.3.xii, 58.

57. Ibid., I.3.xii, 58.

58. Ibid., I.3.xii, 58.

59. Locke, *Two Treatises of Government,* I7.lxvii, 78; II.2.vi, 197.

60. Locke, *An Essay Concerning Human Understanding,* I.1.5, 57.

61. Ibid., I.1.5, 57.

62. Ibid., I.1.5, 57.

63. Locke, *Two Treatises of Government,* II.5.xxv, 215.

64. Ibid., I.9.lxxxvi, 101–2.

65. Waldron, *The Right to Private Property,* 143.

66. Locke, *Two Treatises of Government,* II.3.xvi, 207; II.2.vii, 198.

67. Matthew Kramer, *John Locke and the Origins of Private Property,* 95.

68. Locke, *Two Treatises of Government,* II.5.xxxii, 221.

69. See also Olivecrona, "Locke's Theory of Appropriation," 228.

70. On land ownership and particular duties, see Robert Lamb, "Locke on Ownership," 133.

71. Locke, *Two Treatises of Government,* II.5.xxxiii, 221.

72. See, for instance, Elizabeth Grant, "Private Property in America."

73. On how right-libertarians account for Locke's provisos, see Walter Horn, "Libertarianism and Private Property." On the debate over "world ownership" between right- and left-libertarians, see Peter Vallentyne, Hillel Steiner, and Michael Otsuka, "Why Left-Libertarianism Is Not Coherent, Indeterminate, or Irrelevant: A Reply to Fried"; and Richard Arenson, "Self Ownership and World Ownership."

74. For the relation between Grotius and Adam Smith, see John Salter, "Adam Smith and the Grotian Theory of Property."

75. Alasdair MacIntyre and Paul Ricoeur, *The Religious Significance of Atheism,* 15.

76. Heidegger, *Being and Time,* 193/*151.*

77. Paul Samuelson and William D. Nordhaus, *Economics,* 29–30. Despite this, Samuelson endorses a land value tax, but for economic and not philosophical reasons; Samuelson and Nordhaus, *Economics,* 243–44.

78. In her study of the history of economic models, Mary Morgan identifies two features of economic modeling—maximization and equilibrium. They both give "*form* to ideas . . . but at the same time made those ideas *formal* or rule bound"; Morgan, *The World in the Model,* 394, italics in original; see also 239.

79. Geoffrey Ingham, *Capitalism,* 147. As expressed in a textbook form, see John Sloman, *Economics,* 249 and 261.

80. Christopher Ryan, "Land as a Factor of Production," 18.

81. Taylor, *A Secular Age,* 3.

82. Blaug, *Economic Theory in Retrospect,* 85. Other historians of economics are not so generous. See, for example, Niehans, *A History of Economic Theory,* 93–97. Peddle discusses neoclassical adaptations of rent with respect to John B. Clark; Peddle, "Distributism and Marginal Productivity."

83. Blaug, *Economic Theory in Retrospect,* 86.

84. Ibid., 86. Pareto held a similar view; see Renato Cirillo, *The Economics of Vilfredo Pareto,* 120–21.

85. Alfred Marshall, *Principles of Economics,* 421.

86. Say, *A Treatise on Political Economy*, 32.

87. Marshall, *Principles of Economics*, 421, as quoted in Blaug, *Economic Theory in Retrospect*, 432.

88. Marshall, *Principles of Economics*, 421.

89. Florenz Plassmann and Nicolaus Tideman, "Frank Knight's Proposal to End Distinctions," 506.

90. Ricardo, *Principles of Political Economy*, 45.

91. Robert Andelson, "Neo-Georgism," 717.

92. See, for instance, Gunnar Myrdal, *Objectivity in Social Research;* and a summary by Mark Blaug, *The Methodology of Economics*, 114–20.

93. Blaug, *Economic Theory in Retrospect*, 86.

94. See Mei, "An Economic Turn," 315; and Mei, "Economy of the Gift," 453–54.

95. Christopher Ryan, "Land as a Factor of Production," 8, 12.

96. Marshall, *Principles of Economics*, 636.

97. Polanyi, *The Great Transformation*, 146; compare also 75–76. See also Alan Ryan, *Property*, 77–78.

98. Robert Heilbroner, *The Nature and Logic of Capitalism*, 78–106.

99. George, *Progress and Poverty*, 6. George and Marshall debated, and this contrast certainly comes out. See Nahid Aslanbeigui and Adele Wick, "Progress: Poverty or Prosperity?" 61–64.

100. Mirowski, *More Heat Than Light*, 141; and Düppe, *The Making of the Economy*, 139–40.

101. Mirowski, *More Heat Than Light*, 240 and 237, respectively.

102. Peddle, "Distributism and Marginal Productivity," 322.

103. Gaffney, Harrison, and Feder, *The Corruption of Economics*, 29–30.

104. Roy Darwin et al., "Land Use and Cover in Ecological Economics," 157–58.

105. For an extensive discussion of differences between land and capital, see Mason Gaffney, "Land as a Distinctive Factor of Production."

106. Knut Wicksell, *Lectures on Political Economy*, 149 and 150; compare 134. This view was advocated also by George, *Progress and Poverty*, 198.

107. I paraphrase the account of Knight in Plassmann and Tideman, "Frank Knight's Proposal to End Distinctions," 508–9.

108. Philip Wicksteed, *The Common Sense of Political Economy*, 365. Wicksteed is against the use of terminology which creates unnecessary and arbitrary distinctions. He finds the three factors of production to be misleading, and yet ironically he was a supporter of George's land reform initiative and, as indicated in a previous note, set out to prove George's theory mathematically.

109. George, *Progress and Poverty*, 202.

110. Ibid., 202.

111. Ibid., 201.

112. Gaffney, "Land as a Distinctive Factor of Production," 55–56.

Chapter 4

1. For Heidegger's concern for concreteness in critical distinction to Marx, see Laurence Hemming, *Heidegger and Marx.*

2. Martin Heidegger, *Zollikon Seminars*, 274/*342*. References to *Zollikon Seminars* will indicate the pagination of the English translation followed by the pagination in the original German edition in italics.

3. In general, this is ontotheology; see also Iain Thomson, *Heidegger on Ontotheology*, chapter 1. See, for example, Heidegger on ontotheology, "Hegel's Concept of Experience," in *Off the Beaten Track*, 152. See also Thomas Sheehan, "On Movement and the Destruction of Ontology," 541.

4. See, for example, Martin Heidegger, "Letter on Humanism," in *Basic Writings*, 222–23.

5. Compare Martin Heidegger, "The End of Philosophy and the Task of Thinking," in *Basic Writings*, 437. I regard philosophy as still participating in what Heidegger designates as thinking so long as it can think along with being and the history of philosophy; compare Sheehan, "On Movement and the Destruction of Ontology."

6. I am aware of criticisms of this way of reading Heidegger. I address this briefly at the end of chapter 6. For one of the key passages where Heidegger speaks of being itself as giving and as caught within the play of difference, see Heidegger, *On Time and Being*, 6.

7. Martin Heidegger, "Plato's Doctrine of Truth," in *Pathmarks*, 173; and Heidegger, "On the Essence of Ground," in *Pathmarks*, 124.

8. I say "Platonism" because I suspect it was not Plato's intention to systemize a metaphysics of the Idea (as a "science" of the Good) or to construe the Ideas as a transcendent realm.

9. Heidegger, *Zollikon Seminars*, 31/*39*; I have replaced the bracketed "being" with "being itself" for clarity and consistency with my own analysis. For a concise summary of the ontological difference, see Michael Zimmerman, "Rethinking the Heidegger-Deep Ecology Relationship," 200; and in relation to subjectivity, Raffoul, *Heidegger and the Subject*, §5.3. Dreyfus sees the prevalence of beings in terms of our primary concern for practical action in our use of equipment; Dreyfus, *Being-in-the-World*, 107.

10. On the difference between accuracy of concepts and their precision with respect to understanding reality, see Denis McManus, *Heidegger and the Measure of Truth*, 147.

11. Heidegger's philosophy is often associated with subjective idealism, although aspects of his phenomenology, because they reject traditional questions of correspondence, can be associated with direct realism. Such pairings as idealism/realism are of little help when trying to understand Heidegger unless one is attempting to make him relevant to conventional philosophical debate. For more on Heidegger and epistemological problems, see McManus, *Heidegger and the Measure of Truth.* One of the main reasons for this insufficiency is that traditional epistemological problems elide the role of temporality (by which I do not mean time understood as interval—e.g., at T_1, T_2, etc.) as the medium

through which knowledge arises. In this respect, there is no such thing as a direct or indirect realism unless it can account for the ways both observer and observed have a dynamic relation in and through temporal existence. Thus, the problems of the limits of our knowledge are not epistemological by themselves. They are ontological as well. In fact, epistemological problems cannot be solved without recourse to an underlying ontology that allows the limits of knowledge to be productive according to a dynamic mode of existence that can recognize and play with these limits.

12. Martin Heidegger, *History of the Concept of Time*, 42. I am assuming that concepts can be also like a picture-thing representation; see Martin Heidegger, "The Origin of the Work of Art," in *Poetry, Language, Thought*, 31.

13. Compare McManus, *Heidegger and the Measure of Truth*, 179.

14. For a discussion of this in Heidegger and Ricoeur, see Mei, "An Economic Turn," 300–305.

15. Heidegger, *Being and Time*, 238–39/*193–94*.

16. Heidegger later refers to this kind of error as the philosophically most superficial. Martin Heidegger, "On the Essence of Truth," in *Pathmarks*, 151.

17. Heidegger, "On the Essence of Truth," in *Pathmarks*, 149. Compare McManus, *Heidegger and the Measure of Truth*, 114.

18. Heidegger, "Hegel's Concept of Experience," in *Off the Beaten Track*, 102.

19. McManus, *Heidegger and the Measure of Truth*, 139. Compare Heidegger, "On the Question of Being," in *Pathmarks*, 308. Compare Crowell, "Making Logic Philosophical Again (1912–1916)," 66–67.

20. Heidegger, *The Essence of Truth*, 100–104.

21. McManus, *Heidegger and the Measure of Truth*, 196.

22. I paraphrase McManus's reference to Wittgenstein when elaborating on Heidegger, "On the Essence of Truth," in *Pathmarks*, 142; McManus, *Heidegger and the Measure of Truth*, 131. See also Heidegger, "The Origin of the Work of Art," in *Poetry, Language, Thought*, 62; compare 52: "Science is a domain of truth already opened, specifically by apprehending and confirming that which shows itself to be possibly and necessarily correct within that field."

23. Martin Heidegger, *The Principle of Reason*, 111.

24. This is recognizing *Ereignis* (event/appropriation); see Heidegger, "On the Question of Being," in *Pathmarks*, 302. As Malpas notes, in Heidegger's later work, the play of "revealing-concealing" becomes the dominant way of thinking truth; Malpas, *Heidegger's Topology*, 193.

25. I discuss how I understand Heidegger's relation to metaphysics in Mei, "Heidegger and the Appropriation of Metaphysics."

26. See, for example, Heidegger, "On the Question of Being," in *Pathmarks*, 306–11.

27. Foltz, *Inhabiting the Earth*, 134.

28. Heidegger, "On the Essence of Ground," in *Pathmarks*, 132.

29. Ibid., 130.

30. Compare McManus, *Heidegger and the Measure of Truth*, 221.

31. Heidegger, "The End of Philosophy and the Task of Thinking," in *Basic Writings*, 446. Though he also says that the "why" is necessarily bound up with our

experience of ground since it refers to itself and elicits our questions concerning reasons; see Heidegger, "On the Essence of Ground," in *Pathmarks,* 130.

32. Heidegger, "On the Essence of Ground," in *Pathmarks,* 103. I have replaced "predicative" with the bracketed words since Heidegger was speaking specifically of propositional truth.

33. Heidegger, "On the Essence of Truth," in *Pathmarks,* 147.

34. Compare Sheehan, "On Movement and the Destruction of Ontology," 535–36; and McManus, *Heidegger and the Measure of Truth,* 204.

35. Martin Heidegger, "Postscript to 'What Is Metaphysics?'" in *Pathmarks,* 232. I will develop this in the next chapter. Suffice it to say for now, much of Heidegger's later thought is permeated by the question of "how?" though he never says so explicitly. For example, the emphasis given to *Ereignis* as appropriation is predicated on a mode of being appropriate to being. His turn to defining thinking as thanking also raises the question of appropriate response. See Martin Heidegger, *On Time and Being* and *What Is Called Thinking?*

36. It is most thought-provoking and what reverberates in and through being; see respectively, Heidegger, *What Is Called Thinking?* 4; and Martin Heidegger, *Identity and Difference,* 37.

37. Heidegger sees this primarily in how we use the term "nature" to think that which underlies us, whether we see this in relation to spirit, subjectivity, and so on; Martin Heidegger, "On the Essence and Concept of φύσις," in *Pathmarks,* 184–85. Heidegger's discussion of *hupokeimenon* is frequent and persists throughout his career. See, for example, Martin Heidegger, *The Basic Problems of Phenomenology,* 126–27; Martin Heidegger, *The Metaphysical Foundations of Logic,* 70–73; Heidegger, *Being and Time, 72/46*; Heidegger, "The Origin of the Work of Art," in *Poetry, Language, Thought,* 23; Martin Heidegger, "The Age of the World Picture," in *The Question Concerning Technology,* 147–53; and Heidegger, "The End of Philosophy and the Task of Thinking," in *Basic Writings,* 438.

38. Heidegger, *The Basic Problems of Phenomenology,* 124; compare Hemming, *Heidegger and Marx,* 11–12. For a more historically engaged development of this, see Dupré, *Passage to Modernity,* especially chapter 4. On *subjectum* in Kant, see Raffoul, *Heidegger and the Subject,* 113.

39. Heidegger, "The Age of the World Picture," in *Off the Beaten Track,* 67. I have been using Lovitt's Heidegger translation throughout, but here I prefer Young's. For a study devoted to the subject and Heidegger, see Raffoul, *Heidegger and the Subject,* especially 78 on the unity of the "I."

40. Heidegger, "The Age of the World Picture," in *Off the Beaten Track,* 81; compare 82, again preferring Young's translation.

41. Heidegger, "What Is Metaphysics?" in *Pathmarks,* 90. The phrase *Das Nichts selbst nichtet* has also been translated as "Nothingness itself nothings" and was famously attacked by Rudolf Carnap for violating the logical form of expression; see Michael Friedman, *A Parting of the Ways,* 11–23. As one may have gathered, my understanding of Heidegger's use of "nothing" involves absence as being co-constituted by the relation between being itself and ourselves. Contra Jean-Luc Marion, being does not actively withdraw by itself, but actively withdraws

with us since our relation to it requires this withdrawal; Marion, *Being Given*, 36. This point seems essential in Heidegger's understanding of the relation between *logos* and being, per below; compare Sheehan, "On Movement and the Destruction of Ontology," 538–39.

42. Heidegger, "What Is Metaphysics?" in *Pathmarks*, 85. See also Malpas, *Heidegger's Topology*, 191; and Hemming, *Heidegger and Marx*, 38.

43. Martin Heidegger, *Discourse on Thinking*, 89–90.

44. Martin Heidegger, "Kant's Thesis about Being," in *Pathmarks*, 340.

45. Compare Sheehan, "On Movement and the Destruction of Ontology"; and Raffoul, *Heidegger and the Subject*, 137, 139.

46. Raffoul, *Heidegger and the Subject*, 16.

47. Heidegger, *Being and Time*, 249/*206*.

48. Heidegger, "On the Essence of Ground," in *Pathmarks*, 104–5.

49. See, for example, Heidegger, "Postscript to 'What Is Metaphysics?'" in *Pathmarks*, 232.

50. Heidegger, "On the Question of Being," in *Pathmarks*, 312.

51. Heidegger, "On the Essence of Ground," in *Pathmarks*, 132; my bracketed comments for clarification; emphasis in the original. The union between being and ground is more overt in his lectures on the principle of reason (1955–56) when he states that being is ground.

52. Martin Heidegger, *The Principle of Reason*, 111.

53. Ibid., 111.

54. Ibid.

55. I discuss the role of unity in difference in Heidegger, in Mei, "Economy of the Gift"; but see also Malpas, *Heidegger's Topology*, 56–63.

56. On the uses of presence in Heidegger, see Malpas, *Heidegger's Topology*, 10–11.

57. Martin Heidegger, *An Introduction to Metaphysics*, 101. See also Heidegger on the Greek term *ergon*; "On the Essence and Concept of φύσις," in *Pathmarks*, 217.

58. Heidegger, "On the Essence and Concept of φύσις," in *Pathmarks*, 188; translator's bracketed insertions; emphasis in original.

59. I discuss aspects of their contributions in the next section.

60. See, for instance, Martin Heidegger, "The Thing," in *Poetry, Language, Thought*, 172; and Martin Heidegger, "Building Dwelling Thinking," in *Poetry, Language, Thought*, 153–55.

61. Heidegger, "Building Dwelling Thinking," in *Poetry, Language, Thought*, 155. On configuring (*Gestalt, Stellen, Ge-stell*), see Heidegger, "The Origin of the Work of Art," in *Poetry, Language, Thought*, 64.

62. Heidegger, "Building Dwelling Thinking," in *Poetry, Language, Thought*, 157.

63. The debates concerning how to translate Dasein into English are numerous. For a concise account and persuasive position on the matter, see Malpas, *Heidegger's Topology*, 47–50. For an argument on translating Dasein as "being-here," see Hemming, *Heidegger and Marx*, 10.

64. Heidegger, *Zollikon Seminars,* 120/*157.*

65. Malpas, *Heidegger's Topology,* 91; I have unhyphenated "dis-tance" for consistency with my use.

66. Heidegger, *The Principle of Reason,* 111–13.

67. McManus, *Heidegger and the Measure of Truth,* 196.

68. Foltz, *Inhabiting the Earth,* 167–69.

69. Martin Heidegger, "Why Poets?" in *Off the Beaten Track,* 232.

70. Edward Casey, *Getting Back into Place,* 36.

71. Jeff Malpas, *Place and Experience,* 26.

72. Casey, *Getting Back into Place,* 357–60; Maria Villela-Petit, "Heidegger's Conception of Space," 139–40; and Malpas, *Place and Experience,* 26, and for the quote, Malpas, *Heidegger's Topology,* 78.

73. Malpas, *Heidegger's Topology,* 126; compare Heidegger, *Being and Time,* 171/*132.* I have simplified the opposition between *Vorhandenheit* and *Zuhandenheit* for the sake of clarity. For more on this pairing and its complexities, see McManus, *Heidegger and the Measure of Truth,* 51–75. McManus also provides an interesting clarification of *Vorhandenheit* as a representation of entities in our speech and practices such that our dealing with them forgets the initial question of the meaning of being and the way being conceals itself; McManus, *Heidegger and the Measure of Truth,* 195–202.

74. Malpas, *Place and Experience,* 25.

75. Ibid., 33.

76. Heidegger, *Zollikon Seminars,* 34/*42.*

77. Casey, *Getting Back into Place,* 350.

78. Malpas's account is very nuanced and in arguing against the idea that *Being and Time* is pervaded by subjectivism, he shows how the difficulties of the work stem from a much subtler problem involving place and space. See especially Malpas, *Heidegger's Topology,* 158–63. On Heidegger's own admission, see Heidegger, *On Time and Being,* 23.

79. See Malpas, *The Place of Landscape*; and Casey, *Getting Back into Place,* 266, 302.

80. Casey, *Getting Back into Place,* 313.

81. Collingwood, *An Essay on Metaphysics,* 14.

82. John Sallis, *Topographies,* 3–4. Compare R. G. Collingwood, *An Autobiography,* 31–43, on the situational context necessary for analyzing propositions.

83. Casey, *Getting Back into Place,* xiv–xv; and Malpas, *Heidegger's Topology,* 7.

84. Casey, *Getting Back into Place,* 264.

85. Ibid., 32, 35.

86. Ibid., 212.

87. Ibid., 262.

88. This omission is true of the more recent studies of landscape; see Malpas, "Place and the Problem of Landscape" which I note below and in which Casey's concern is more about liminality than land.

89. Edward S. Casey, "Mapping the Earth in Works of Art," 268.

90. Casey remarks that Heidegger's failure to think of land and its liminality

is due to his wish to avoid Hegelian third terms; Casey, "Mapping the Earth in Works of Art," 263. While this may be true generally of Heidegger's philosophy, my interpretation of his failure (if it can be called that) is due to an absence of thinking through his accounts of earth and world more concretely in relation to specific practices. This criticism generally informs the argument of this chapter as well as the next.

91. Malpas, *Place and Experience,* 1. The concept of land figures even less in Malpas, *Heidegger and the Thinking of Place.*

92. Malpas, *Heidegger's Topology,* 174.

93. Ibid., 177.

94. Jeff Malpas, "Introduction," ix.

95. Malpas, "Place and the Problem of Landscape," 15–21.

96. Malpas, *Place and Experience,* 40–41.

97. This is stated by Edward S. Casey, "The Edge(s) of Landscape: A Study in Liminology," 99.

Chapter 5

1. Paul Ricoeur, *The Conflict of Interpretations,* 6; and Ricoeur, *The Rule of Metaphor,* 313.

2. I am aware of the argument that Heidegger is against metaphysics because of its conception of being as production, or what Zimmerman discusses in terms of "productionist metaphysics"; Zimmerman, *Heidegger's Confrontation with Modernity,* 222. Here I mean something different by production, where the things produced are not simply extant objects. The basis for this will be evident in my discussion of *aition.* In short, the ancient Greek understanding of cause retains a meaning of production wed to the idea that humans are in debt to that which is prior to them. For the historical complications of this idea due to medieval metaphysics and modern technology, see Foltz, *Inhabiting the Earth,* 72, 101, 136, 145.

3. Martin Heidegger, *On Time and Being,* 18.

4. For a discussion on existential spatiality, see Malpas, *Heidegger's Topology,* 78–83, 92–96.

5. Martin Heidegger, "Science and Reflection," in *The Question Concerning Technology,* 161; see also Martin Heidegger, "The Question Concerning Technology," in *The Question Concerning Technology,* 26.

6. Heidegger, "The Question Concerning Technology," in *The Question Concerning Technology,* 10.

7. Heidegger, "On the Essence and Concept of φύσις," in *Pathmarks,* 98, 188. See also Heidegger, "The Question Concerning Technology," in *The Question Concerning Technology,* 7; and Richard Rojcewicz, *The Gods and Technology,* 15–19.

8. MacIntyre discusses this in the historical context where the scientific method of experimentation begins from a basic empiricism and then moves toward a method of investigation which looks behind the appearance of things. MacIntyre, *After Virtue,* 80; compare Collingwood, *The Idea of Nature,* 12.

9. Martin Heidegger, "Phenomenology and Theology," in *Pathmarks*, 58.

10. Martin Heidegger, "Nietzsche's Word: 'God Is Dead,'" in *Off the Beaten Track*, 194.

11. Heidegger, "Nietzsche's Word: 'God Is Dead,'" in *Off the Beaten Track*, 195. Compare Heidegger, *Being and Time*, 137/*104*, 465–66/*412–13*.

12. Heidegger, "On the Essence and Concept of φύσις," in *Pathmarks*, 188.

13. See, for example, Don Ihde, *Heidegger's Technologies*. For an interesting critical engagement with post-phenomenological and empirical criticisms of classical philosophy of technology, see Dominic Smith, "Rewriting the Constitution"; and Smith, "The Internet as Idea," respectively.

14. Raffoul, *Heidegger and the Subject*, 150, quoting Martin Heidegger, "Letter on Humanism," in *Basic Writings*, 254.

15. Heidegger speaks of this meaning of nature in terms of causality and calculability. I stress "conventionally" and do not preclude a substantially meaningful use of the term; Heidegger, *Zollikon Seminars*, 18/*21*–22, 25/*30*–31. For the different senses of nature, see Foltz, *Inhabiting the Earth*, chapter 7. To be sure, much literature in the area of environmental ethics has criticized and explored the human relation to nature, drawing on anthropological and historical analyses to rethink how we should treat it. And while much of the literature deals only superficially with the ontology of nature, a portion of these studies draws on phenomenology. In particular, those building upon the work of Maurice Merleau-Ponty offer analyses of a nature similar to what I will argue in relation to Heidegger's later thought. Much of the literature takes inspiration from Aldo Leopold's "The Land Ethic" (1949) in which he attempts to redefine our obligations to nature. Environmental ethicists critical of our use of nature tend to emphasize the problematic role of human and/or male dominance (anthropocentrism and andocentrism, respectively) and how such views can be corrected by alternative conceptions of care, nonintervention, or rights and obligations. For a discussion of environmental ethics and land, see Grant, "Private Property in America." Studies employing a phenomenological approach in some manner tend to note our essential bond to the earth or, conversely, earth's otherness in relation to wilderness, or that which cannot be placed under the dominion of humans. On the former, see for example, David Abram, "Earth in Eclipse"; Foltz, *Inhabiting the Earth*; John Llewellyn, "A Footnote in the History of Φύσις"; Renaud Barbaras, "Merleau-Ponty and Nature"; and Zimmerman, "Rethinking the Heidegger-Deep Ecology Relationship." On the latter, most notable is the discussion of wilderness in Casey, *Getting Back into Place*, part 4. Barbaras and Llewllyn develop a reading of nature as "non-constructed, non-instituted" through Merleau-Ponty's phenomenology which parallels to some extent my claim that land is *hupokeimenon*. However, Barbaras's analysis rests to some degree on the otherness of nature, which would resist my move to derive an economics from it. Llewellyn's study focuses on our concrete relation to nature through dwelling. I refer to Foltz throughout this study.

16. Heidegger, "On the Essence and Concept of φύσις," in *Pathmarks*, 200.

17. Heidegger, "The Origin of the Work of Art," in *Poetry, Language, Thought*, 42.

18. Heidegger, *What Is Called Thinking?* 200, as quoted in Foltz, *Inhabiting the Earth,* 74. Foltz notes there are many senses to *hupokeimenon,* and that the sense I employ in terms of primordial source is "the strictest."

19. Joseph Fell, *Heidegger and Sartre,* 197, as quoted in Malpas, *Heidegger's Topology,* 197.

20. Heidegger, "On the Essence and Concept of φύσις," in *Pathmarks,* 221; and Heidegger, "The Origin of the Work of Art," in *Poetry, Language, Thought,* 59. See also Mei, "Heidegger in the Machine," on the difference between nature, machine, and artefact.

21. For more on this, see Mei, *Heidegger, Work, and Being;* and Hemming, *Heidegger and Marx,* 88.

22. See also Heidegger, "Letter on Humanism," in *Basic Writings,* 243.

23. Heidegger, "The Origin of the Work of Art," in *Poetry, Language, Thought,* 47.

24. Heidegger, "The Origin of the Work of Art," in *Poetry, Language, Thought,* 42; and Heidegger, *Zollikon Seminars,* 176 / *222.* Compare Foltz, *Inhabiting the Earth,* 163.

25. Heidegger, "The Origin of the Work of Art," in *Poetry, Language, Thought,* 47. Compare Martin Heidegger, *The Fundamental Concepts of Metaphysics,* 26.

26. Heidegger, "The Origin of the Work of Art," in *Poetry, Language, Thought,* 42; my emphasis.

27. Compare the translation of this passage by Julian Young and Kenneth Haynes in Heidegger, *Off the Beaten Track,* 24.

28. Heidegger, "Building Dwelling Thinking," in *Poetry, Language, Thought,* 154.

29. Martin Heidegger, "Aletheia (Heraclitus, Fragment B 16)," in *Early Greek Thinking,* 113; and Heidegger, "The Origin of the Work of Art," in *Poetry, Language, Thought,* 42.

30. Heidegger, "The Origin of the Work of Art," in *Poetry, Language, Thought,* 48.

31. Foltz, *Inhabiting the Earth,* 136.

32. Heidegger, "The Origin of the Work of Art," in *Poetry, Language, Thought,* 63. Compare *dike* in Martin Heidegger, "The Anaximander Fragment," in *Early Greek Thinking,* 41–48.

33. Heidegger thus equates human work with production deriving from earth's self-secluding nature. See Heidegger, "The Origin of the Work of Art," in *Poetry, Language, Thought,* 47.

34. This is referred to by Heidegger in terms of the strife between earth and world; "The Origin of the Work of Art," *Poetry, Language, Thought,* 63; see also Michael Zimmerman, *Contesting Earth's Future,* 129–30. But here I emphasize this strife in terms of bringing about the end of entities within a life cycle.

35. Heidegger, "On the Essence and Concept of φύσις," in *Pathmarks,* 194.

36. I include under the term "technics" not just entities we produce, but also practices which give rise to institutions. For an examination of the appropriateness of the technics involved in liability insurance to the question of being, see Mei, "Heidegger and the Appropriation of Metaphysics."

37. Arendt, *The Human Condition*, prologue.

38. Heidegger, "The Origin of the Work of Art," in *Poetry, Language, Thought*, 75.

39. Heidegger, "The Origin of the Work of Art," in *Poetry, Language, Thought*, 74; and Martin Heidegger, "Why Poets?" in *Off the Beaten Track*, 239–40. I elide the essential and primary role language has for Heidegger. Suffice it to say, it is consistent with the ancient Greek notion that *logos* is a constituent of the cosmos, already inhering in the fabric of things.

40. Foltz, *Inhabiting the Earth*, 161.

41. In *Heidegger, Work, and Being*, I argued that Heidegger conceives of a hermeneutical unity between *theoria*, *praxis*, and *poiesis*. How strongly Heidegger wants to emphasize the poetic over against the others remains debatable. I regret to say that I erroneously leave out references to Heidegger's *Plato's Sophist* where he discusses the three Aristotelian intellectual virtues. My thanks to Laurence Hemming for pointing this out. References to *Plato's Sophist* can be found in an earlier version of my book which was my Ph.D. thesis at the University of Kent, completed in 2008.

42. Achievement refers to *praxis* where doing the action is the end. Production refers to *poiesis* where the action arrives at an end separate from the action.

43. Heidegger, *What Is Called Thinking?* 16–17.

44. Martin Heidegger, ". . . Poetically Man Dwells . . ." in *Poetry, Language, Thought*, 228.

45. To what extent Heidegger "forgets air" and therefore the passage of the Other is questionable. His emphasis on earth and ground arises from his concern to understand the place in which recognition of the Other can occur. On this view, the passing of air is intimately related to the air manifesting in a specific locality between, for example, two people. Air is not void or space; it is breath. Heidegger comments on Herder's *Reflections of the Philosophy of the History of Mankind*: "The ones who by a breath risk more risk it with language. They are the saying ones who are saying more. For this one breath by which they risk more is not just saying in general; rather, the one breath is an other breath, a saying other than what human saying usually is. The other breath no longer solicits for this or that objective thing; it is a breath for nothing; Heidegger, *Off the Beaten Track*, 238." Suffice it to say, "nothing" in Heidegger's thought is not without merit and is an unfathomable abundance.

46. Heidegger, "Building Dwelling Thinking," in *Poetry, Language, Thought*, 147–48.

47. Casey, "Mapping the Earth in Works of Art," 268.

48. See, for example, Casey, *Getting Back into Place*, 55, 60, 62.

49. My thanks to Nicholas Davey for bringing these examples to my attention. Even for those who love the sea, it is not uncommon for sailors returning to land to express gratitude by kissing the land or to deem those unworthy of the sea, or landlubbers, as those who are too clumsy with their landed existence to understand how the sea is navigated. My thanks to Patricia Baker for mentioning these examples.

50. Heidegger, *Zollikon Seminars*, 164/*210*.

51. I assume here Heidegger's argument about *dunamis* being a capacity as both potential and actual; see Heidegger, *Aristotle's "Metaphysics" θ 1–3,* in particular, §22.

52. But not the sole reason. While interested in practice in Heidegger, I do not adhere to the claim that practice and the practical hold a preeminent status over the theoretical. See McManus's *Heidegger and the Measure of Truth* for a refutation of the "primacy of practice claim" as well as Scharff, "Rorty and Analytic Heideggerian Epistemology," 498; and Foltz, *Inhabiting the Earth,* 34 n.3.

53. I discuss this in terms of human vocation in Mei, *Heidegger, Work, and Being,* 123–36. See also Malpas, *Heidegger's Topology,* 176.

54. See, for example, Tim Ingold's discussion of taskscape and landscape in archaeological and anthropological theory; Ingold, "The Temporality of Landscape," 158.

55. Heidegger, "Letter on Humanism," in *Basic Writings,* 242.

56. Heidegger, "Building Dwelling Thinking," in *Poetry, Language, Thought,* 161.

57. Ibid., 161.

58. Mill, *Principles of Political Economy,* 237.

59. On this view, concerns about overpopulation may derive from an incorrect relation to land. See my discussion of scarcity in chapter 8.

60. For historical problems of this kind in the United States, see Grant, "Private Property in America," chapter 2.

Chapter 6

1. Heidegger, *Being and Time,* 385/*336.*

2. Albert Camus, *The Myth of Sisyphus,* 4.

3. Foltz, *Inhabiting the Earth,* 154–76.

4. Heidegger, *Being and Time,* 68/*42.*

5. Raffoul, *Heidegger and the Subject,* 16.

6. Heidegger, *Being and Time,* 68/*42*; compare 275/*232* on potentiality-for-being.

7. Heidegger, *Being and Time,* 186/*145.*

8. Raffoul, *Heidegger and the Subject,* 9; capitalization of "Being" has been omitted.

9. Paul Ricoeur, *Husserl,* 209. Hermeneutic phenomenology seeks to describe finite conditions that both limit and enable human understanding. The limiting conditions of, for example, embodiment, the passions, and otherness provide access to the world that cannot be grasped otherwise. It makes mediation through these specifically human features meaningful as opposed to being inimical or extraneous to reason. I leave untreated the difference between hermeneutic and existential phenomenologies, the latter of which can be said to focus mainly on the primacy of perception. In contrast, Ricoeur's hermeneutic phenomenology, for example, takes a linguistic turn. Being-landed is, in this sense, another form of relation which encompasses perception.

10. Raffoul, *Heidegger and the Subject,* 22; capitalization of "Being" has been omitted.

11. Heidegger, *Being and Time,* 329/*284.*

12. Ibid., 185/*145.*

13. Michael Dummett, *The Origins of Analytic Philosophy,* 23.

14. Edmund Husserl, *Cartesian Meditations,* 10–11, 58.

15. Ibid., 11.

16. Dummett, *The Origins of Analytic Philosophy,* 38.

17. Husserl, *Cartesian Meditations,* 57.

18. Joseph Kockelmans, *Edmund Husserl's Phenomenology,* 83; see also Ricoeur, *Husserl,* 101; and Ian James, *The New French Philosophy,* 22.

19. Heidegger, *Identity and Difference,* 65.

20. Jean-Luc Marion, *In Excess,* 46; Shane Mackinlay, *Interpreting Excess,* 16.

21. Marion, *In Excess,* 47. Raffoul would disagree that this reduction is exclusionary in a detrimental sense; Dasein brackets out "the ontical characteristics of existence"; Raffoul, *Heidegger and the Subject,* 243.

22. Marion, *Being Given,* 52; compare Emmanuel Levinas, *Totality and Infinity,* 77. See James, *The New French Philosophy,* 26, and Mackinlay, *Interpreting Excess,* 17. Heidegger's later thought is not really a solution to this problem since Marion sees it as a flawed attempt to move beyond phenomenology by turning to what does not appear; Marion, *In Excess,* 110.

23. Marion, *Being Given,* 147.

24. Ibid., 148.

25. Marion, *In Excess,* 112.

26. Ibid., 37–38.

27. For a summary of this controversy, see Oliver Davies, "The Challenge of the Past"; James, *The New French Philosophy,* 17–38; and Shane Mackinlay, "Exceeding Truth." Obviously, Marion does not claim to follow Husserl strictly, given the former's emphasis on the saturated phenomena; Mackinlay, *Interpreting Excess,* 37.

28. Marion, *Being Given,* 17.

29. For an account and clarification of this, see Mackinlay, *Interpreting Excess,* 35–56. I am aware that Derrida accuses Marion of breaking with Husserl's definition of givenness as neutral; see for instance Davies's concise summary of the debate; "The Challenge of the Past." My hermeneutical leanings should indicate where I stand on this. I do not think neutrality is viable as a methodological claim. Ricoeur's hermeneutic phenomenology can, in this sense, act as a potential mediator between the Derrida-Marion debate.

30. Jean-Luc Marion, *Reduction and Givenness,* 203; my emphasis.

31. Marion, *In Excess,* 31–32.

32. Compare Sheehan, "A Paradigm Shift in Heidegger Research," 193. I leave undiscussed the relation between "there" and the constitution of "there." Sheehan argues that humans open thereness through their participation with it. My comments in this section refer to a similar relation in which humans play an integral role, where their participation reshapes reality. However, I do emphasize that it is land which grants the possibility for any kind of "there" to be seen. So in one sense, "thereness" exists prior to humans, yet in terms of some place still

yet to be more fully revealed. Hence in chapter 5, I referred to land as actual potential-for-use.

33. This example is taken from Leon MacLaren, who provides an extended analysis of its implications in relation to ground rent; MacLaren, *Nature of Society*, 55–64. The example originally comes from George, *Progress and Poverty*, 347–48.

34. I will not go into detail about this justification. I find it fatally flawed on the grounds it excludes past, present, and future generations from the land. Claims that owning land in perpetuity benefits society by means of providing employment is also fallacious if it can be shown that these benefits are only *relative* when assuming a state of affairs where laborers do not have access to employment, which tends to involve not having access to land. For more conventional rejections of original acquisition, see Waldron, *The Right to Private Property*, 253–83.

35. In cases where the business owner is not the landlord, the fee of rent is felt by the business owner which, in turn, acts as a cost affecting the amount of wages that can be paid. I discuss this later on.

36. Opponents might raise the point that the same is true of air and water—that is, that a laborer is in some sense bound by access to these elements. One should not forget, however, that elemental specificity is one that still takes shape according to our being-landed. Deprivation of air and water occur in relation to how its respective space or area can be withheld on the land. If we bracket land, what effect does this have? "Absolute and pure," Nietzsche might say, "an act [of living] is imagined here which does not really occur at all"; Nietzsche, *Will to Power*, 7–8, as quoted in Ricoeur, *Oneself as Another*, 14 n.2.

37. Smith, *The Wealth of Nations*, 1:168. It is unfortunate Smith did not adhere to this view more consistently and strongly; see Mei, "An Economic Turn," 313–15.

38. I play on Foucault's own words; *Discipline and Punish*, 244.

39. This sketch derives from a classic Georgian perspective. For more on this, see Maclaren, *Nature of Society*; George, *Progress and Poverty*, and George, *Social Problems*; and Harrison, *The Power in the Land.*

40. Levinas, *Totality and Infinity*, 40. Casey, *Getting Back into Place*, 65, defines site pejoratively as "simple location" and "just there."

41. Jacques Derrida, "The Principle of Reason," 5–6, 17.

42. Heidegger, *Being and Time*, 171/*133*.

43. Paul Ricoeur, "The Function of Fiction in Shaping Reality," in *A Ricoeur Reader*, 133. Prior to this quote I draw on Ricoeur's analysis of utopia as a meaningful type of nowhere; see Paul Ricoeur, *Lectures on Ideology and Utopia*, 309–10.

44. For a detailed study of the relation between necessity and supra-necessary ends with regard to human work, see Mei, *Heidegger, Work, and Being.*

45. Simone Weil, *Gravity and Grace*, 2–3.

46. Ibid., 58: "To love purely is to consent to distance, it is to adore the distance between ourselves and that which we love."

47. Marion, *Being Given*, 131.

48. Casey, *Getting Back into Place*, 118.

49. Heidegger, *Being and Time*, 412/*361*, recalling my discussion of Heidegger and science in chapter 6.

50. Derrida, "The Principle of Reason," 6.

51. Heidegger, ". . . Poetically Man Dwells . . ." in *Poetry, Language, Thought,* 221.

52. Ibid., 221.

53. Raffoul, *Heidegger and the Subject,* 230; capitalization of "Being" has been omitted.

54. Ibid., 231; capitalization of "Being" has been omitted.

55. Steven Galt Crowell, "Subjectivity," 131.

56. It seems instead they cohere as the facticity of our being.

57. Heidegger, *Being and Time,* 329/*284.*

58. Compare Ricoeur, *Oneself as Another,* 329–43.

59. Arendt, *The Human Condition,* 137.

60. Georges Bataille, *The Accursed Share,* 7.

61. Ibid., 21.

62. Bataille seems to miss this point and instead focuses on how the human organism has the globe as its field of equilibrium while other organisms are confined to particular environments; Bataille, *The Accursed Share,* 33. Likewise, he only mentions in passing the role of technology and more highly developed industry; *The Accursed Share,* 119.

63. Bataille, *The Accursed Share,* 31–32.

64. Ibid., 119.

65. Heidegger, *Plato's "Sophist,"* 7.

66. Heidegger, *What Is Called Thinking?* 148 and 142, respectively.

67. Heidegger, *On Time and Being,* 23.

68. Steven Galt Crowell, "What Gives? Getting Over the Subject?" 94.

69. I assume an understanding of this term here, though I address its meaning in more detail in chapter 7.

Chapter 7

1. On ecological economics and Henry George, see Herman Daly, *Ecological Economics,* 45, 111; and Brian Czech, "The Neoclassical Production Function."

2. Roy Darwin et al., "Land Use and Cover in Ecological Economics," 158.

3. Ibid., 158.

4. See, for example, Anastasios Xepapadeas, "Ecological Economics," 744; and Herman Daly, *Beyond Growth.* Daly argues elsewhere for "strong sustainability" in which natural resources cannot be confused with or substituted by man-made capital goods. He states, "The main idea behind sustainability is to shift the path of progress from growth, which is not sustainable, toward development, which presumably is"; Daly, *Ecological Economics,* 15.

5. Czech also notes the importance of land in more typical neoclassical economists; Czech, "The Neoclassical Production Function," 2194 and 2197.

6. H. William Batt, though attempting to draw links between ecological economics and Henry George's economics, notes that energy (its production, consumption, and conservation) is the central term on which ecological ap-

proaches focus; Batt, "The Compatibility of Georgist Economics and Ecological Economics."

7. Ricoeur, *The Conflict of Interpretations,* 441.

8. Ibid., 455–56.

9. See, for example, Christoph Cox, *Nietzsche,* 235–38.

10. Arendt, *The Human Condition,* 96–97.

11. Düppe, *The Making of the Economy,* 189.

12. George, *The Science of Political Economy,* 323–24. Compare Mirowski, *More Heat Than Light,* 143.

13. George, *The Science of Political Economy,* 324.

14. I here make no distinction between production and service. I use the term "production" to include service since in the end I see the provision of services as ultimately involved in the production of wealth, though it presupposes the existence of object commodities. In many instances production of wealth cannot be said to be complete without the involvement of various services—for example, transportation, exchange, etc. Compare George, *The Science of Political Economy,* 325–26.

15. Jevons, as quoted in Mirowski, *More Heat Than Light,* 219.

16. George, *The Science of Political Economy,* 303.

17. Mei, *Heidegger, Work, and Being,* 74–91.

18. I think this is possible if we can speak of a commodity's disposition or capacity. I do so in the next section but without explicit discussion. For more on capacity and disposition, see Mei, "Heidegger in the Machine."

19. For an account of the origins of this debate, see James S. Coleman, "Social Capital in the Creation of Human Capital"; and Alejandro Portes, "Social Capital."

20. There is an obvious debt here to Sen's discussion of commodities and capabilities, though it is apparent here that I link commodities strongly to the actualization of capacities; see Sen, *Commodities and Capabilities.* This does not mean, however, that I think economic well-being can be measured on the basis of commodities and utilities. This is because while use of commodities is necessary to ontological actualization, simply measuring commodities does not mean these commodities link to actualization in reality. Hence, Sen's discussion of real freedom and opportunity becomes invaluable; Sen, *The Idea of Justice,* 225–38.

21. Heidegger, *Being and Time,* 99–100/ *70.*

22. Opting for Stambaugh's translation of *Being and Time,* 66/ *71.*

23. Compare Raffoul, *The Origins of Responsibility,* 259–60.

24. Opting for Stambaugh's translation of *Being and Time,* 66/ *71.*

25. Opting for Stambaugh's translation of *Being and Time,* 66/ *71.*

26. Walter Brogan, "The Community of Those Who Are Going to Die," 237–48.

27. George, *The Science of Political Economy,* 295–96.

28. Heidegger, *Being and Time,* §71.

29. Ibid., 423/ *371.*

30. Mei, "Heidegger in the Machine."

31. George, *The Science of Political Economy,* 351–52.

32. Ibid., 352.
33. Ibid., 99–104.
34. Ibid., 329.
35. Ibid., 330.
36. Ibid.
37. Ibid.
38. Ibid., 331.
39. Ibid., 353.
40. Ibid., 78. I use this quotation rhetorically since George poses the question in order to show that pursuing it would lead us to religion or metaphysics. Nevertheless, the reason for my use of the quote is in the same spirit as George observes—that is, that political economy must address the material necessity of human agency.
41. Polanyi, *The Great Transformation,* 187; compare 188.
42. I play on the words in Polanyi when commenting about the primacy of social relations over the economic; Polanyi, *The Great Transformation,* 60.

Chapter 8

1. My account of Keith Tribe's analysis of land in chapter 2 is of this type. I discuss shortcomings of post-structural criticisms of economics to some extent in Todd Mei, "Ricoeur *Economicus.*"
2. George, *Progress and Poverty,* 168; my emphasis.
3. Marglin, *The Dismal Science,* 47.
4. Suffice it to say that grace and gift are not necessarily identical in meaning. For a discussion of these topics with respect to theology, see Mei, "Economy of the Gift."
5. Sen talks about the difference in "self-assessed morbidity rates" between the affluent and the poor, where the latter are less aware of morbidity rates despite low life expectancy in their urban area; Sen, *The Idea of Justice,* 164–66. For a more classic analysis, see Marshall Sahlins, "The Original Affluent Society."
6. John Bellamy Foster, "Malthus' Essay on Population at Age 200."
7. Compare Spencer Banzhaf and Nathan Lavery, "Can the Land Tax Help Curb Urban Sprawl?"; and Fred Foldvary, "Geo-Rent," 124. Tideman argues that a tax on ground rent can help to balance population growth through incentive. By figuring a nation's total growth rate in its total appropriation of natural resources, one can determine whether the appropriation exceeds that of other nations with slower growth. Nations of slower growth can claim financial compensation for the pressure to set aside more resources; Tideman, "Applications of Land Value Taxation."
8. There is also the complementary effect where an increase in wages will tend toward a rise in land value. This is because the more one earns and cannot own land, the more financial resource there is to pay for access to land.
9. Colin Clark, *Population Growth and Land Use.* This phenomenon occurred, of course, in the land enclosure movements from the fifteenth to nineteenth cen-

turies in England where peasants were removed for the land and forced to find a living in the cities. Suffice it to say, the question of when enclosures occurred ideologically and not just legally is complex. See Marglin, *The Dismal Science*, 80–95.

10. George, *Progress and Poverty*, 256–57.

11. Or what is essentially holding land from use during the interim before houses are built. Tescos in the United Kingdom has been accused of this. Gaffney discusses how land speculation figures into the growth strategy of corporations; Mason Gaffney, "The Adequacy of Land as a Tax Base," 167.

12. Veblen, "On the Nature of Capital," 524. See also Veblen, *Absentee Ownership*, 139–40.

13. George, *Progress and Poverty*, 365–66.

14. Economist Fred Foldvary is perhaps an exception as he endorses a tax on ground rent while being somewhat conservative in his libertarian beliefs; see, for instance, Foldvary, "Geoism and Libertarianism." Left libertarianism is a different matter because it favors strong notions of common ownership while attempting to respect individual rights. See, for instance, Michael Otsuka, *Libertarianism without Inequality*; Hillel Steiner, "Left Libertarianism and the Ownership of Natural Resources"; and Peter Vallentyne, "Left-Libertarianism as a Promising Form of Liberal Egalitarianism." Economists supporting left-libertarian views, such as Tideman and Vallentyne, endorse a version of a tax on ground rent; "Left-Libertarianism and Global Justice." My disagreements with libertarianism in general, however, is its overdetermination of the individual as the foundation for conceiving moral and political matters. In other words, it ignores the kind of ontological and phenomenological analysis I have proposed and underdetermines the thesis that land is subject.

15. Liam Murphy and Thomas Nagel, *The Myth of Ownership*; Waldron, *The Rule of Law*; and Lewis Hyde, *Common as Air*.

16. George, *Progress and Poverty*, 408.

17. Ibid., 360–61. For more recent arguments addressed to specific economic rebuttals, see Nicolaus Tideman, "The Economics of Efficient Taxes on Land"; and Gaffney, "The Adequacy of Land as a Tax Base."

18. Nicolaus Tideman, "Private Possession as an Alternative," §III.

19. Arendt, *The Human Condition*, 177.

20. I admit being intrigued by Dries Deweer's account of personalist republicanism styled after Ricoeur's philosophy; Deweer, "Ricoeur on Citizenship."

21. Foltz, *Inhabiting the Earth*, 161.

22. Philip Goodchild, *Theology of Money*, 237.

23. Arendt, *The Human Condition*, 176–77.

24. For an account of how George has been misrepresented by academic economists, see Gaffney, Harrison, and Feder, *The Corruption of Economics*. For a discussion of specific misunderstandings of George's view, see Jürgen Backhaus, "Henry George's Ingenious Tax," 454–60.

25. Tideman, "Private Possession as an Alternative," §I. Critics might argue that private ownership of land is more beneficial than renting it since the former involves a sense of personal attachment and responsibility. There are two responses: first, such a sense of accountability is probably not possible when land

is owned by a corporation, as it is in many cases of speculation. Accountability to land would then be secondary to the desire for the rent it generates. Second, the case I have made for understanding land as subject involves a decisive shift away from the kind of philosophical imaginary in which one sees oneself as an individual who can own land like one can other entities. Land's subjectivity gives it priority; and so by implication, there is already figured into our relation to land a sense of appropriateness and accountability. Accordingly, renting land is not an instance of temporary use without care, but rather a practice that arises from the acknowledgment that land provides an ontological foundation for existence that cannot be privately controlled or captured.

26. Usufruct systems have their own problems. For a discussion of the complexities relating to property and time, see Andrew Reeve, *Property*, 152–78. Nonetheless, the simplicity of the tax on ground largely avoids these because the decision to use land and pay a fee is based on the potential possessor's intentions and expectations.

27. George, *Progress and Poverty*, 347.

28. Ibid., 360–61.

29. Foldvary, "Geo-Rent," 110–12.

30. Compare George, *Progress and Poverty*, 450; Foldvary, "Geo-Rent," 109; and Tideman, "Private Possession as an Alternative," §II.

31. For more on this, see Tideman, "Private Possession as an Alternative," §II.

32. Compare Collingwood, "Economics as a Philosophical Science," 173–74; and Foldvary, "Geo-Rent," 109.

33. Foldvary, "Geo-Rent," 109.

34. Otherwise known as the "Henry George Theorem" presented by Atkinson and Stiglitz, *Lectures on Public Economics*, as discussed in Foldvary, "Geo-Rent," 115–16.

35. Tideman, "The Economics of Efficient Taxes on Land."

36. Backhaus, "Henry George's Ingenious Tax," 463–64.

37. George, *Progress and Poverty*, 255, as quoted in Tideman, "George on Land Speculation," 1095.

38. Tideman, "George on Land Speculation."

Conclusion

1. Tolstoy, *How Much Land*, 108.

2. Ibid., 110.

Bibliography

Abram, David. “Earth in Eclipse.” In *Merleau-Ponty and Environmental Philosophy: Dwelling on the Landscapes of Thought*, edited by Sue L. Cataldi and William S. Hamrick, 149–76. Albany: SUNY Press, 2007.

Andelson, Robert. “Neo-Georgism.” In *Critics of Henry George: An Appraisal of Their Strictures on “Progress and Poverty,”* edited by Robert Andelson, 705–29. Malden, Mass.: Blackwell, 2004.

Anderson, Elizabeth. *Value in Ethics and Economics.* Cambridge, Mass.: Harvard University Press, 1993.

Araujo, Marcelo de. “Hugo Grotius, Moral Scepticism and the Use of Arguments in *Utramque Partem*.” *Veritas* 56, no. 3 (2011): 145–66.

Arendt, Hannah. *The Human Condition.* 2nd edition. Chicago: University of Chicago Press, 1958.

Arenson, Richard. “Self Ownership and World Ownership: Against Left-Libertarianism.” *Social Philosophy and Policy* 27 (2010): 168–94.

Aslanbeigui, Nahid, and Adele Wick. “Progress: Poverty or Prosperity? Joining the Debate between George and Marshall on the Effects of Economic Growth on the Distribution of Income.” *American Journal of Economics and Sociology* 60, no. 5, Supplement (2001): 33–54.

Atkinson, Anthony, and Joseph Stiglitz, *Lectures on Public Economics.* London: McGraw-Hill, 1987.

Backhaus, Jürgen. “Henry George’s Ingenious Tax: A Contemporary Restatement.” *American Journal of Economics and Sociology* 56, no. 4 (2006): 453–74.

Banzhaf, H. Spencer, and Nathan Lavery. “Can the Land Tax Help Curb Urban Sprawl? Evidence from Growth Patterns in Pennsylvania.” *Journal of Urban Economics* 67 (2010): 169–79.

Barbaras, Renaud. “Merleau-Ponty and Nature.” *Research in Phenomenology* 31, no. 1 (2001): 22–38.

Barbosa, Luiz C. “Theories in Environmental Sociology.” In *Twenty Lessons in Environmental Sociology*, edited by Kenneth A. Gould and Tammy Lewis, 24–44. New York: Oxford University Press, 2009.

Bataille, Georges. *The Accursed Share,* volume 1. Translated by Robert Hurley. Brooklyn, N.Y.: Zone Books, 1989 [1967].

Batt, H. William. “The Compatibility of Georgist Economics and Ecological Economics.” Presentation at the United States Society for Ecological Economics. Saratoga Springs, N.Y., 2003. http://www.wealthandwant.com/docs/Batt_GEE.html.

Benson, Peter, and Stuart Kirsch. "Capitalism and the Politics of Resignation." *Current Anthropology* 51, no. 4 (2010): 459–86.

Blaug, Mark. *Economic Theory in Retrospect.* 3rd edition. Cambridge: Cambridge University Press, 1978.

———. *The Methodology of Economics: Or How Economists Explain.* 2nd edition. Cambridge: Cambridge University Press, 1992.

Blundell, Boyd. *Paul Ricoeur between Theology and Philosophy: Detour and Return.* Bloomington: Indiana University Press, 2010.

Bourdieu, Pierre. *Outline of a Theory of Practice.* Translated by R. Nice. Cambridge: Cambridge University Press, 1977.

Brogan, Walter. "The Community of Those Who Are Going to Die." In *Heidegger and Practical Philosophy*, edited by François Raffoul and David Pettigrew, 237–48. Albany: SUNY Press, 2002.

Browning, Gary, and Andrew Kilmister. *Critical and Post-Critical Political Economy.* Houndsmill, Eng.: Palgrave Macmillan, 2006.

Bryan, Dick. "'Natural' and 'Improved' Land in Marx's Theory of Rent." *Land Economics* 66, no. 2 (1990): 176–81.

Buckle, Stephen. *Natural Law and the Theory of Property: Grotius to Hume.* Oxford: Clarendon, 1991.

Burkett, Paul. *Marx and Nature: A Red and Green Perspective.* New York: St. Martin's, 1999.

Camus, Albert. *The Myth of Sisyphus and Other Essays.* Translated by Justin O'Brien. New York: Vintage Books, 1955 [1942].

Cantillon, Richard. *Essai sur la nature du commerce en general.* London: Frank Cass, 1959 [c. 1730].

Carchedi, Guglielmo. *Beyond the Crisis: Marx's Dialectics of Value and Knowledge.* Leiden: Brill, 2001.

Carrette, Jeremy. *Religion and Critical Psychology: Religious Experience in the Knowledge Economy.* London: Routledge, 2007.

Casey, Edward S. "The Edge(s) of Landscape: A Study in Liminology." In *The Place of Landscape: Concepts, Contexts, Studies*, edited by Jeff Malpas, 91–109. Cambridge, Mass.: MIT Press, 2011.

———. *Getting Back into Place: Toward a Renewed Understanding of the Place-World.* 2nd edition. Bloomington: Indiana University Press, 2009.

———. "Mapping the Earth in Works of Art." In *Rethinking Nature: Essays in Environmental Philosophy*, edited by Bruce Foltz and Robert Frodeman, 260–69. Bloomington: Indiana University Press, 2004.

Churchman, Nancy. "David Ricardo on Public Policy: The Question of Motive." *Journal of the History of Economic Thought* 17, no. 1 (1995): 133–52.

Cirillo, Renato. *The Economics of Vilfredo Pareto.* London: Frank Cass, 1979.

Clark, Brett, and John Bellamy Foster. "Marx's Ecology in the 21st Century." *World Review of Political Economy* 1, no. 1 (2010): 142–56.

Clark, Colin. *Population Growth and Land Use.* London: Macmillan, 1977.

Coleman, James S. "Social Capital in the Creation of Human Capital." *American Journal of Sociology* 94, Supplement (1988): S95–S120.

Collingwood, R. G. *An Autobiography.* Oxford: Clarendon, 1978.

———. "Economics as a Philosophical Science." *International Journal of Ethics* 36, no. 2 (1926): 162–85.

———. *An Essay on Metaphysics.* Revised edition. Oxford: Clarendon, 1998 [1940].

———. *The Idea of Nature.* Oxford: Clarendon, 1945.

Cox, Christoph. *Nietzsche: Naturalism and Interpretation.* Berkeley: University of California Press, 1999.

Crowell, Steven Galt. "Making Logic Philosophical Again (1912–1916)." In *Reading Heidegger from the Start: Essays in His Earliest Thought,* edited by Theodore Kisiel and John van Buren, 55–72. Albany: SUNY Press, 1994.

———. "Subjectivity: Locating the First-Person in *Being and Time.*" In *Heidegger's "Being and Time": Critical Essays,* edited by Richard Polt, 117–39. Lanham, Md.: Rowman and Littlefield, 2005.

———. "What Gives? Getting Over the Subject?" *Continental Philosophy Review* 33 (2000): 93–105.

Czech, Brian. "The Neoclassical Production Function as a Relic of Anti-George Politics: Implications for Ecological Economics." *Ecological Economics* 68 (2009): 2193–97.

Daly, Herman. *Beyond Growth: The Economics of Sustainable Development.* Boston: Beacon, 1996.

———. *Ecological Economics and Sustainable Development: Selected Essays of Herman Daly.* Cheltenham, Eng.: Edward Elgar, 2007.

Darwin, Roy, Marinos Tsigas, Jan Lewandrowski, and Anton Raneses. "Land Use and Cover in Ecological Economics." *Ecological Economics* 17 (1996): 157–81.

Davies, Oliver. "The Challenge of the Past: Meister Eckhart, Reasoning and Contemporary Philosophy." *Medieval Mystical Theology* 20, no. 1 (2011): 9–27.

Deléage, Jean-Paul. "Eco-Marxist Critique of Political Economy." In *Is Capitalism Sustainable?* edited by Martin O'Connor, 37–52. New York: Guilford, 1994.

Derrida, Jacques. *Given Time: I. Counterfeit Money.* Translated by Peggy Kamuf. New York: Columbia University Press, 1992.

———. "The Principle of Reason: The University in the Eyes of Its Pupils." *Diacritics* 13, no. 3 (1983): 2–20.

Deweer, Dries. "Ricoeur on Citizenship: A Picture of a Personalist Republicanism." In *Paul Ricoeur and the Task of Political Philosophy,* edited by Greg S. Johnson and Dan R. Stiver, 35–50. Lanham, Md.: Lexington Books, 2013.

Dix, Guus. "Ricardo's Discursive Demarcations: A Foucauldian Study of the Formation of the Economy as an Object of Knowledge." *Erasmus Journal for Philosophy and Economics* 7, no. 2 (2014): 1–29.

Dreyfus, Hubert. *Being-in-the-World: A Commentary on Heidegger's "Being and Time," Division I.* Cambridge, Mass.: MIT Press, 1991.

———. "Can There Be a Better Source of Meaning Than Everyday Practices? Reinterpreting Division I of *Being and Time* in the Light of Division II." In *Heidegger's Being and Time: Critical Essays,* edited by Richard Polt, 141–54. Lanham, Md.: Rowman and Littlefield, 2005.

Dreyfus, Hubert, and Harrison Hall. "Introduction." In *Heidegger: A Critical Reader,* edited by Hubert Dreyfus and Harrison Hall, 1–25. Oxford: Basil Blackwell, 1992.

Dummett, Michael. *The Origins of Analytic Philosophy.* Cambridge, Mass.: Harvard University Press, 1993.

Düppe, Till. *The Making of the Economy: A Phenomenology of Economic Science.* Lanham, Md.: Lexington Books, 2011.

Dupré, Louis. *Marx's Social Critique of Culture.* New Haven, Conn.: Yale University Press, 1983.

———. *Passage to Modernity: An Essay in the Hermeneutics of Nature and Culture.* New Haven, Conn.: Yale University Press, 1993.

———. *The Philosophical Foundations of Marxism.* New York: Harcourt, Brace and World, 1966.

Eckelund, Robert B., Jr., and Robert D. Tollison. *Mercantilism as a Rent-Seeking Society: Economic Regulation in Historical Perspective.* College Station: Texas A&M University Press, 1981.

Elliott, John E. "The *Grundrisse* as Social Theory: Link between Young Marx and Mature Marx." *Social Science Quarterly* 59, no. 2 (1978): 239–56.

Evans, Michael. "Karl Marx's First Confrontations with Political Economy: The 1844 Manuscripts." *Economy and Society* 13, no. 2 (1984): 115–52.

Fell, Joseph. *Heidegger and Sartre: An Essay on Being and Place.* New York: Columbia University Press, 1979.

Fine, Ben. "On Marx's Theory of Agricultural Rent." *Economy and Society* 8, no. 3 (1979): 241–78.

Fine, Ben, and Alfredo Saad-Filho. *Marx's "Capital."* 5th edition. New York: Pluto, 2010.

Foldvary, Fred E. "Geoism and Libertarianism." *The Progress Report.* 2007. http://www.progress.org/tpr/foldvary-geoism-and-libertarianism/.

———. "Geo-Rent: A Plea to Public Economists." *Econ Journal Watch* 2, no. 1 (2005): 106–32.

Foltz, Bruce. *Inhabiting the Earth: Heidegger, Environmental Ethics, and the Metaphysics of Nature.* Atlantic Heights, N.J.: Humanities, 1995.

Foster, John Bellamy. "Malthus' Essay on Population at Age 200: A Marxian View." *Monthly Review: An Independent Socialist Magazine* 50, no. 7 (1998). http://monthlyreview.org/1998/12/01/malthus-essay-on-population-at-age-200/.

———. *Marx's Ecology: Materialism and Nature.* New York: Monthly Review, 2000.

Foucault, Michel. "About the Beginning of the Hermeneutics of the Self." In *Religion and Culture,* by Michel Foucault, edited by Jeremy Carrette, 135–52. London: Manchester University Press/Routledge, 1999 [1993].

———. *Archaeology of Knowledge.* Translated by A. M. Sheridan Smith. London: Routledge, 1972.

———. *Discipline and Punish: The Birth of the Prison.* Translated by Alan Sheridan. New York: Vintage, 1977.

———. *Dits et écrits* 1–4. Paris: Gallimard, 1994.

———. *Essential Works of Foucault 1954–1984.* Volume 3, edited by James D. Faubion. New York: New Press, 2000.

———. *The Order of Things: An Archaeology of the Human Sciences.* London: Routledge, 1970.

———. *Society Must Be Defended: Lectures at the Collège de France, 1975–76.* Translated by David Macey. London: Penguin, 2003 [1975].

Friedman, Michael. *A Parting of the Ways: Carnap, Cassirer, and Heidegger.* Chicago: Open Court, 2000.

Friedmann, Harriet. "Household Production and the National Economy: Concepts for the Analysis of Agrarian Formations." *Journal of Peasant Studies* 7, no. 2 (1980): 158–84.

Gaffney, Mason. "The Adequacy of Land as a Tax Base." In *The Assessment of Land Value,* edited by Daniel Holland, 157–212. Madison: University of Wisconsin Press, 1970.

———. "Land as a Distinctive Factor of Production." In *Land and Taxation,* edited by Nicolaus Tideman, 38–102. London: Shepheard-Walwyn, 1994.

———. "The Role of Ground Rent in Urban Decay and Revival: How to Revitalize a Failing City." *American Journal of Economics and Sociology* 60, no. 5, Supplement (2001): 57–83.

Gaffney, Mason, Fred Harrison, and Kris Feder. *The Corruption of Economics.* London: Shepheard-Walwyn, 1994.

Gagnon, Marc-André. "Capital, Power and Knowledge According to Thorstein Veblen: Reinterpreting the Knowledge-Based Economy." *Journal of Economic Issues* 41, no. 2 (2007): 593–600.

Galbraith, J. K. *The Affluent Society.* New edition. London: Penguin, 1998.

George, Henry. *Progress and Poverty.* New York: Robert Schalkenbach, 1992 [1879].

———. *The Science of Political Economy: A Reconstruction of Its Principles in Clear and Systematic Form.* New York: Robert Schalkenbach, 1992 [1898].

———. *Social Problems.* New York: Robert Schalkenbach, 1996 [1883].

Ghosh, Jayati. "Differential and Absolute Rent." *Journal of Peasant Studies* 13, no. 1 (1985): 67–82.

Goodchild, Philip. *Theology of Money.* London: SCM, 2007.

Grant, Elizabeth. "Private Property in America: Land Use and the Ethics of Owning Land." M.A. thesis in Environmental Philosophy, University of North Texas, 2005. http://www.cep.unt.edu/theses/grant.pdf.

Grotius, Hugo. *The Freedom of the Seas, or, The Right Which Belongs to the Dutch to Take Part in the East Indian Trade* [*Mare liberum*]. Translated by Ralph van Deman Macgoffin. New York: Oxford University Press, 1916 [1608].

———. *The Rights of War and Peace* [*De jure belli ac pacis libri tres*]. Translated by John Morrice. Indianapolis: Liberty Fund, 2005 [1625].

Gutting, Gary. *Thinking the Impossible: French Philosophy since 1960.* Oxford: Oxford University Press, 2011.

Haakonssen, Knud. *Natural Law and Moral Philosophy: From Grotius to the Scottish Enlightenment.* Cambridge: Cambridge University Press, 1996.

Han, Lixin. "Marxism and Ecology: Marx's Theory of Labour Process Revisited." In *Eco-Socialism as Politics: Rebuilding the Basis of Our Modern Civilisation,* edited by Qingzhui Huan, 15–31. Dordrecht: Springer, 2010.

Harrison, Fred. *The Power in the Land: Unemployment, the Profits Crisis and the Land Speculator.* London: Shepheard-Walwyn, 1983.

———. *Ricardo's Law: House Prices and the Great Tax Clawback Scam.* London: Shepheard-Walwyn, 2006.

Harvey, David. *The Limits of Capital.* Oxford: Basil Blackwell, 1982.

Heering, Jan Paul. *Hugo Grotius as Apologist for the Christian Religion: A Study of His Work "De veritate religionis christianae"* (1640). Leiden: Brill, 2004.

Heidegger, Martin. *Aristotle's "Metaphysics" θ 1–3: On Essence and Actuality of Force.* Translated by Walter Brogan and Peter Warnek. Bloomington: Indiana University Press, 1995 [1981].

———. *The Basic Problems of Phenomenology.* Revised edition. Translated by A. Hofstadter. Bloomington: Indiana University Press, 1982 [1927].

———. *Basic Writings.* Translated by David Farrell Krell. San Francisco: HarperSanFrancisco, 1993.

———. *Being and Time.* Translated by Joan Stambaugh. Albany: SUNY Press, 1996 [1927].

———. *Being and Time.* Translated by John Macquarrie and Edward Robinson. Oxford: Blackwell, 1962 [1927].

———. *Discourse on Thinking: A Translation of Gelassenheit.* Translated by John M. Anders and E. Hans Freund. New York: Harper and Row, 1966 [1959].

———. *Early Greek Thinking: The Dawn of Western Philosophy.* Translated by David Farrell Krell and Frank A. Capuzzi. San Francisco: HarperSanFrancisco, 1984.

———. *The Essence of Truth.* Translated by Ted Sadler. New York: Continuum, 2002 [1988].

———. *The Fundamental Concepts of Metaphysics.* Translated by William McNeill and Nicholas Walker. Bloomington: Indiana University Press, 1995 [1983].

———. *History of the Concept of Time.* Translated by Theodore Kisiel. Bloomington: Indiana University Press, 1985 [1979].

———. *Identity and Difference.* Translated by Joan Stambaugh. Chicago: University of Chicago Press, 1969 [1957].

———. *An Introduction to Metaphysics.* Translated by Ralph Manheim. New Haven, Conn.: Yale University Press, 1959 [1953].

———. *The Metaphysical Foundations of Logic.* Translated by Michael Heim. Bloomington: Indiana University Press, 1984 [1978].

———. *Off the Beaten Track.* Translated and edited by Julian Young and Kenneth Haynes. Cambridge: Cambridge University Press, 2002.

———. *On Time and Being.* Translated by Joan Stambaugh. New York: Harper and Row, 1972 [1969].

———. *Pathmarks.* Edited by William McNeill. Cambridge: Cambridge University Press, 1998.

———. *Plato's "Sophist."* Translated by Richard Rojcewicz and André Schuwer. Bloomington: Indiana University Press, 1997 [1992].

———. *Poetry, Language, Thought.* Translated by Albert Hofstadter. New York: Harper and Row, 1971.

———. *The Principle of Reason.* Translated by Reginald Lilly. Bloomington: Indiana University Press, 1991 [1957].

———. *The Question Concerning Technology*. Translated by William Lovitt. New York: Harper and Row, 1976.

———. *What Is Called Thinking?* Translated by J. Glenn Gray. New York: Harper and Row, 1968 [1954].

———. *Zollikon Seminars: Protocols—Conversations—Letters*. Translated by Franz Mayr and Richard Askay. Evanston, Ill.: Northwestern University Press, 2001 [1987].

Heilbroner, Robert. *The Nature and Logic of Capitalism*. New York: W. W. Norton, 1985.

———. *The Worldly Philosophers: The Lives, Times and Ideas of the Great Economic Thinkers*. New York: Simon and Schuster, 1986.

Hemming, Laurence. *Heidegger and Marx: A Productive Dialogue over the Language of Humanism*. Evanston, Ill.: Northwestern University Press, 2013.

Hodge, Joanna. *Heidegger and Ethics*. London: Routledge, 1995.

Honneth, Axel. *Pathologies of Reason: On the Legacy of Critical Theory*. Translated by James Ingram. New York: Columbia University Press, 2009.

Horn, Walter. "Libertarianism and Private Property in Land: The Positions of Rothbard and Nozick, Critically Examined, Are Disputed." *American Journal of Economics and Sociology* 43, no. 3 (1984): 341–55.

Horner, James H. "Seeking Institutionalist Signposts in the Work of Henry George." *American Journal of Economics and Sociology* 52, no. 2 (1993): 247–55.

Howard, M. C., and J. E. King. "Marx, Jones, Rodbertus and the Theory of Absolute Rent." *Journal of the History of Economic Thought* 14, no. 1 (1992): 70–83.

Husserl, Edmund. *Cartesian Meditations: An Introduction to Phenomenology*. Translated by Dorion Cairns. Dordrecht: Kluwer, 1999 [1931].

Hyde, Lewis. *Common as Air: Revolution, Art and Ownership*. New York: Union Books, 2010.

Ihde, Don. *Heidegger's Technologies: Postphenomenological Perspectives*. New York: Fordham University Press, 2010.

Ingham, Geoffrey. *Capitalism*. Cambridge, Eng.: Polity, 2008.

Ingold, Tim. "The Temporality of Landscape." *World Archaeology* 25, no. 2 (1993): 152–74.

James, Ian. *The New French Philosophy*. Cambridge, Eng.: Polity, 2012.

Kennedy, Geoff. "Capitalism, Contextualisation and *The Political Theory of Possessive Individualism*." *Intellectual History and Political Thought* 1, no. 1 (2012): 228–51.

Kockelmans, Joseph. *Edmund Husserl's Phenomenology*. West Lafayette, Ind.: Purdue University Press, 1994.

Kologlugil, Serhat. "Michel Foucault's Archaeology of Knowledge and Economic Discourse." *Erasmus Journal for Philosophy and Economics* 3, no. 2 (2010): 1–25.

Kramer, Matthew H. *John Locke and the Origins of Private Property: Philosophical Explorations of Individualism, Community, and Equality*. Cambridge: Cambridge University Press, 1997.

Kresge, Stephen, and Leif Wenar, eds. *Hayek on Hayek: An Autobiographical Dialogue.* London: Routledge, 1994.

Krugman, Paul. *The Accidental Theorist.* London: Penguin, 1999.

Lamb, Robert. "Locke on Ownership, Imperfect Duties and 'the Art of Governing.'" *The British Journal of Politics & International Relations* 12, no. 1 (2010): 126–41.

LeDoeuff, Michèle. *The Philosophical Imaginary.* Translated by Colin Gordon. London: Continuum, 2002.

Leshem, Dotan. "Oikonomia Redefined." *Journal of the History of Economic Thought* 35, no. 1 (2013): 43–61.

Levinas, Emmanuel. *Totality and Infinity: An Essay on Exteriority.* Translated by Alphonso Lingis. Pittsburgh, Pa.: Duquesne University Press, 1969.

Llewellyn, John. "A Footnote in the History of φύσις." *Research in Phenomenology* 31, no. 1 (2001): 39–61.

Locke, John. *An Essay Concerning Human Understanding.* London: Penguin, 1997 [1689].

———. *Two Treatises of Government.* London: A. Millar et al., 1764 [1690].

MacIntyre, Alasdair. *After Virtue.* 2nd edition. Notre Dame, Ind.: University of Notre Dame Press, 1984.

———. *Three Rival Versions of Moral Enquiry: Encyclopedia, Genealogy, and Tradition.* Notre Dame, Ind.: University of Notre Dame Press, 1990.

MacIntyre, Alasdair, and Paul Ricoeur. *The Religious Significance of Atheism.* New York: Columbia University Press, 1966.

Mackinlay, Shane. "Exceeding Truth: Jean-Luc Marion's Saturated Phenomena." *Pacifica* 20 (2007): 40–51.

———. *Interpreting Excess: Jean-Luc Marion, Saturated Phenomena, and Hermeneutics.* New York: Fordham University Press, 2010.

MacLaren, Leon. *Nature of Society and Other Essays.* London: School of Economic Science, 2010.

Macpherson, C. B. *The Political Theory of Possessive Individualism: Hobbes to Locke.* Oxford: Oxford University Press, 1962.

Malpas, Jeff. *Heidegger and the Thinking of Place: Explorations in the Topology of Being.* Cambridge, Mass.: MIT Press, 2012.

———. *Heidegger's Topology: Being, Place, World.* Cambridge, Mass.: MIT Press, 2006.

———. "Introduction." In *The Place of Landscape: Concepts, Contexts, Studies,* edited by Jeff Malpas, vii–xiii. Cambridge, Mass.: MIT Press, 2011.

———. *Place and Experience: A Philosophical Topography.* Cambridge: Cambridge University Press, 1999.

———. "Place and the Problem of Landscape." In *The Place of Landscape: Concepts, Contexts, Studies,* edited by Jeff Malpas, 3–26. Cambridge, Mass.: MIT Press, 2011.

———, ed. *The Place of Landscape: Concepts, Contexts, Studies.* Cambridge, Mass.: MIT Press, 2011.

Malthus, Thomas. *The Nature and Progress of Rent.* Charleston, S.C.: BiblioBazaar, 2006 [1815].

Mandel, Ernest. *Marxist Economic Theory*. Translated by Brian Pearce. London: Merlin, 1968.

Marglin, Stephen A. *The Dismal Science: How Thinking Like an Economist Undermines Community*. Cambridge, Mass.: Harvard University Press, 2008.

Marion, Jean-Luc. *Being Given: Toward a Phenomenology of Givenness*. Translated by Jeffrey L. Kosky. Stanford, Calif.: Stanford University Press, 2002.

———. *In Excess: Studies of Saturated Phenomena*. Translated by Robyn Horner and Vincent Berraud. Fordham, N.Y.: Fordham University Press, 2002.

———. *Reduction and Givenness: Investigations of Husserl, Heidegger, and Phenomenology*. Translated by Thomas A. Carlson. Evanston, Ill.: Northwestern University Press, 1998.

Marshall, Alfred. *Principles of Economics*. 8th edition. London: Macmillan, 1890.

Marx, Karl. *Capital: A Critique of Political Economy*. Volume 1. Translated by Ben Fowkes. London: Penguin Books, 1976 [1867].

———. *Capital: A Critique of Political Economy*. Volume 3. Translated by David Fernbach. London: Penguin Books, 1981 [1894].

———. *Economic and Philosophical Manuscripts of 1844*. Translated by Martin Milligan. Amherst, Mass.: Prometheus Books, 1988 [1844].

———. *Grundrisse*. Translated by Martin Nicolaus. London: Penguin Books, 1973 [1857–58].

Marx, Karl, and Friedrich Engels. *Collected Works*. Volume 38. London: Lawrence and Wishart, 1982.

———. *Collected Works*. Volume 41. London: Lawrence and Wishart, 1985.

———. *The German Ideology*. Amherst, Mass.: Prometheus Books, 1998 [1845].

McManus, Denis. *Heidegger and the Measure of Truth*. Oxford: Oxford University Press, 2012.

Mei, Todd S. "An Economic Turn: A Hermeneutical Reinterpretation of Political Economy with Respect to the Question of Land." *Research in Phenomenology* 41, no. 3 (2011): 297–326.

———. "Economy of the Gift: Rethinking the Role of Land Enclosure in Political Economy." *Modern Theology* 25, no. 3 (2009): 441–48.

———. "Heidegger and the Appropriation of Metaphysics." *The Heythrop Journal* 50, no. 2 (2009): 257–70.

———. "Heidegger in the Machine: The Difference between *Techne* and *Mechane*." *Continental Philosophy Review* (2015): 1–26. doi: 10.1007/s11007-015-9319-3.

———. *Heidegger, Work, and Being*. London: Continuum, 2009.

———. "Insurance in Between: A Critique of Liability Insurance and Its Principles." *Literature and Theology* 21, no. 1 (2007): 82–98.

———. "The Pre-eminence of Use: Reinterpreting the Relation between Use and Exchange in Aristotle's Economic Thinking." *The Journal of the History of Philosophy* 47, no. 4 (2009): 523–48.

———. "Ricoeur *Economicus*: Can Economic Exchange Involve Mutual Recognition?" In *Paul Ricoeur and the Task of Political Philosophy*, edited by Gregory R. Johnson and Dan R. Stiver, 65–84. Lanham, Md.: Lexington Books, 2013.

Meikle, Scott. "Quality and Quantity in Economics: The Metaphysical Construction of the Economic Realm." *New Literary History* 31 (2000): 247–76.

Milbank, John. *Theology and Social Theory: Beyond Secular Reason.* Oxford: Blackwell, 2005.

Milios, John, Dimitri Dimoulis, and George Economakis. *Karl Marx and the Classics: An Essay on Value, Crises and the Capitalist Mode of Production.* Aldershot, Eng.: Ashgate, 2002.

Mill, J. S. *Principles of Political Economy.* Amherst, Mass.: Prometheus Books, 2004 [1848].

Mirowski, Philip. *More Heat Than Light: Economics as Social Physics, Physics as Nature's Economics.* Cambridge: Cambridge University Press, 1989.

Morgan, Mary. *The World in the Model: How Economists Work and Think.* Cambridge: Cambridge University Press, 2012.

Munzer, Stephen. *A Theory of Property.* Cambridge: Cambridge University Press, 1990.

Murphy, Liam, and Thomas Nagel. *The Myth of Ownership: Taxes and Justice.* Oxford: Oxford University Press, 2002.

Myrdal, Gunnar. *Objectivity in Social Research.* London: Gerald Duckworth, 1969.

———. *The Political Element in the Development of Economic Theory.* London: Routledge and Kegan Paul, 1953.

Nelson, Robert H. *Economics as Religion: From Samuelson to Chicago and Beyond.* University Park: Pennsylvania State University Press, 2006.

Niehans, Jürg. *A History of Economic Theory: Classic Contributions, 1720–1980.* Baltimore: Johns Hopkins University Press, 1990.

Nietzsche, Friedrich. *Untimely Meditations.* Edited by Daniel Breazeale, 59–123. Cambridge: Cambridge University Press, 1983 [1874].

———. *Will to Power,* volume 15 of *Complete Works.* Translated by Anthony M. Ludovici. Edinburgh: T. N. Fowlis, 1910.

Niman, Neil B. "Henry George and the Development of Thorstein Veblen's Theory of Capital." *Journal of the History of Economic Thought* 32, no. 3 (2010): 419–31.

Olivecrona, Karl. "Locke's Theory of Appropriation." *The Philosophical Quarterly* 24, no. 96 (1974): 220–34.

Otsuka, Michael. *Libertarianism without Inequality.* Oxford: Clarendon, 2003.

Pareto, Vilfredo. *Manual of Political Economy.* Translated by Ann S. Schwier. London: Macmillan, 1971 [1921].

Peddle, Francis K. "Distributism and Marginal Productivity: The Application of Natural Law to Public Finance." *Science et Esprit* 63, no. 3 (2011): 315–31.

Petty, William. *A Treatise of Taxes and Contributions.* London: Angel in Cornhill, 1662.

Plassmann, Florenz, and Nicolaus Tideman. "Frank Knight's Proposal to End Distinctions among Factors of Production and His Objection to the Single Tax." *History of Political Economy* 36, no. 3 (2004): 505–19.

Plato. *Republic.* Translated by Joe Sachs. Newburyport, Mass.: Focus Publishing, 2007.

Polanyi, Karl. *The Great Transformation: The Political and Economic Origins of Our Time.* Boston: Beacon, 2001 [1944].

Portes, Alejandro. "Social Capital: Its Origins and Applications in Modern Sociology." In *Knowledge and Social Capital: Applications and Foundations,* edited by Eric L. Lesser, 43–67. Woburn, Mass.: Butterworth-Heinemann, 2000.

Pufendorf, Samuel. *Of the Law of Nature and Nations, Eight Books.* Translated by Basil Kennett. Oxford: L. Lichfield, 1710 [1672].

———. *The Whole Duty of Man, According to the Law of Nature.* Translated by David Saunders. Indianapolis, Ind.: Liberty Fund, 2003 [1673].

Raffoul, François. *Heidegger and the Subject.* Translated by David Pettigrew and Gregory Recco. Atlantic Highlands, N.J.: Humanities, 1998.

———. *The Origins of Responsibility.* Bloomington: Indiana University Press, 2010.

Ramirez, Miguel. "Marx's Theory of Ground Rent: A Critical Assessment." *Contributions to Political Economy* 28 (2009): 71–91.

Rancière, Jacques. *Dissensus: On Politics and Aesthetics.* Translated and edited by Steven Corcoran. London: Continuum, 2010.

Reeve, Andrew. *Property.* Basingstoke, Eng.: Macmillan, 1986.

Ricardo, David. *Principles of Political Economy and Taxation.* 3rd edition. Amherst: Prometheus Books, 1996 [1812].

Ricoeur, Paul. *The Conflict of Interpretations.* Edited by Don Ihde. Evanston, Ill.: Northwestern University Press, 1974.

———. *Hermeneutics and the Human Sciences.* Translated and edited by J. B. Thompson. Cambridge: Cambridge University Press, 1981.

———. *Husserl: An Analysis of His Phenomenology.* Translated by Edward G. Ballard and Lester E. Embree. Evanston, Ill.: Northwestern University Press, 1967.

———. *Lectures on Ideology and Utopia.* Edited by George H. Taylor. New York: Columbia University Press, 1986.

———. *Oneself as Another.* Translated by Kathleen Blamey. Chicago: University of Chicago Press, 1992.

———. *A Ricoeur Reader: Reflection and Imagination.* Edited by Mario J. Valdés. New York: Harvester Wheatsheaf, 1991.

———. *The Rule of Metaphor.* Translated by Robert Czerny, Kathleen McLaughlin, and John Costello. London: Routledge and Kegan Paul, 1977.

Rojcewicz, Richard. *The Gods and Technology: A Reading of Heidegger.* Albany: SUNY Press, 2006.

Routh, Guy. *The Origin of Economic Ideas.* London: Macmillan, 1975.

Ryan, Alan. *Property.* Milton Keynes, Eng.: Open University Press, 1987.

Ryan, Christopher K. "Land as a Factor of Production." *The American Journal of Economics and Sociology* 61, no. 5 (2003): 7–25.

Sahlins, Marshall. "The Original Affluent Society." In *The Politics of Egalitarianism: Theory and Practice,* edited by Jacqueline Solway, 79–98. New York: Berghahn Books, 2006.

Sallis, John. *Being and Logos: Reading the Platonic Dialogues.* 3rd edition. Bloomington: Indiana University Press, 1996.

———. *Topographies.* Bloomington: Indiana University Press, 2006.

Salter, John. "Adam Smith and the Grotian Theory of Property." *The British Journal of Politics and International Relations* 12 (2010): 3–21.

Samuelson, Paul. "Wages and Interest: A Modern Dissection of Marxian Economic Models." *The American Economic Review* 47, no. 6 (1957): 884–912.

Samuelson, Paul, and William D. Nordhaus. *Economics*. 15th edition. New York: McGraw-Hill, 1995.

Say, Jean-Baptiste. *A Treatise on Political Economy: Or the Production, Distribution, and Consumption of Wealth*. Translated by C. R. Prinsep. Kitchener, Ont.: Batoche Books, 2001 [1803].

Schabas, Margaret. *The Natural Origins of Economics*. Chicago: University of Chicago Press, 2005.

Scharff, Robert C. "Rorty and Analytic Heideggerian Epistemology—and Heidegger." *Man and World* 25 (1992): 483–504.

Schneewind, J. B. *The Invention of Autonomy: A History of Modern Moral Philosophy*. Cambridge: Cambridge University Press, 1998.

Sen, Amartya. *Commodities and Capabilities*. New Delhi: Oxford University Press, 1999.

———. *The Idea of Justice*. Cambridge, Mass.: Belknap, 2009.

Sheehan, Thomas. "A Paradigm Shift in Heidegger Research." *Continental Philosophy Review* 34 (2001): 183–202.

———. "On Movement and the Destruction of Ontology." *The Monist* 64, no. 4 (1981): 534–42.

Sloan, Pat. *Marx and the Orthodox Economists*. Oxford: Basil Blackwell, 1973.

Sloman, John. *Economics*. 6th edition. Harlow, Eng.: Prentice Hall, 2006.

Smith, Adam. *The Wealth of Nations*, I–V. Edited by A. Skinner. London: Penguin, 1999 [1776].

Smith, Dominic. "The Internet as Idea: For a Transcendental Philosophy of Technology." *Techne* 19, no. 3 (2015): 381–410.

———. "Rewriting the Constitution: A Critique of 'Postphenomenology.'" *Philosophy & Technology* (2014): 1–19. doi: 10.1007/s13347-014-0175-6.

Steiner, Hillel. "Left Libertarianism and the Ownership of Natural Resources." *Public Reason* 1, no. 1 (2009): 1–8.

Stigler, George J. "Ricardo and the 93% Labor Theory of Value." *American Economic Association* 48, no. 3 (1958): 357–67.

Taylor, Charles. *A Secular Age*. Cambridge, Mass.: Belknap, 2007.

Thompson, James. "Buildings Destroyed after Rate Relief Abolished." *The Independent*, August 13, 2008. http://www.independent.co.uk/news/business/news/buildings-destroyed-after-rate-relief-is-abolished-892966.html.

Thomson, Iain D. *Heidegger on Ontotheology: Technology and the Politics of Education*. Cambridge: Cambridge University Press, 2005.

Thumfart, Johannes. "On Grotius's *Mare Liberum* and Vitoria's *De Indis*, Following Agamben and Schmitt." *Grotiana* 30 (2009): 65–87.

Tideman, Nicolaus. "Applications of Land Value Taxation to Problems of Environmental Protection, Congestion, Efficient Resource Use, Population, and Economic Growth." In *Land Value Taxation: Can It and Will It Work*

Today? edited by Dick Netzer. Cambridge, Mass: Lincoln Institute of Land Policy, 1998. https://sites.google.com/site/nicolaustideman/research.

———. "The Economics of Efficient Taxes on Land." In *Land and Taxation,* edited by Nicolaus Tideman, 103–40. London: Shepheard-Walwyn, 1994.

———. "George on Land Speculation and the Winner's Curse." *American Journal of Economics and Sociology* 63, no. 5 (2004): 1091–95.

———. "Private Possession as an Alternative to Rental and Private Ownership of Land" (in Russian). *Agrarnaya Nauka* (*Agrarian Science*) 2, no. 93 (1993): 22–24. English version of the text, https://sites.google.com/site/nicolaustideman/research.

Tideman, Nicolaus, and Peter Vallentyne. "Left-Libertarianism and Global Justice." In *Human Rights in Philosophy and Practice,* edited by Burton M. Leiser and Tom D. Campbell, 453–57. Burlington, Vt.: Dartmouth, 2001.

Tolstoy, Leo. *How Much Land Does a Man Need? and Other Stories.* Translated by Ronald Wilks. London: Penguin, 1993 [1886].

Tribe, Keith. *Land, Labour and Economic Discourse.* London: Routledge and Kegan Paul, 1978.

Tuck, Richard. *Natural Rights Theories: Their Origin and Development.* Cambridge: Cambridge University Press, 1979.

Tucker, G. S. L. "Ricardo and Marx." *Economica* 28, no. 111 (1961): 252–69.

Vallentyne, Peter. "Left-Libertarianism as a Promising Form of Liberal Egalitarianism." *Philosophical Exchange* 39, no. 1 (2009): 56–71.

Vallentyne, Peter, Hillel Steiner, and Michael Otsuka. "Why Left-Libertarianism Is Not Coherent, Indeterminate, or Irrelevant: A Reply to Fried." *Philosophy and Public Affairs* 33, no. 2 (2005): 201–15.

Veblen, Thorstein. *Absentee Ownership: Business Enterprise in Recent Times: The Case of America.* New edition. New Brunswick, N.J.: Transaction, 1997 [1923].

———. "On the Nature of Capital." *Quarterly Journal of Economics* 22, no. 4 (1908): 517–42.

Villela-Petit, Maria. "Heidegger's Conception of Space." In *Critical Heidegger,* translated and edited by Christopher Macann, 134–57. London: Routledge, 1996.

Viner, Jacob. *The Role of Providence in the Social Order: An Essay in Intellectual History.* Philadelphia: American Philosophical Society, 1966.

Waldron, Jeremy. *The Right to Private Property.* Oxford: Clarendon, 1988.

———. *The Rule of Law and the Measure of Property.* Cambridge: Cambridge University Press, 2012.

Weber, Max. *The Protestant Ethic and the Spirit of Capitalism.* Translated by Talcott Parsons. Minneola, N.Y.: Dover, 1958 [1905].

Weil, Simone. *Gravity and Grace.* Translated by Emma Craufurd. London: Routledge and Kegan Paul, 1963.

Wenzer, Kenneth C. *An Anthology of Tolstoy's Spiritual Economics.* Volume 2. Rochester, N.Y.: University of Rochester Press, 1997.

Westphal, Kenneth R. "Do Kant's Principles Justify Property or Usufruct?" *Annual Review of Law and Ethics* 5 (1997): 141–94.

Wicksell, Knut. *Lectures on Political Economy: Volume 1: General Theory*. London: Routledge and Kegan Paul, 1934.

Wicksteed, Philip. *The Common Sense of Political Economy*. London: Routledge and Kegan Paul, 1933 [1910].

Winch, Donald. *Economics and Policy: A Historical Study*. London: Hodder and Stoughton, 1969.

Xepapadeas, Anastasios. "Ecological Economics: Principles of Economic Policy Design for Ecosystem Management." In *The Princeton Guide to Ecology*, edited by Simon A. Levin, 740–47. Princeton, N.J.: Princeton University Press, 2012.

Zimmerman, Michael E. *Contesting Earth's Future: Radical Ecology and Postmodernity*. Berkeley: University of California Press, 1994.

———. *Heidegger's Confrontation with Modernity: Technology, Politics, Art*. Bloomington: Indiana University Press, 1990.

———. "Rethinking the Heidegger-Deep Ecology Relationship." *Environmental Ethics* 15 (1993): 195–224.

Index